Akashic *Records*

Case Studies of Past Lives

Lois J. Wetzel, MFA

Akashic Records

Case Studies of Past Lives

© 2009 Lois J. Wetzel, MFA
ISBN 978-0-9832002-0-8

Lois J. Wetzel, MFA
Hot Pink Lotus Pod
Box 571742
Houston, Texas 77257
www.hotpinklotuspod.com
info@hotpinklotuspod.com
713-384-8764

Acknowledgments

I acknowledge and appreciate all the clients who continue to come to me for past life readings. Without them, I could not fulfill my Soul contract in this lifetime. I am grateful to my early teachers, William David Dimitru (now called Elias de Mohan), and the late Martha Garrett, for their teaching, support and wisdom. I am grateful to Melissa Lockwood, friend and owner of the "Ruby Rabbit," who believed in and encouraged me giving me the opportunity to begin doing large numbers of past life readings in the early 1990s.

Without Becky Hannah, my friend, transcriptionist and editor, this book would never have been written. Thank you, Becky.

Most of all, I am deeply grateful to my two steadfast, loving sons, Austin and Stuart, for incarnating upon Earth and allowing me the joy both of being their mother and of watching them grow into two such amazing men.

Table of Contents

Foreword

In 1952, amateur hypnotist Morey Bernstein put ordinary housewife Virginia Tighe into a trance using a process called hypnotic regression. He gradually took her back to childhood, but then Morey got adventurous. Curiosity got the best of him as he attempted to take Virginia one step further—to the time before birth. Without warning, he found himself talking to a woman named Bridey Murphy, who claimed to be a 19th-century Irishwoman reincarnated in the US 59 years later.

The concept of reincarnation has been around much longer than Morey and Virginia's time. It's speculated that since the Iron Age Greek pre-Socratics talked of reincarnation, and the Celtic Druids adhered to its doctrine. The philosophical traditions in India date back to the 6th century BC. Tibetan Buddhism actually developed a process, a 'science' of death and rebirth, as it were, which was recorded in detail in *The Tibetan Book of the Dead*.

In this new culture of the evolution of human consciousness, understanding the multidimensional nature of self can literally be a lifesaver. As our multiple aspects are waking up to each other, more and more of us are experiencing what Lois refers to as past life "blowback"—a condition wherein the thoughts, feelings, senses and memories of a past life come alive within our present body. This phantom psyche can take over the mechanism and create an out-of-context perspective that can go from baffling to debilitating.

What brings about our deepest phobias—fear of heights, water or tight places? Why does someone drive us crazy, making us say and do things we seemingly can't control? More often than not, understanding the drama and story behind the phantom psyches of past lives can bring clarity and freedom, and allow us to forgive each other and ourselves.

Lois Wetzel has written a definitive book on the subject. Her past life readings have helped countless people get their present lives back, me included. Lois' reading opened a new pathway of forgiveness and integration at a time it was most needed.

Read this book and consider your own stories and dramas. Learn from others who were guided to accept and unite all parts of their lives. Then be inspired to take your own journey into wholeness. That's what this book helped me do, may it so inspire you.

Barbara With

Introduction

It has been both my honor and my joy to have been allowed to work with the Akashic Records for over twenty years. I was given the Records by a Luminous Being in a dream in the mid-1980s, and gradually this work began to unfold from that point on. It was a few years before I actually did my first past life reading. This reading was for Bruce, who in 1990 had come in for a bodywork session. And about a year later, a past life spontaneously arose with Carol, who was on my table getting bodywork at my office on Bee Caves Road in Austin, Texas. We both simultaneously and spontaneously saw the identical past life in which we had been together.

It was not until a few years later when I moved to Houston—in 1994— that I began to do past life readings on a regular basis. This happened during a "dark night of the soul" following a painful breakup with a man whom I had thought I would marry. After slightly over year of deeply grieving, I began to ask myself, "What else is there for me to do in the world, besides crash and burn from a broken heart?" Fortunately, an acquaintance, dear, sweet Brenda, suggested that I begin to advertise some of the other wonderful things I knew how to do, like shamanic journeying and past life readings. There were a couple of false starts advertising directly to massage therapists, a few of whom turned out to be religious fanatics. Two even took the time to write and tell me that I was going to burn in hell as their response to my direct mail marketing about things not religious, but spiritual. So I decided to approach the task differently.

I began reading a locally owned magazine, the *Indigo Sun*, in which I had also been placing ads. An advertisement for a new shop caught my eye, and I eagerly drove the thirty minutes out to the west side of Houston to check things out. When I walked into this shop, the Ruby Rabbit, a metaphysical store and teaching center, a strangely happy feeling came over me. I felt as though I had, after years of wandering alone in a hostile environment, entered a safe haven. I knew from that feeling I was on the right track. The owner, Melissa, had recently opened the shop, and was excited to have me do Soul retrievals and teach shamanic journeying. She advertised this in her direct mail newsletter. This was several years before the age of email newsletters. It surprised me to discover that we had no takers for this class. It was a bit too early for such things, I now realize. The timing was wrong. No one could understand the relevance in their lives of what it was that I was offering. It just did not "click."

Melissa, who had immediately felt very familiar, like an old friend, asked what else I could do. I said I could do past life readings. Her eyes lit up, and she scheduled me on Sundays for four hours a day to do one after another. We had scores of people interested in that every month! I began to get the practice I had needed. Additionally, my heart began to heal, since I was doing one of those things which makes my Soul sing. My confidence in what I was doing skyrocketed as I watched the lights come on in people's faces as they said, "Ah, yes…That explains why...." over and over again. I was always precisely on target about the most bizarre details in the lives of complete strangers. It was gratifying for them and for me. Some of their realizations were immediate some came later, after they left the shop. They would come by later and share their insights. I felt like I was providing, at a nominal fee, a much-needed service. My clients were delighted and brought their friends the next Sunday.

After about a year of doing these readings, I wrote an article for the *Indigo Sun* magazine, and began to get regular clients for the past lives at my office. It never occurred to me to record these readings. When they did get recorded by the clients, I did not keep a copy. So the vast majority of those past lives are forever lost to me. I cannot remember what I saw while in a trance for very long afterward. It is like waking from a dream, we think we will remember, but then shortly thereafter, we do not. I was solely interested in healing the clients. Over the past two years or so have I begun to record all the sessions and keep copies for my own files.

The reader will notice that there are a lot of lifetimes in Atlantis, Lemuria and Egypt. This is because these civilizations lasted for thousands of years, and usually the advanced spiritual seekers who come to me for readings have been reincarnating for quite a while. Each healer will attract clients who resonate with their energy. Mine are usually other healers and teachers, but whatever the occupation, they are almost always fairly highly evolved spiritual beings. So they have indeed had many lifetimes in these cultures.

This is also true for Native American lives, because this was a culture in which one could have a very spiritual experience, and so many advanced Souls have opted to live during those times. There are many lifetimes living on the coast or on islands, because that is where most people settle to this day! And there are several lifetimes traveling in wagons to sell things or entertain, because that was the only mode of inland transport for many centuries. Agricultural lifetimes are prominent because for a very long time, humans were far more involved in agriculture than they currently are.

Some of my clients came from other planetary or star systems, and fell into the reincarnation cycle on Earth accidentally, some on purpose.

Sometimes I have been allowed to see lovely, harmonious and balanced civilizations about which we know not. They have been completely lost, and all traces of them utterly disappeared in the sands of time. It is such an honor to be allowed to see these thrilling, vanished worlds, with their unique and fascinating clothing, architecture and machinery, or technology which did not utilize machines. (Some highly advanced civilizations from a cultural standpoint have very little happening in the way of machines!) I have seen unusual buildings, transport vehicles, clothing and adornments that I could never, ever have made up myself. I am grateful for my academic background as a painter, with all those hours of art history, so that I can appreciate the rarity, uniqueness and true beauty of what I am continuously being allowed to see. It is as though I have my own personal window onto ancient civilizations which hardly anyone now alive on the planet has ever seen! I feel deeply honored and privileged to have been given permission to see such magical, glorious, exotic, heavenly and sometimes bizarre scenes. With that comes the necessity of also seeing ugly, frightful, nauseating and horrible ones as well, for the purpose of helping others heal themselves.

Over the ensuing years since I started doing readings at the Ruby Rabbit, I have been allowed to witness thousands of past lives. Working with past lives is definitely not for the faint of heart. It takes a great deal of courage to allow myself to actually see some of these things, so inglorious, which have happened to people. These are events and situations which, if unresolved, continue to haunt them in the present, and which will still haunt them in future lives, if unaddressed. All these lifetimes are connected to each other, and if we heal something in one of them, it affects all of them. Wondrously, just remembering these past lives and understanding what the point of knowing about them is, will heal the person. The Guardians of the Akashic Records always let me know what the point of learning about each lifetime is. The result is rather like lancing a boil, which drains, and then can finally heal.

Many people have indicated that I must have done something in the past to earn the right to see the Akashic Records, and I think that may be true. However, I have not been curious enough yet to check and see what it was that I did. Perhaps I will get around to it one day. In the meantime, though, there seem to be much more important past lives to see, so that people can understand who they really are, and know about their accomplishments, talents, good deeds, as well as their mistakes, unlearned lessons, and the tribulations or horrors visited upon them, and why. These events were all lessons the Soul chose before incarnating, either to learn from or with which they were to teach others in their lives, and whether or not the lessons were learned is the primary issue. We need to understand the lessons, and to finally learn them.

My clients have especially needed to understand about their mistaken conclusions drawn during the last few moments before death. These moments are distinctly significant to the Soul, as they are permanently imprinted, like light imprints itself on an unexposed photographic negative, more so than events or conclusions drawn at any other point in the lifetime.

Recurring patterns in lifetime after lifetime need to be examined, so they can be healed and not further repeated. Past lives with loved ones as well as those with enemies require that a bright light be directed upon them. In that way these Souls can see the full picture while in human form, and these Souls can finish their karma together. The other choice is continuing to repeat the same karmic "games" repeatedly, sometimes for millennia. In the way that I understand it, we can heal the karma only while we are in human form. Just knowing about these things in our spirit state, between lives, is not enough. We must work through these issues and clear up the karma while incarnated. And the time is right now to get that done.

I wish to express my deepest and most profound gratitude to my clients, the individuals who have agreed to allow their stories to be told on the following pages. By so doing, they are being of important spiritual service to others, so that the reader may learn from their experiences, and have the chance to learn, grow and be healed themselves.

As I said earlier, for the first several years, I kept no records of the past life readings which I had done. My only goal was helping individuals and their families to heal. I made a few recordings of the Akashic Records readings starting in 2005, but became more diligent about it in 2008. On the following pages, I will tell about some of the more interesting past lives I have seen in that time period, both in the form of case studies of people for whom I have done Akashic Records readings of past lives, as well as those which have come up spontaneously, or in the context of doing an energy medicine session, such as a BodyTalk session.

We are Immortal Souls, returning again and again for learning and growth. It is my hope that you, the reader, will take from these past lives of others, the deep understanding that our past lives are part of the complex web of everything we are. From the viewpoint of the Soul, they are all occurring at the same time. All of them are impacting each other. To fully heal, I believe we must look deeper than is our custom. Hopefully one day all healers, including psychotherapists, psychologists and psychiatrists will, as a matter of course, consider past life therapy, the ongoing journey of the Soul, as a crucial piece of the healing process. After all, the word "psyche" does mean "Soul".

1
The Pyramid, the Book, and the Dream

This is how I remember it. I was sitting in a semi-darkened room studying at a library table. Also sitting at this table was Joy, one of my friends. As we sat studying quietly, I realized that a woman of about my age had come to stand beside the table and was looking straight at me. She had on a plain brown homespun, belted dress. Her shiny brown hair was pulled back into a bun; her face was expressionless, but she had warm, kind brown eyes. She spoke to me telepathically, when I looked at her, and indicated with her arm softly outstretched, palm and fingers slightly turned upwards, that I was to leave this spot, and walk away. As I began to look around, I realized that I was sitting at a library table on one tier of a theatre in the round. There were no other people there I could see besides Joy, the brown-clad woman, and me.

Following this woman, I walked down the curved wooden tiers toward the center of the stage, where there was a brightly lit, internally glowing golden pyramid, measuring about fifteen to twenty feet high at the apex. As I approached the pyramid, the woman gestured toward a door in the pyramid with her hand, and then faded into the background. A flush, trapezoidal-shaped door in the side of the golden pyramid gently opened outward on its own. From the inside of the structure came a white light so intense that I was blinded by it at first.

As I moved inside, my eyes gradually became accustomed to the light. There was an unusual looking box inside the center of the pyramid. It was shaped rather like a low wooden bookcase. It was long, narrow, enclosed, and without shelves. The box was open at the top, and brilliant, intense white light flooded out.

Standing beside the box was a barefoot man, wearing only a white loincloth. He had curly, short blonde hair, intense but reassuring blue eyes that gave off a deep, profound sense of peace, and fine curling golden hair all over his body. His body was thin like a swimmer's body, or a yogi's. There was absolutely nothing sexual about this person's demeanor. I intuitively took him to be the Archangel Gabriel.

The most amazing thing about him was that he emitted light. His whole body glowed like a candle whose wick is below the uppermost edge of the candle, and is causing all the wax of the entire candle to emit a soft glow. I could not see the flame, just the overall bright, warm glow coming from his entire being. This Luminous Being made eye contact with me, and the soft yet intense look in his eyes both mesmerized and reassured me. I felt safe, comforted and surrounded by his loving, compassionate energy field.

He smiled just a little, and then bent over slightly, reaching down into the box with both hands, and drew out from it a very ancient-looking, large book. The big, heavy book was encased in old brownish leather, with some mild wear at the corners. I could smell the soft, warmly scented leather. The edges of the book's casing were piped in red. The head of a lion was perched at the top of the case, and it was made of solid gold. There were brown leather straps and copper-colored buckles at the bottom, so that the book's leather case could be opened to remove the book by sliding it out the bottom. The lion's head faced two ways, both outward from the front as well as facing again outward from the back of the book; thus the lion looked both forward and back, simultaneously, like the god Janus. The glowing man extended his arms to nearly their full length, handing the book to me, and with the slightest downward inclination of his head, almost bowing. I took the heavy book in my hands, and carried it in front of my chest just as he had, with both hands. He then indicated with a slow, gentle nod and a slight lift of his eyebrows in the direction of the door to the pyramid, that I should follow him. All communication was utterly telepathic and gestural. No words were ever spoken. They were not necessary.

This perfectly-formed, glowing Being turned and walked out of the pyramid. He continued across the theatre floor and on up to the many leveled tiers of the theatre in the round. From there he walked slowly yet steadily up all the levels. I followed him unswervingly. We walked past Joy, who did not notice us at all, but kept toiling away at her reading. We continued upwards, toward an exit which looked very much like a subway exit, and began walking up the long stairs toward the bright light coming from above. At this same moment I realized I was simultaneously outside of my body watching myself as I followed this luminous being. I observed with pleasure that the ends of my hair had begun to glow in the same way that he glowed, because I was following him. I knew that one day I would glow from within just as he was if I continued to follow his lead. Then I awoke.

More real than my waking life, this dream was one of the most powerful spiritual experiences I have ever had. I awoke that sunny morning bubbling from deep inside with excitement, but over precisely what I was unsure. Although I could think of almost nothing else for days, I could not discuss this at home. I had learned to keep such information from my husband. Therefore I went to two of my spiritual teachers separately, William and Martha, who did not know each other. I asked each of them what they thought this exciting dream of mine meant. Both of them immediately stated that this luminous person was the Ascended Master known as Jesus, who also had an incarnation as Lord

Sananda, among others. This was based upon his physical description. They both volunteered without prompting that the book I had been given was the Akashic Records. They both volunteered without prompting that the book was the Akashic Records and they were both deeply impressed with the gift I had been given. I had never before heard of Lord Sananda, but I took their words to be true.

I have since learned that this book, called the Akashic Records, contains the records of all the lifetimes of all Souls who have ever incarnated on the Earth plane or ever will. These records are not just of past lives, but probable future ones as well. When I asked why I had been given this book, William and Martha both said I had doubtless earned access to it in a past life. I went to two separate people for confirmation that what I was hearing was true, not that I doubted anyone, but just because when something significant happens, I like to get confirmation. And I did. They said the same thing, and they did not know each other, so they could not have compared notes.

At the time, I drew the conclusion that this dream meant that I would be getting past life readings. That was pretty exciting for me! I had never had one before. And shortly thereafter I did get a reading from my teacher, William. It was a powerful experience; I learned a lot from several of the lifetimes that were covered. One that sticks in my mind was as a female diagnostician in the Healing Temples of Atlantis who was punished horribly for being too good at what she did. These past lives explained certain things about me which I had not understood before, things William could not have known about me. Afterward, I did not think much more about having been given the Akashic Records book in this dream until couple of years later, when a bodywork client just out of the blue asked me if I could do past life readings.

One of the most thrilling moments of my life occurred upon awakening from that dream. It was one of those dreams that we only have a few times in our lives. And perhaps some people never have them. Breathlessly awakening, I was bubbling over with excitement, joy and wonder. Yet I could not begin to articulate why. I would not know for several years why the thrill was so intense. Even so, I had an amazing endorphin high for over three days. Something powerful was happening that was beyond my conscious mind's ability to understand. Yet I could feel it.

I had begun studying metaphysics about a year earlier. By the time that I had this dream, it was clear to me that if I did not follow my heart and study spirituality, my life was simply not going to work. There was an ever-growing chasm between who I was on the inside, and who I was out in the world. I had realized that until the gap was closed, I would never be okay. I also knew that this would necessitate that I defy society, my husband, and almost everything

I had ever been taught. At that point in time, I was a successfully exhibiting painter, a trial lawyer's wife, and a mother of two school aged children. I also owned my own business restoring historic commercial properties on the Strand in Galveston, and was a member of the Junior League, a nationwide volunteer organization. Yet I was also a Reiki Master. The night that I had this dream was in the mid 1980s, and I was in my mid-thirties.

2
Doing My First Past Life Reading

I assimilated the past lives that William had told me about in the reading he did for me after the dream, and did not think much more about the dream for a while. I became quite busy with an overdue divorce, relocating myself and my sons to Austin, Texas, and attending massage school there. I had become so stressed out from living a life that was totally incongruous with my true inner being, that I had to change almost everything, just to stay alive. I had developed a serious stress-related illness. Both going to massage school and living in semi-rural Lakeway, just outside Austin, had a profoundly calming effect. After living there for about a year, I finished massage school and immediately opened a Reiki and bodywork practice. Not long after I started my practice, a surprising client showed up who triggered my memory of the pyramid dream.

Bruce was a client who came to see me for the first time in 1990. He had been referred to me by a nearby chiropractor, having sustained injuries in a fall from a roof. One day while on my treatment table, Bruce shocked me by asking out of the blue if I could do past life readings. Immediately as he asked it, I knew that I could. Even more surprising, I knew the precise details of how to do it. Somehow this data had been "downloaded" to me at some point without my realizing it!

So I did a reading for him, right then and there, since he had asked for it. I closed my eyes, and utilizing certain symbols I already knew in a different way, I was able to access his Akashic Records. I found that I could easily see the one particular lifetime that was relevant for him in that moment. From my perspective, the experience was like a movie playing in my head, and as I watched it, I narrated what I was seeing. Bruce's eyes were closed, too. In this lifetime, Bruce was in the process of getting a divorce from a woman who was leaving him, and he did not understand why she was going. They had been together about six years. She had a seven-year-old son from a prior relationship to whom he had become very deeply attached, and his sorrow at losing both of them ran deep.

The past life which I saw that day was one that had occurred in Ancient Egypt, and Bruce was a slave master who had fallen for a slave. This old love had come back as his wife, Jenny. She had become pregnant by him in the past life in Egypt, and he knew this would spell serious trouble for both of them when her pregnancy began to show. So he arranged safe passage for her to another land, where she could start over. Due to heavy family obligations, he could not join her. On the evening they were to part, during the darkest part of the night, they were quietly rushing down a pier toward a boat she was to board. As I described this, I noticed that the pier was made of a strange building material. Lashed together underfoot were stalks of what looked like bamboo. I commented that the pier was made of an odd material when Bruce, whose eyes were also closed, said that it indeed looked strange, like bamboo or something. Imagine my shock that Bruce also saw bamboo, when I had not yet said what the odd material was! It was then, in that first past life reading, I realized without a doubt that I was seeing something real, something I was not just making up. This was enormous for me. A reasonable person naturally has doubts about such matters, but this certainly quieted one of mine.

I finished the past life reading, which ended with Jenny and the baby she carried being killed by Bruce's enemies, who were lurking in the shadows on the dock, and Bruce being captured and imprisoned for breaking "slave relations protocols." There was a violent fight. He was injured in the process, in a manner similar to the injuries for which he had come to see me for treatment. He had a wound to the hip, and was hit on the head very hard, and injured his wrist. In this lifetime he had fallen off a roof while doing home repairs, and had received almost the exact same injuries.

Whatever or whomever was allowing me to read the Akashic Records was also explaining things to me at the same time. I now know that these are the Guardians of the Akashic Records. They explained the point of knowing about each past life, and they still do that. The point of the past life between Bruce and Jenny in Egypt, and its relationship to the current situation was this: it was important for Bruce to let Jenny and her son go this time, and start over somewhere else, because Jenny had not been able to do that in the past life. She still had a Soul-level longing to complete this task of leaving him and standing on her own two feet, which she had never done, even in the current lifetime. She had always been cared for by her father or a husband, and needed to learn independence. This was a pattern for her over many lifetimes. Bruce was also supposed to maintain contact with the boy, who thought of him as a father, and who had been his unborn son in Egypt. Knowing this made it easier for Bruce to let go of Jenny.

When Bruce told Jenny about the reading, it helped her to allow Bruce to stay in touch with her son. She was already inclined to do so, but could not understand why she felt that way, since the boy was not his child. All that changed when she heard about the past life in Egypt so long ago, which resonated with her as well. She felt deeply in her heart that this reading was true. It explained a lot about how she felt, and about their situation. She decided not to listen to her mother who was telling her to cut off all contact with Bruce so the boy would not be confused. It was clear her mom did not have enough information when she gave that advice. This experience taught Jenny to trust her instincts. Bruce and Jenny still went their separate ways, but in a gentler fashion than they might have prior to the reading with me, and with greater understanding. Bruce did stay in touch with the boy. On the whole, this was a more positive outcome than the one they would have had without the reading. They were at peace; Bruce and his "son" did not lose touch; Jenny could trust her instincts. She could also leave, and it was still sad, but easier for Bruce to accept.

The benefits of this first reading to me were many. First, it gave me the opportunity to realize that I knew how to do a past life reading from the Akashic Records. Second, it allowed me the experience of having a client see something I was seeing before I had described the scene. Because of this, I always know I am actually seeing something real, and not something I made up. And lastly, this first reading allowed me to see how knowing about past lives can have verifiable, positive healing effects both in an individual's life, and in the life of a family.

3
When, Where, and How

With that first past life reading for Bruce, I had started on my path of doing past life readings from the Akashic Records. This is still one of the more important tools in my shamanic healing bag.

Healing the Soul has many facets. One facet is that in order to heal the Soul, the ego needs to become aware of who the Soul is, as much as is possible. In other words, I do the readings in part so that people can get to know themselves better. That includes getting in touch with forgotten aspects of themselves, including their hidden talents and abilities, and their heroic deeds in the past. I also do them so people can consciously remember that they have certain tendencies to make the same mistakes repeatedly, thereby allowing them the chance to make different decisions in the present life. In this way they can avoid making those same mistakes, if they so choose.

Another reason is so that the clients can learn about misunderstandings they had in the past, know more details about some of the events or situations they misunderstood, see the past from a different vantage point (that of being in a new body/personality), and have the opportunity to draw different conclusions about past events.

Further, I do these readings so my clients can understand their relationships over many lifetimes with certain other people/Souls. Sometimes when they get this larger picture, they make different decisions about their lives and relationships, or perhaps they finally appreciate the other person/ Soul. Enhanced past life knowledge can help us develop both compassion and affection for others. Past life readings also give us the opportunity to balance karma consciously. It is not always easy, but the person who steps up to the challenge is profoundly rewarded.

Due to the intensely personal nature of these readings, I never do them to entertain anyone, or to prove anything to anyone (like how psychic I am, or that this phenomenon is real). This is an important ethical consideration. Before I do the reading, I speak with the client for a while, and make certain that they know this is not entertainment or a parlor trick. I am told the day might come when I will need to do a reading in class as a demonstration, with safeguards and permissions in place. But unless I am guided to do so for some reason which I cannot imagine at this point in time, I would not do this at a party, nor in front of a third person, except in very rare cases, and only if that were in the best interest of the client. Everyone has the right to privacy in a situation like this, and normally if a third party insisted on being there, I would refuse to do the reading until he/she left. If the client wants to share the information I give, he/she can choose to do that. Often they do not want the third party present, but will not admit that they do not, until that person has left the room. I have realized it is part of my job to protect the client in this way, to create a safe atmosphere in which to perform such a sacred act as reading from the Akashic Records.

Yes, I do regard these readings as a sacred form of spiritual work, which has the capacity for profound healing, depending upon how the client receives the information. I know it is very important for me to be neutral about what I see, report it without getting emotional, and soften the impact of any horrific situations I might see. It is not for me to judge anyone, neither the client nor anyone else. It is sometimes my job to warn someone, when the Guardians of the Records ask me to do that. Primarily, I am there to help the client understand the past. I trust that I will be shown what the client most needs to see, regardless of what they have asked to see or learn about. Their Higher Self and Guides, in concert with the Guardians of the Akashic Records, will make sure of that. I give the client the chance to ask questions at the end of each lifetime I am reporting, but not during the reporting. It is too hard to shift gears between doing the reading and answering questions, as different states of consciousness are used for the two. I ask the client to keep his/her eyes closed during the reading, if I am doing it in person, because for some reason if their eyes are open, it is like having the lights on in a movie theater! I cannot "see" the past life very well.

When I am finished narrating all the lifetimes for that session, I talk to the person some more, to help them begin to process what they just heard. Sometimes the healing they experience is instantaneous. But it is also possible that it will take up to a few months to fully assimilate the past lives. The client may have more memories surface in dreams, or even in the waking state, related to those past lives. Personally, I once had small bits of a past life come up in a reading done for me by a woman who was channeling Moses. The next morning I awoke having seen detailed visions of the entire last two years of that lifetime. It "explained a lot" including myriad tiny details relating to certain puzzling actions one of my own children had performed when very small. Dozens of minute, seemingly unrelated events fell into place, and I got the full picture. It all made sense at last!

Assimilation will have to do with acceptance, understanding the past events, learning the lessons, and not being affected by the past life any longer. In other words, if a fear of drowning came from a particular past life, the client would cease to be afraid of the water or of drowning once all the past lives necessary to hear about on this topic were assimilated. Then the client will not get emotional talking about the past life, nor while thinking about it.

I allow the client to email me up to a couple of days after the session with more questions. After that, I ask them to listen to the recording again, as I will have probably forgotten most of what I had seen. If the client wants further counseling, or has ongoing questions about the session, she/he can schedule another appointment with me to discuss their questions. This seldom happens, though.

There are also those rare clients who will "test" the past life therapist by seeing if the past life they already know about will come up. Sometimes these do, actually, but usually not. And why do they not? Usually they will not come up again because the client already knows about that lifetime. In fact, it may have been previously assimilated, and no longer an issue for the Soul. Remember, these readings are not done to prove anything to anyone. The client's Higher Self and Guides will be so excited about the reading that they take the current opportunity to tell the client about more of their lifetimes, in order to maximize the experience of past life therapy. After all, it is not often that one comes for Akashic Records readings! In my experience, the only way anything will be "proven" to the client, is when a past experience surfaces in the reading which explains something to them about themselves, about which the reader did not previously know. And the past life therapist is not in control of that. It happens all by itself, and it happens, it seems to me, only when we are doing the reading with the pure, clear spiritual intent of helping the client heal himself.

To ready myself to do any reading, I always acknowledge the Creator Source, my Higher Self and Guides, my "I AM" presence, and those of the client. Then silently I pray the following:

"Creator-Source Matrix: Please assist me in putting my own personal judgments, issues and restrictions out of the way, and do the best reading I possibly can for the highest good of all concerned. Thank you. Amen."

And then I proceed with the session, using the symbols given to me to open the individual's portal to the Akashic Records.

4
Spontaneous Past Life Recall

After the past life reading which I had done for Bruce, I did not think often about doing past life readings, it just slipped right out of my mind. I assume now that the time was not yet right for me to do more readings.

About a year later as I was doing bodywork on my friend Carol, something strange happened. Below is what she wrote to me later about her experience of that day in my office in Austin. I had known Carol only a few months when this occurred. I include this because it is a prime example of how a past life can just pop into a person's mind, if the conditions and timing are correct, and their Guides want it to happen.

Carol was a wife and mother, who had set aside her career to stay home and raise her two sons, a choice that was not all that popular at the time. Most women were vigorously pursuing their careers. I had done the same thing a few years earlier, being a few years older than she, so I could identify with her. Her husband was earning quite a bit at that time. Their money came from a highly successful business which the two of them, along with a couple of friends, had started together a few years prior. After the children arrived, she had chosen to devote herself to her family because she could. Here is her accounting of that day on my healing table, in her own words:

> In the fall of 1991 I had one of the most amazing experiences of my life. I had decided to come to my friend Lois for my first professional massage. I was so pleased to relax and take time for myself from my busy life of taking care of others. The room was comfortably cool and dimly lit as I lay down on the massage table and settled into the face cradle. A beautiful array of crystals danced in the candlelight on the floor below me.
>
> We spoke softly of our lives with our busy little boys as my knots of tension slipped away. I closed my eyes. As we quieted down, I suddenly felt a warm, dry breeze waft across my face and body. Then I became aware that a late afternoon sun beat down on my head and shoulders. As I opened my eyes, with my inner vision, I was looking across a deep blue sea stretching endlessly before me. I was standing on a white stone cliff, and I was not alone. I saw my feet in leather sandals and long gauzy robes fluttering about my legs. I felt strong and young and sure of my purpose.

I looked to my right and saw the steps of a temple looming behind us on the cliff. And I knew that it was my home, my work and my heart. As I looked to my left, my friend stood beside me. Our long, dark curls mingled in the sea breeze. I knew in my heart that it was Lois, and we were sisters in every sense of the word.

Then in the distance, I heard the voice of the Lois of today say, "you know...we were priestesses in Atlantis together". With her voice my vision cleared and once again the crystals flashed in the candlelight. Shocked, I knew that we had shared the time of my vision of Atlantis, and with that knowledge my life would never be the same.

Indeed I had seen the same vision, while my eyes were closed, and I was giving her a massage. Carol's reaction was that she was shocked and amazed. It had a paradigm-shifting effect on her. For me it was confirmation of something I already hoped was true; people come together again from the same Soul families.

My dear friend Carol and I have become, and remain, extremely close "sisters" in this lifetime. Fifteen years after the shared vision of that past life memory, when Carol's first-born and beloved son, Erich, was tragically killed at the age of twenty-four, I was the first person she called, aside from her immediate family. We are still quite close, talking several times a month, although we have not lived in the same city for over thirteen years. We are there for each other, as sisters are, in good times and bad.

5
Past Lives and Energy Medicine Sessions

The past lives which come up in the context of energy medicine, such as BodyTalk, EDINA or Psych-K sessions, only come up as little brief fragments. Just enough information is revealed to allow the client to get the issue balanced. In the case of BodyTalk, the BodyTalker sees the past life fragment, and tells the client before balancing it. With Psych-K the past life will sometimes flash before the person being balanced while they are repeating their phrase silently to themselves. With EDINA energy medicine, the past life will appear either as a brief flash of imagery, or as a full-blown memory, suddenly downloaded directly to the client, depending upon what the client needs at that time.

Later, as I begin to write the past lives down, subsequently taking session notes, the larger picture often reveals itself to me. I move into the altered state easily where I can see the past lives again. The client does not necessarily hear all these details during their session, but many have reported remembering the details themselves spontaneously, or having a dream that shows them all of the details soon after the session.

Post-Partum Depression

One of the most memorable past lives which surfaced in the context of a BodyTalk session is that of Kevin, a seven-year-old boy whose mother Mindy, a nurse, had come to see me complaining of a sore knee. When Mindy saw what BodyTalk did for her knee, she asked if I thought I could help her little boy, who she said was horrified of the dark. I told her that I believed I could. She added she had two older children who did not have this problem.

The following week, she brought this adorable, sweet-faced little boy with red hair in to see me. He was so cute I wanted to squeeze him, but decided to show him the proper respect due another spirit having a human experience. The situation we were addressing was serious for him, and I did not want him to feel minimized.

Kevin reported he was so frightened of the dark and of being behind a closed door alone, that he would wake up in the night shaking, and need to get into bed with his mother and father. He said he would just wake up utterly terrified for no apparent reason. The worst part was that he could never, neither awake nor asleep, bear being alone behind a closed door. I asked if he had any other issues to work on, like problems with any subjects at school, or with friends or sports, questions I always ask the child clients, and he said that he had trouble with math. So except for these fears, he seemed a very normal child.

I began the session, and activated whichever formulae that the innate wisdom of his body indicated it needed balanced. This is how BodyTalk is done. We ask the innate healing wisdom of the individual's body what it needs help balancing, so it can heal itself, using a muscle response technique. Then after balancing about three formulae, in the first session I had with Kevin, a past life came up to be balanced in which he had been a female.

This young married woman was about eighteen years of age when she had a baby. This was in the mid-1800s in the northeastern United States. She had an intense hormonal reaction after childbirth, which caused her to have post-partum depression so severe that she experienced a temporary psychotic break. In those days, of course, they did not know to give hormone supplementation; they just locked crazy people up forever. She was chained to a wall, on an eight-to-ten-foot-long chain, in a locked room, wearing a ratty white nightgown with tiny purple flowers on it. The flowers were ridiculous-looking in the context of the rest of the scene, almost cruel in their silliness, with their implied reference to sweetness and normalcy.

The only furniture in that prison of a hospital cell was a metal bed with springs running from side to side to support the sleeper, and no mattress or covers. One horizontal window with bars was near the ceiling. The window was long, narrow, and far too high for this tiny woman to see out. At night it was completely dark in her cell, and no one in the facility was allowed to make a sound, for fear of painful retribution by the attendants, who behaved like prison guards.

Every day these attendants would hose her and the room down from outside, through the bars in the door to her room. There was a drain in the center of the floor. She was hosed down to wash out the urine and fecal matter that was all over her and the room. No one ever touched her, in all those years she was in the asylum. No one ever tried to help her or heal her. She was considered permanently insane, and no claims by her that she was over it were ever listened to, even when she obviously got better, used the drain in the floor as a toilet, and tried to engage the guards in conversation. Twice a day food and water were slipped through a slot at the bottom of the door. This woman lived to be about thirty-five years old, chained to the wall, with no mattress, no toilet or shower, and worst of all, no human touch. There were no books to read, no one to talk to, no view of the outside. She ultimately died of influenza, her immune system destroyed by years of abuse, depression and lack of touch.

When this Soul reincarnated this time as a little boy, she chose a snuggly, warm, loving mother who would be patient with the need for excessive touching, and calm about with his inability to tolerate being behind a closed door, like the young mother had been at the asylum, or in the dark alone.

Hearing about the past life helped the mother understand better why Kevin was always in her lap, and could not sleep alone, or be behind closed doors.

Kevin heard about the past life, too, although the details were spared. The gory parts were glossed over. He said that it sounded familiar, and wanted to know if he would ever get over it. I said now that he knew about it, he would just automatically get better. And he did.

The mother reported about ten days later when she came for her next session that over the period of a few days he had begun to calm down. He was not sitting in her lap or up beside her on the couch every time she sat down. After about three days, he could go to bed alone and fall asleep without a light on in his room. A week after the session he was able to sleep through the night and not wake up to crawl into bed with his parents. He came back for another couple of sessions, but the largest shift occurred after that first one. It was a profound change, and one for which his mom was deeply appreciative.

This BodyTalk experience happened over five years ago, and Kevin's changes have held. He has had no further issues with trouble sleeping alone, fear of the dark, nor being behind closed doors. He closes his door every day after school to do homework, play on his computer, build model airplanes, or listen to his music. He lives life as other children do.

Serial Monogamy

Brandon came to see me on a regular basis for energy medicine sessions, and had been doing that for some years. His main objective was spiritual growth. One day when he came for his regular session, he said that he was quite upset with himself. Brandon was a tall, single man in his late thirties, and he was both good-looking and fit. The problem facing him was that he had a very difficult time dating more than one woman at a time. He behaved as if he were married to every woman he went out with more than a couple of times. This was very irksome to him since there were no rules anywhere against dating several women at the same time. He wanted to see several women until he gradually narrowed the field, and decided which one he wanted to have as a steady girlfriend. He had not had a special woman in his life for a couple of years. The guilt of dating more than one woman at a time seemed so illogical to both of us. He thought about the guilt constantly.

I did a BodyTalk session for Brandon. Among other things, a past life came up for balancing. It was one in which Brandon had been a woman. The year was 1458; the location was Italy. She was married to a wealthy older man, whom she loved, but who was not virile any longer. The husband, in fact, was quite unable to perform at all. She was a young, beautiful woman with all her hormones functioning, and thus she had certain needs. She spontaneously started having an affair with a virile younger man whom she met while visiting at a cousin's country estate one summer. This man sought her out when she got back to her own town. The sex between them was both satisfying and intense, and she had her very first orgasms with him. This was because the young man knew certain tricks, having been trained by prostitutes. The older man, her husband, would never have dreamed of doing such things to a lady, and his wife was a lady.

The wife was having more fun than she had ever dreamed possible, and so she continued the affair. The husband looked the other way. He loved his wife, and wanted her to be happy. He trusted her to not wander too far from home.

The wife did not take the lover seriously; he was just a lot of fun for her. The young man, on the other hand, fell madly in love. She was the most delicate, sweet-smelling creature he had ever had the honor to ravish. He would refuse to wash to keep the scent of her on him for days because he was so obsessed with her. Certain they would be together one day as husband and wife, he thought of her day and night. This continued for many months.

Late one sad night though, the lover became a bit drunk, and used the key she had given him for their basement trysts to sneak into their home. Instead of going to the basement, he made his way to her bedroom. There lying on the bed was his true love, with her grey-haired, snoring husband. He went insane with jealousy when he saw the old man sleeping, his arm casually draped over the bosom of his beloved. Before he had time to think, he had picked up a heavy bronze sculpture and smashed in the husband's head. The wife woke and began screaming. Her lover was arrested after the servants found him standing drunk over their dying master. The unfortunate man was quickly hanged for the murder.

The wife was so wracked with guilt she could not function for over a year. She just lay in bed, sobbing. She had loved her kindly older husband, and she never got over the deep, gut-wrenching guilt for having been the reason he had died early. Their children's hearts were broken as well. Everyone thought the lover was just a robber who broke in, but she knew better.

Additionally, she felt guilty over the fate of the lover. Even though the lover was just a dalliance, still she felt wretched that he had died. This situation had imprinted itself so strongly upon the Soul that even in the current lifetime as a male, Brandon could not even go out on dates with more than one woman in the same time period. He had to stop seeing one woman before he could begin to see another. He was committed to whomever he was dating, no matter what, even if it was just a casual relationship. When he did not act committed, he obsessed and felt guilty. As any man can attest, this is not normal for a male.

A few weeks after this session, Brandon reported with delight that his guilty feelings seemed to be gone, and he was definitely not obsessing over dating two women any more. He knows he will easily commit to monogamy when finally he does get married, but feels he will no longer suffer such debilitating guilt when dating casually. And this came as a tremendous relief for him.

Fear of Drowning

Nina reports that this past life came up for her during a BodyTalk session with me about two years ago:

In this particular lifetime, she was a man who worked underwater repairing the outside of the glass-looking dome of a healing temple, which had been constructed about thirty feet under the sea. His job was to regularly swim around outside these temple domes and do the repair work that was inevitably required of such structures. With prolonged practice, he gradually became able to hold his breath for longer and longer periods of time. He became something of a celebrity, performing acrobatics in the water outside the domes. This young man had a powerful, handsome body, and looked quite attractive on land or in water. It was no surprise that the women who worked inside the domes enjoyed stopping what they were doing to watch him swim around above their workplace. He gained a certain amount of notoriety.

One such day he was drawing an especially large crowd of young, nubile women as an audience. It had become very gratifying to impress them with how long he could stay underwater, blending gymnastics with repair work. This time he miscalculated how long he could do that feat, and because of that, he drowned feeling deeply humiliated at having all those women watch him die so ignobly.

When this past life was related to Nina, she said it totally explained why she had such a terror of drowning in the current lifetime. It also helped her understand why the fear was more intense when there were large numbers of people about, like at a public pool or at the beach.

About a month later, Nina emailed to say that she had gone swimming in the Gulf of Mexico, and actually allowed herself to both float on its surface, and dive below the surface of the water, holding her breath for a few seconds. She was able to do this for the first time in her entire life without debilitating fear. Nancy felt quite certain it was because of the BodyTalk session which included balancing for the lifetime when she drowned in front of her group of admirers. Any summertime Sunday in Galveston comes with thousands of people crowding noisily onto the beach with their umbrellas, coolers, children and dogs. Even though she went swimming in the Gulf at that time, on a Sunday afternoon in July, the crowd of people on the beach did not make her nervous, either.

Tortured Back

Marlene, a forty-one year old school teacher, had ongoing back pain which had started mysteriously when she was about twenty-two years of age. There did not seem to be any particular event in her current life which could have caused the onset of these symptoms. There really seemed to be absolutely no cause at all. However, the pain was real, quite harsh, and ever present. I know from experience with past lives that this sometimes just happens at the same age we were in another lifetime when an accident, or other mishap, occurred.

During the course of an EDINA energy medicine session, a memory emerged of a past life in which she had been tortured during a wartime experience in an Asian country. She had been a young officer who was taken prisoner. The captors believed the soldier possessed information which he actually did not have. The torture was focused upon his back, and involved bamboo stakes. This pain and questioning had gone on for weeks, until he died in his sleep as a direct result of an infection caused by the torture. He was captured, tortured and died - all when he was twenty-two years of age in the prior life.

After this session, the pain in her back gradually began to recede. After a couple of months, Marlene was utterly free of this pain which had been with her for almost twenty years.

This concludes the examples of the ways in which a past life might make itself known in the context of an energy medicine session. This is a different experience than that of an Akashic Records reading, which has a specific procedure and formal setting. Many lifetimes come up in that setting, and in greater immediate detail, along with certain explanations. The Guardians of the Akashic Records are available to explain to me the point of seeing each lifetime that emerges in a formal reading.

What follows are a series of what I call "Case Studies". These are formal past life readings from the Akashic Records. I have alphabetized them by first name, not by last name or by date. Neither dates nor time really matter, especially to the Soul or Higher Self, since all the past lives are happening simultaneously from their point of view. Time and space are only illusions we have as a consequence of being on a spinning planet.

Naturally, the client's names and identifying information have been changed to protect my clients, their families and friends.

6
The Individual Case Studies

Past Life Reading: Bob Sandford: October 11, 2008

Bob has come in for an Akashic Records reading to learn more about certain patterns in this current lifetime. He tells me that his spiritual journey began not long ago with a visit to his old Army buddy in Canada, who is a First Nations shaman. Bob talks about his aversion to organized religion, and about being easily distracted from what he is studying, quickly moving from one spiritual discipline to another. He would like to be able to focus on something and stick with it, to become "a distance runner instead of a sprinter," as he puts it. He says the wife finds him wish-washy, and it bothers him that he is. He wants to find out what he came here to do in this lifetime, and get busy doing it.

Lois: Bob, here is one reason why I do the past life readings. I learned while studying psychology in grad school that certain memories repressed from childhood can affect you in bizarre ways which you cannot imagine. Once there was a woman I worked with briefly, who after she remembered that her grandfather had sexually molested her, was able to date men who were her own age. This was a woman in her early forties. Thank goodness she was not in her sixties before she learned this, because once a man got grey hair, she felt repulsed at the thought of being touched by him. She said it felt "incestuous," which did not make logical sense even to her. Yet soon after she remembered her grandfather, who had grey hair, had molested her, all of that changed. Grey-haired men were no longer repulsive, only her grandfather's behaviors were. Repressed memories of trauma, particularly, can affect you in ways that you cannot imagine. This is true of the current lifetime, and also of past lives.

Another reason I do these readings is that sometimes we have abilities and talents that cause us to have a yearning to do something for which we have no training or background in this lifetime. If we became aware that we have mastered this in the past, we would not think, "Oh, that's out of my range. I am interested in that but I am not smart enough, big enough, strong or young enough, or whatever, to do that." We are not as much learning something new, as remembering something previously known.

A different and acutely important reason for having past life readings is that sometimes people need to know the origins of recurring patterns with certain people. They need to know what it is that they meant to resolve with that person when they incarnated this time. A variety of things might need to happen to balance the karma with that other person.

Sometimes what needs to be resolved is just to get out of the relationship without being killed, or to figure out how get out of the relationship safely, so no one is harmed, or waiting all our lives for them to die. It also is common recurring theme for some people, just to trust being in a certain relationship, and not being afraid of getting in, or being fully engaged and making a commitment. A person, for example, might have an irrational fear of being with some person to whom they are also drawn. Why might they have this irrational fear? Because in past lives, one or the other has committed suicide due to the relationship not working out they way they had desperately wanted it to work out. Just think of Romeo and Juliet. Do you think those two would not have second thoughts about coming together again? Look how it ended! It may be that they incarnated this time to joyfully be together without committing suicide, but if one is too afraid of the other because of this unrecalled past, the coming together may never happen.

Also, knowing about past lives can help you to understand why someone is making life miserable for you, even though you never did anything to harm them. Was it because they went to jail, and you did not help bail them out in some other lifetime? Maybe you could have testified on their behalf, and got them released from jail, but you were too afraid, or too selfish to become involved. They might be getting even with you for something neither of you consciously recalls ever happening. This is often what is going on when you meet someone you instantly despise; you "remember" them from a past life.

Additionally, there are huge numbers of people who would benefit from knowing about their acts of heroism, bravery, selflessness, or courage in past lives. Occasionally that kind of thing will come up in a reading. Sometimes people need to hear about that for their self-esteem. So, those are some of the reasons why I do these readings. They can help people grow, stretch, and become everything they were meant to be.

I next give instructions to Bob; what to expect and how the actual reading works. I then close the window blinds, saying it is easier to see these images of the lifetimes if it is not bright in the room. I explain that I read somewhere the word shaman actually means "the one who can see in the dark." I tell Bob that I will place my hands on the back of his head to access the past lives, as that is where they are stored. I also joke that if it were up to me, the past lives would be stored on the sides of the head, as that would be easier to reach, but no one consulted with me as to where they should be stored. Bob said no one consulted with him, either. We both have a hearty laugh. (Then I pause to view the first lifetime.)

<u>Lois:</u> I am now seeing something which has never occurred to me could happen. I am seeing Roman soldiers marching in the snow. You are there as

some sort of commander. You are wearing a short skirt, a little thing, and it has metal all over it, and that is definitely not comfortable in the snow. You all are in England, which makes sense about the snow; or I should say that you were in what we would now call England. The soldiers customarily took spoils of war: Saxon slaves and whatever else they desired. Rome considered this part of the soldiers' payment for their work

Apparently, you traveled constantly. It was a very satisfying lifetime for you because you really loved seeing what was over the next hill. You did have a slave for a while—a Saxon slave. It bothered you that she seemed to be so unhappy all the time. Eventually after a few years, in the middle of the night, you set her free. That was hard for both of you. She did not want to be a slave, she did not want to leave her family, and at the same time, she did not want to leave you. This is the Soul you are married to in this lifetime, so in some ways it makes sense that you are feeling wishy-washy about her. You had eventually set her free, having also felt a bit guilty about having taken a slave for sex.

You could not communicate with her very well, so this caused problems. You two did not speak the same language, so she could not fully understand your setting her free. She left you, but she left without ever understanding why you let her go. She was not sure if she displeased you, or if you did it out of love. Yet she left because she wanted to go home, and you could not tell her about your reasons. This explains a lot about her concern regarding your "seeming to be" unpredictable as you have mentioned.

After that you just kept on moving—over the next hill, to the next vista. You were going where you were instructed by the higher command to go, and were feeling all right about that. However, this slave woman was the closest thing to a wife you ever had. Ultimately you died in battle in your late thirties, which was kind of old for those days. She never knew what happened to you. Do you have any questions about that lifetime?

<u>Bob:</u> There are no questions, but there are some good parallels to my present life. It explains a lot.

<u>Lois:</u> They are telling me that lifetime of constant moving, constantly seeing what is over the next hill was to break you of the pattern of being stuck in one place—to get you to enjoy adventure and seeing new vistas, having new experiences. You had quite a few lifetimes where they could not have blasted you out of the town you lived in, even if they had dynamite. So you decided between incarnations, with the help of your Guides, that you needed new experiences with travel. But at the same time, it may have made you get easily bored and want to move on to the next thing, too. Let me see about the next lifetime.

This is early 1800s and you are riding a camel, and at first I thought you were an Arab, but you are not. You are some white guy who wound up in the desert somehow…almost by accident. I would say a plane crash, but they did not have planes back then. I need to see this more clearly. (Pause)

You were traveling from one location to another, and through the desert was the shorter way to get there. The people who were guiding your caravan came down with some kind of disease, and you turned out to be the only one immune to it. At one point this experience was petrifying, because you thought you would die in the desert, not knowing where to go and not having the proper equipment. The others had drunk almost all of the water. You kept thinking they would get well eventually, and so did they. But they did not recover. A few days after the last of your party died, another caravan came along and picked you up, just as you were about to run out of water. You could not communicate with them, because you did not know their language, and they did not know yours, either. They just took you along with them. It was an act of mercy on their part.

Still, there was a real feeling of fear in your heart, because it was unclear whether you were a prisoner or not. They gave you clothes to wear that would protect you from the sun. No one could tell you were a foreigner, which was also for your protection. They took you into the next village with them, thinking you would find some people who were like you eventually. But no one spoke English or French, which were your two languages. The tribe would go on to the next location, and still you could not find anybody who could speak either of your languages.

This went on for a couple of years. The tribe would give you tasks to do, and then you began to wonder if you were a slave, until one day they went into a town where there happened to be an English woman walking down the street. You started talking to her which frightened her initially, because you were so well disguised by the tribe that she thought you were some kind of fierce nomadic raider about to harm her. Then she listened for a moment and realized you were an Englishman—actually a Welshman.

She helped you find your way back to civilization as you knew it to be, but you were not anywhere near the city where you needed to be. You really were alive only because of the kindness of strangers. First the tribe saved you, and then the strange Englishwoman. By this time, your whole family had concluded that you were dead. When finally you got home, everything had changed. Your wife had sold the home, because you were not earning an income any more. The company you worked for left her high and dry. She was living in the country with a cousin. Your two small children could not remember you. This was so painful for you. Your wife was initially traumatized when she saw you. She thought she was seeing a ghost. She screamed and ran the other way. And so you wondered, "Do I just go someplace else and start over again?" You had discovered that you really loved the nomadic life, as it turned out. You really took joy in that way of life.

Confused as to what to do next, you went to a monastery to meditate. It was one of those places where people are silent. Your plan was to meditate, decompress from your adventure in the desert, and gain the clarity to decide what to do next. You were in the monastery for a couple of months when the monks began to put pressure on you to become one of them. It just seemed like the easy way out, so you decided to become a monk. You left your wife and kids and became a monk.

Apparently the experience in the desert had been a deeply traumatic one. You suffered from post-traumatic stress disorder, but no one knew what that was. At that point, you needed someplace to feel safe, and to readjust to life in your native country. This is how you ended up in the monastery. In the first place, you only went in to meditate and figure out what to do next. You realized it felt safe there, and they held out that they were going to take care of your family. Once they had some sort of binding agreement, you were trapped. It was an agreement from which you could not get free, having had signed over to them whatever else you happened to still own.

They agreed that they would then take care of your wife and kids, and you found out later that they were not doing what they had promised regarding your family. You lived another ten years as a monk, and were given menial jobs to do. You developed a deep bitterness toward the Church as a result of their failure to honor their agreement where your wife and children were concerned. When you died, you swore that you would never have anything to do with another church again no matter how many lifetimes you lived.

I just asked the Guardians of the Akashic Records a question, "What was the purpose of you knowing that this lifetime?" The first answer I am hearing is that you needed to know why you have such a strong aversion to the Church. This lifetime is one of the reasons, but certainly not the only one. Again, the wife in that lifetime is the one you are married to now, so her fear is explained. She viewed you in that lifetime again as being unpredictable. In her mind it looks like this: you are dead but then you are not dead; you come home, and then leave for a while, saying you are coming back, but you do not. You become a monk. This was very disturbing on a deep level for her, this level of unpredictability. And you were deeply saddened at the string of events that resulted in your family not being together, nor cared for properly. Questions?

Bob: No. It all seems pretty clear. Thank you.

Lois: (Long pause while I begin to see the next lifetime.) This lifetime seems to be in the early 1700s. You are a Native American, and I am unclear which tribe it is. I may get that later, but I am not getting that information just yet. You are a young man, a warrior, fighting against another tribe. The first thing I am seeing is that you are doing a war dance in a circle, preparing yourself for battle. You then go into battle and have a near-death experience. You were wounded, and left your body. You walked around looking at all the other wounded and dead people. Seeing a light, you moved toward it feeling the peace and immense joy in the Light, and were told that you had to go back. You were coming back into your body and deeply knowing that never again would you go into battle and injure or kill anyone. You needed to be healing people, not killing people. As a result, you had a complete personality change. Your own people had thought you were dead. They had checked your body, and left you there. The opposing tribe left you, too. When you awakened—and you had been unconscious for maybe an hour—your wound was spontaneously healed. There was still some tenderness and redness, remnants of a wound, but it healed so fast, that there was no trace of the wound by the time you walked home.

When you got home, from that point on you began studying with a nearby shaman. Your tribe had no shaman, so you went to another tribe, where there were a lot of familial connections. This shaman was a cousin. It took about two years, but you became a full-fledged shaman-healer and lived to be quite old for a Native American. You lived to be fifty-five, and passed on your wisdom to many other people. You had a special talent for healing war wounds quickly. You would just put your hand over the wound, and do whatever else it was you did with the rattles, the drums, the smoke and the herbs, and people healed miraculously. This was because you became a shaman by healing your own war wound, after having a near-death experience. Anything we have healed in ourselves we can more easily heal in others, according to shamanism.

Do you have questions about that lifetime?

Bob: Could I ask one about the previous one? Is any of the sadness from the previous lifetime coming through to now and affecting me physically?

Lois: Yes, this happens often. It happens especially if you are unaware of the past life situation. Once you know about it, it begins to heal. The sadness begins to heal, along with its physical manifestations. Now, you may feel it again for a few days after the reading, and remind me to tell you about apple cider vinegar baths, as they will help you in releasing the emotion quickly. We are going to move onto the next lifetime now if that is okay with you.

Bob: Yes. I am ready.

Lois: (Pause) I am seeing Atlantis, specifically the city of Poseida. Again, there you were a healer, this time in a temple. You are among the most elite of the healers, and your specialty was diagnostics. People came from far and wide to be diagnosed by you, when other people could not figure out what was wrong with them. You would tell them what was out of balance and which healer, or which temple to attend, and in what order they should attend them. It was rather like writing a prescription. You were extremely efficient. You saw a lot of people every day. It was a satisfying lifetime, but you were something of a workaholic, obsessed with the work. You overdid it. Knowing about that will be helpful to you so that you do not repeat that because there is nothing beneficial about obsessive behavior. Period. A person needs to be balanced. That is the main reason for you to know about that lifetime.

You lectured before huge crowds of healers on diagnostic techniques, regarding how you did it. You were also a teacher of diagnostics. You were not married but you did have—there was serial monogamy in Atlantis. In other words, you would be with somebody for a few years then that would finish. Everyone would eventually reach a time when a relationship was completed, and move on to somebody else. They had a completely different culture. They did not think they were supposed to be together for their entire lives. The best relationships you had were with other healers, because they understood that you had little time for a relationship. You had one child.

Questions about that particular life?

Bob: What were my duties as a diagnostician, what did I do?

Lois: Being a diagnostician means that you have to take a collection of details that do not seem like they have anything to do with each other, and see the pattern, see the relationships, and make a diagnosis (which is really just a guess). You try to come up with what needs to be balanced to heal that person.

Bob: I am good at spotting patterns mathematically, symbolically. My wife always tells me that she always sees me in front of a crowd teaching.

Lois: Well, it seems that she was there in one of those serial relationships, and was a healer as well. I keep waiting for her to have another relationship with you like parent/child or something but I have not seen that yet. (I pause again, looking at the next lifetime.)

Oh, my, this is nice! Every now and again we have something called "vacation lifetimes" for the Soul's rest and recreation. It is not that you have to accomplish or learn anything, but just relax and enjoy life on Earth because of the beauty and the pleasure and the joy of it. This is on the island of Bali. You were a healer and skilled artisan; you made exquisite ritual objects. You favored making sacred objects for other healers, and you did it for the pure pleasure and joy of producing gorgeous objects. This is how a true artist works, just for the joy of creating something beautiful. You did the work in a sacred and respectful way for how the objects would be used. You were married, this time, to somebody else. I do not see many married lifetimes for you, which is interesting. We usually see a little of both single and married lives. You had thirteen children in this life on Bali. You were playing catch up in the children department, I suppose. Before you came into this life, you said you had to have some kids.

This was just a lovely, relaxing, joyous lifetime, and your Guides wanted you to hear about that, because your lives have not all been filled with "trial and tribulation." They want to be sure that you know that you have also had some fun. You did win awards for the quality of your handwork. You were honored in front of crowds for the quality of your sacred objects which people used in healing...like magic wands, but not like that. I am seeing discs of some kind. And your Guides definitely wanted you to know about your great skill as an artisan of handcrafted items. This was a very long time ago...maybe a couple of thousand years ago.

Questions about that one?

<u>Bob:</u> No, I cannot think of any.

<u>Lois:</u> I am being told those are the lifetimes you need to see today. I feel like we addressed a lot, but not all, of the things you asked about in the beginning of the session. You need to assimilate these lifetimes before you get another past life reading. You will have a sense of when you get it all assimilated and are ready to do more of this kind of work.

<u>Lois' Notes:</u> Bob called a few months later to say things were definitely smoother between him and his wife since the reading. He explained to her about the past lives they had had together. She seemed to relax about his being unpredictable, telling him that she had always feared he would simply disappear and never come back, or banish her for no reason. Now she understood why she had felt that way. The past lives resonated with her strongly. Bob has studied some healing classes, and is planning to begin doing this spiritual healing work part-time as a way to fulfill his need to express his healing and spiritual tendencies. He has been practicing on friends, and is very excited about this new direction. A few months later he reported that the undercurrent of sadness he had been feeling was gone and he thought it was because he now knew about the life as a Roman soldier.

<u>Past Life Reading: Bobbie Tresor: February 11, 2008</u>

Bobbie wanted an Akashic Records past life reading because she was curious to learn more about herself. I had known Bobbie casually for a number of years as a client, but she lives in a different state, well over a thousand miles away. What follows is a long-distance reading.

Lois: The first past life that I am seeing is in Greece, at the Temple of Athena. You are a high priestess with thick, curling black hair, wearing flowing brightly colored robes which are cinched with a twisted belt that looks like a rope, but is made of a silky, soft fiber. This is ancient Greece, and it is approximately 450 BCE. What I am first seeing is that you are doing the ritual lighting of some kind of lamp on the altar to Athena. Oh, interesting. As I look around I see other priestesses. There are several people there whom you know from this lifetime, and one of them is me. I was one of the priestesses. One of them is your former daughter-in-law from this lifetime, Paige. She was also one of the priestesses. There were many other priestesses in your care, and you were our teacher, our leader and our healer. You were wise, strong and beautiful. We all loved you like a mother, and idolized you.

The Goddess Athena carried a sword. She represented the warrior spirit in women, and was assigned the duty of protecting the military among other things. A lot of the high ranking Greek military personnel came to you as High Priestess for advice and for protection, and you would pray with them before they went into battle. You also would create protective amulets for them, and for their soldiers, and you led something similar to prayer vigils on behalf of them and their armies.

I see you living a very long life, and retiring at an advanced age. These particular priestesses did not ever marry. So the younger priestesses functioned like your family. You remained on the temple grounds in a special house until the end of your days, taken care of and honored by the younger women. Spare time in retirement was spent mostly with consulting with the younger women, and gardening. It was a long and happy life. You wanted to know, out of curiosity, about some of your past lives, so this is the first one I have seen. If you were here I would let you ask questions, but you are not so you might want to jot some questions down as you listen to the recording. If it is not too long after I have done the reading, I can probably go back in and answer the questions. Okay, let us go on into the next lifetime...You were happy in that lifetime by the way. You were deeply fulfilled, doing that job. Okay, I am going to move on to the next lifetime. (There is a long pause.)

Next I am seeing you addressing your troops. You are a man in this lifetime. I see you on horseback, preparing to lead a charge into battle. You are what we would call an Englishman now. This is about the thirteenth century. You are seriously weighed down with heavy armor, and sweating profusely inside of it. It seems most uncomfortable. I am not sure precisely when this occurred, but I identify the era usually by looking at the costumes. At this point in time you are trying to repress a Scottish uprising. Eventually Scotland became free, but this is when they were not; they were under British rule or the rule of the King of England somehow. You were successful to a point but ultimately that war was lost—not this particular battle, but the war. I am not getting your name. Yet I am getting that you had a loyal following, and that your men loved you. You were an outstanding leader in battle. Never would you ask your men to do anything you would not do yourself, and you yourself always led the charge.

You married and had six children. You had a good deal of money. The king compensated you very well; yours was a high ranking. You were not killed in battle, but lived to a ripe old age, happily and safely on your country estate. There were many grandchildren. You lived to be about sixty-five years of age, which was old for those days. (Long pause)

So now I am seeing your next lifetime. From time to time we have what we call "vacation" lifetimes where there is not anything in particular you are trying to accomplish; you just get to reap your rewards. I am seeing you again as a man living in a rural setting. It was far from anybody else. Your wife was the man you are married to now. Patrick was a woman then. You had three children. Hand weaving was your wife's trade, and twice a year you would travel a great distance to the nearest town with an open-air market. Many people would come there. It was a semi-annual event, spring and fall. You would sell your wife's woven goods there, which were unusually soft and colorful. She had made a name for herself with these exceptional woolen weavings. You had animals which look rather like large goats, and that is where the fibers came from for the weaving. That was the source...that and some plant you grew. A small amount of the woven fibers came from the plant.

At home your main job was to plow the fields with some kind of animal... this is a very long time ago. I simply do not recognize these animals. They seem to be rather a cross between a hairy ox and a cow. This was a beautiful climate. It never got deeply cold or terribly hot. You had a gentle, pastoral experience, and just raised your children.

There was no war, there was no pestilence nor was there famine. It was an idyllic lifetime. You both lived to be old, given what was considered old at that time. This looks like a semi-tropical climate, but there were mountains in the distance, and not a lot of jungle around, but it was that kind of warm climate.

Oh, I see! This is rural Lemuria. Of course, this is a long time ago. No wonder I do not recognize anything. Far away in those mountains was a sacred cave where the whole family went every year and other families joined them for a ceremony which celebrated rebirth. You would go down deep into a cave, reminiscent of returning to the womb, and emerge on the surface at dawn on the first day of spring. Everybody would emerge together and celebrate. There was some sort of astrological event where the light of a certain star would align in a special way to the cave. (pause) Sirius is the star, as it turns out. The light would hit the back wall of the cave in a certain spot on that day, and there was a major celebration. Everyone looked forward to it each year.

Mostly all around you, I see nothing but huge expanses of meadows and fields. There are few roads, but the roads which they do have are paved with beautifully decorated, hand-carved stones which have been hand laid in intricate patterns. These were laid quite a long time ago, way before your time. Mostly people walk, but they can also ride these strange animals which look like a cross between an ox and a cow, and also they plow with them. That is all I am seeing for that lifetime. That countryside and civilization is breathtaking; the air is pristine and the sky so clear! I wish I could make a film of that. It is visually stunning. Okay, let me see what other lifetime you may have had that you need to know about. (Long pause)

This is most unusual. This is fairly rare, and I am always surprised to see this kind of thing. I am actually seeing what may be one of your future lives, or else a lifetime from the distant past, one in which we have no record of the civilization. There is some kind of space vehicle which you are aboard, but it does not look even remotely like anything I have ever seen before.

The craft is sort of like an orbiting man-made object. It has a most long orbit and is extremely large. You are female, and in charge of this strange craft. The shape of this spacecraft is somewhat like a bowl with wings, as viewed from the outside. It is silvery in color. The wings do not move; they are fixed. On the inside, it has its own ecosystem; its own recycling, self-renewing air supply, as well as small bodies of water, which are fresh-water lakes. This ship is quite like a small moon. It is absolutely huge. People live inside of it, and it has gardens, trees, fields, such. Its long orbit takes many thousands of years, passing through numerous different galaxies.

The people are human-looking, and on this craft, they live to be quite old. As they go past certain planets, they can stop and get off to visit for a while. They go shopping, and sell some of their goods as well. Plus they do a lot of teaching. They have small, short-range transport aircraft that come out of the main spaceship, and people utilize them to come and go from this craft to other planets. This is one of those situations where people live to be one to two thousand years old, so you really get a lot done in each lifetime. The civilization is quite advanced as a result of the great wisdom people are able to garner over having such long lifetimes each time they incarnate. Their fine arts are extremely sophisticated, too, and they place great importance upon art. The designs of the architecture, furnishings and clothing are exquisite! I wish I had time to just study these. Artists are highly valued and respected.

You have a specific mission on this orbiting "moon" spacecraft—to spread civilization throughout the cosmos. So make of that what you will. You have a family; three husbands, or three men with whom you have children, and there is no sense of "ownership," or possessiveness. Because you are such a high-ranking officer and important person, you can have as many husbands as you desire—only they are not husbands in the way we understand the term "husband." They are men who are devoted to you, but not exclusive to you. They do see other women. Husband in their context is like a committed supporter, or a permanent alliance. They support you in every way, and they father your children. Because people live to be so old, it is considered rather ridiculous to think that one person is going to stay married to just one other person alone for two thousand years, so these people are interchangeable. Sometimes you are with one man, sometimes you are with another one. They have special friends on the side, too. I see that this is also a long and happy life. Now I will be moving to the next lifetime. (Long pause)

I am seeing you on board a sailing ship, and it is a very unusual sailing ship. You are a woman. You are an Egyptian female, and wealthy. This is an opulent setting. I am not sure when the time frame was, but I am seeing this big, pleated-looking sail and the boat itself is made up of very tiny planks of what looks like bamboo strips. This is a most handsome craft. You are taking a pleasure cruise down the Nile into the sea and going to visit some of your far-flung settlements. The group is taking a tour. You were a powerful, important political figure, a member of the Pharoah's family. In other words, there was a male and you were the female counterpart. A Queen, sort of, but what I am hearing is that you were also a Pharaoh. The man and the woman were both Pharaohs. At least that is what they considered it then. It may not be what the history books say now, though. I am unsure. You have six children. All of them are healthy. One of them died before he reached adulthood. He was poisoned, but it was accidental. He went on a hunting excursion and somebody mistook one plant for another plant, and they were eating the berries and several people were killed, so he was not targeted. It was an accident. He came back as your son in this lifetime, too. He is the younger son in this lifetime.

The man, your partner, who was the male Pharaoh in that lifetime you do not know in this lifetime. You did meet him in passing once, actually, in Washington, DC. He was a very high-ranking official and you knew there was some sort of recognition like, "I know you from somewhere." He felt it too, but I do not think there was any conversation to speak of other than, "How do you do. It is nice to meet you." It was all business. There was not supposed to be a connection made in this lifetime. Your karma with that person is finished, which is why you felt that intense feeling, but nothing happened. He just passed through, because we do not usually want to get involved again with somebody with whom karma is completed. It is rather like backtracking, because unfortunately, you can always create new karma with them. And then you would have to spend who knows how much time balancing your karma all over again.

He may have been there, in Washington, to support you in some way. He may have helped you, or been there to promote your career, but it would have been at arm's length, whatever he did. You might have not even realized that he did anything for you. I am unable to tell if he is a high-ranking government official, but I want to say that he might have been military, too. But I am not quite positive, you know; he might have been in the federal government and ex-military, I feel it is some combination of the two. It is hard to say. A long, happy life again was your experience in Egypt.

I am getting that this is all you need to hear at this time. Usually people get past lives where they drew an incorrect conclusion and they need to know about it so they can get some healing done, and what I keep getting from your Guides and from mine is that this is not what you asked for nor what you needed at this point in time. You just needed to know more about yourself.

Email me if you have specific questions, and please do so within the next twenty-four hours if you can. The after-experience for me is that it is like waking up from a dream, and the longer you wait, the fewer details of the dream I will be able to recall from the reading without going into a trance again.

Lois' Notes: Bobbie emailed me that she found the reading fascinating, since she seemed to have had a lot of lives involved with the military and that is what her life has revolved around this time, too. She said a lot is going on in her private life right now, and she did not know if she would have been able to integrate anything difficult, but she did want to know more about herself, and that is what she got. Next time she gets a reading, who knows what will show up.

Past Life Reading: Candi Petrovski: April 11, 2007

Candi, who had short, curly, dark brown hair and a slight frame, walked with a barely perceptible limp due to her having been injured as a child. She was a married, middle-aged woman with two adolescent sons. She was an accomplished sculptor who also had academic training in a technical field. In explaining what she wanted from the reading, Candi said that she was simply curious about her past lives with her two teenaged sons, her husband, and her good friend who lives in Iowa, Bertha. She was also open to whatever else her Guides wanted her to hear at this point in time.

(I explain what to expect during the reading, that the most important to know about will show up first, and I pause to begin seeing the past lives.)

<u>Lois:</u> The first thing I am seeing is you as a lovely, quiet young girl, alone in a rowboat. It is a very calm body of water, as clear as glass. Hardly anyone ever goes out here, which makes it quite peaceful. There are large round rocks all over the bottom. You are dressed in peasant garb, but it is tidy and clean. You are not a fancy lady. This appears to be somewhere in the 1600-1700s. (Pause) Late 1600s is what I am getting, and in what is now known as Great Britain—England. It is your day off from work, and you are rowing on this little fishing pond; you dearly love doing this. You adore the peace, the serenity, and the calm. You are trailing your hands in the water and the water is not deep. You could stand up in it if you wanted to. You are just floating gently along, relaxed and allowing yourself to be in a deeply altered state.

You see something very strange. At first you think you might be dreaming. It seems to be a woman, lying on the bottom of the lake. You realize what you are seeing, that the person on the bottom of the lake is a very fine lady who has apparently killed herself by drowning. The water is so shallow, that this could not have been accidental. You are the first to see this corpse. It is very upsetting for you, causing immediate trauma. You are not sure what to do about it. Finally, you gather your wits about you, and decide to row back to shore and tell somebody about it. You were a small woman, and not strong enough to lift her into the boat. And besides, the boat was too little to hold the both of you. You went around excitedly telling people that there was a very fine, dead lady on the bottom of the lake. I am thinking you must have been young—thirteen to fifteen—and you repeated to everyone that something must be done. Nobody believed you.

This is shocking. Absolutely nobody believed you; not one person ever went out on that lake to see for themselves, and there were certainly no fine ladies around those parts. They all thought you were imagining things, or making up a wild story. It was not until perhaps a couple of years later before people found out that a woman from a neighboring estate—it was far enough away that nobody in your neighborhood had heard that she was missing—had simply disappeared one night and nobody understood why, or what had become of her. In the meantime, you went out there several more times over a period of weeks, and looked at her. You were just forlorn, because you could not get anyone to believe you. In the meantime she was decomposing. You could not get down to the body, and were frightened to try anyway, and the long and short of it is that you went mad. Every time you went out there the body would be a little bit more decomposed, and you just did not know what to do. It drove you slowly mad, and ultimately you fell into the water and drowned, because you completely fell apart mentally and emotionally.

The reason you need to know about this, is that it is extremely important for you always to trust your own perception, and not listen to other people.

You are on the brink of things beginning to happen in your life that you again cannot prove using conventional means, and most of the people close to you are not going to believe you. This is because these things that are coming to you are of a metaphysical or spiritual nature, and you must be careful whom you tell about these things. At the same time, it is extremely important that you trust your own perceptions, and know that what you perceive is perfectly valid. You are to remember that your perceptions are more important than what other people have to say about what you have perceived. Trust yourself!

Do you have any questions about that lifetime?

Candi: Do people know where I am? Important people? Or does my body just decompose there as well?

Lois: Of course they found you, because they knew you were missing. Your family knew you were gone, and then there was that lonely little rowboat out on the lake and empty. But where you fell in was a different spot than the fine lady's location. So it was still a while before they found out why you had gone mad, and then the whole village grieved that they had not listened to your story.

Candi: What was my name?

Lois: Let me see if I can get that information. Your first name was Ellen, but they called you Ellie. McWhorter was the last name.

Candi: What did I do for a living?

Lois: You did something with your hands like weaving or spinning. This caused a lot of calluses to form on your fingers, which is why you liked leaning over the edge of the boat, trailing your hands in the water. It was so cool and comforting. (I pause as I see the next lifetime come into focus.)

I do not know if you have ever heard of this before, but it is widely believed that large numbers of people incarnating on the planet at this time came from other star systems, and for that reason have many past lives on other planets. What I am seeing right now is you coming from somewhere else to Earth in a spaceship, not to incarnate, though, but to colonize. Your group is from the Pleiades and doing genetic experimentation, not in any kind of negative way, but in a "trying to be helpful" kind of way. They are doing this with the permission of Earth's Planetary Logos.

You functioned like the ship's psychologist almost, but not exactly. You were one who helps everybody stay in balance on long voyages. Also you worked with people on the ethics of how to treat beings which are not as technologically advanced, beings from other planets. On the ship with you is Arnold (Candi's husband in this lifetime). As a matter of fact, he is in the command center with three other people and two junior persons. There are three people who make the big command decisions, if these are ever needed. So, he is in charge. You work for him, and that is all I am getting. You had a past life aboard a spaceship with Arnold and he is your lover. Your name is Zara. This was a passionate love that you two had, and the passion lasted an extraordinarily long time. But I do not think anyone on the ship was married as we understand marriage. The culture does not appear to sustain that kind of thing. Apparently, the people lived to be very, very old—like a thousand years, so nobody makes a lifetime commitment, but they do have long-term relationships and he was a very dear one of yours.

Questions about that one?

Candi: Was I a female?

Lois: Yes. He was a male and you were a female.

Candi: The other people on the ship, were they anybody I know?

Lois: No.

Candi: Anything about... actually we came to Earth, did we not?

Lois: Yes, you came to help the beings on the planet evolve by sharing some RNA/DNA with them, so this must have been a long time ago. I am getting that this was approximately ten to twelve thousand years ago.

Candi: Did we give our own personal genetic material, or some we had with us in vials from our planet, or what?

Lois: No, The Guardians are not going into that kind of detail... but they are saying that as a result, we Earthlings are not monkeys anymore! (Laughing) I know they worked with us, but that is the extent of the information I am being allowed to see. I am not getting any more than that. That is what you needed to know about him. That is one of the places you have known your husband before. (I pause before going on to the next lifetime.)

In the next life I am seeing you are in a group of three young men going off to war together on horseback. This is a period of time which predates anything we are aware of having existed. This period is not anything in our recorded history. These three young men are of about the same age. They are blood relatives, perhaps cousins, and grew up together. These young men are you and your two sons in the current lifetime, Candi. You have apparently been together in multiple lifetimes as equals. It is unusual for you to come in as a parent to one another, so if you have any feelings of camaraderie with them, or if it seems to be more like a friend-based relationship than most people have with their children, this would be why. I see you doing a lot of horse riding in parades, a lot of long-distance trips with large groups of men. It has the appearance of an army, but is more informal than any army I have ever seen. These men rode wherever they want to go unless they are in a parade. There were feathers and scarves and things blowing in the wind behind them, part of the uniform. You three spent a whole lot of time having fun, going to places where people danced and drank alcohol. You also viewed entertainment which was put on by female dancers. It was quite a long time ago, and I am not seeing anything that looks terribly familiar, other than the people on horses, with scarves and feathers. The houses are very strange-looking. They look rather similar to adobe, but they are very rounded. I do not see any right angles anywhere.

Do you have any questions about that lifetime?

Candi: No. But my sons and I do have a wonderful, egalitarian camaraderie. That is definitely true.

Lois: The purpose of that was to let you know one of the situations in which you have been with your sons before.

Candi: Okay, this it is nice to know, and it rings true, but I cannot think of any questions.

Lois: (Pause) I see you in a large building, in which you are doing what looks like some sort of ritual. It is not a religious ritual, but yet it is ritualistic in the sense that what people go through to fire up a submarine when it has been in dock for a while is a ritual, or the checklist pilots go through before taking off in a commercial jet. It is that sort of ritual; a precisely timed thing. (I pause to watch the scene unfold further.) You seem to be making something that has to do with an energy form. Yet you put together things that look inert. They do not seem to have any particular function; they just look like pieces. This is quite hard to describe. It would be like if you saw somebody putting a car's engine together, but if you had never seen a car before, how could you describe what you were seeing? Let me say, you are putting together some very big things. You are with another person, and you both are connecting and assembling this thing. While you are co-workers, there is something more to the relationship than that. It is like you two made a lifetime commitment to some sort of project, and you are doing this together.

I think this might be during the time of Atlantis, but I am not sure what the precise culture was. This is technology I have never seen before, so it is hard to describe, but there is some sort of triangular thing with curved corners, and then from up under the center of it comes this really intense beam of light. Accompanying the light there is a particular, special sound. To get this device to work, you pull on this part really fast, so nobody will know what made it work. This was very secretive work. Later you would hide the parts in different places. One of the locations is inside a cave, and the other two are in places nobody would think to look for sophisticated equipment. They are in a barn or something similar.

It appears as though you are involved with a rebellion. This is equipment that is going to subvert other equipment. This other equipment is being used by the powers that be; corrupt governmental forces it would seem. There are a whole lot of people in the civilization, ordinary citizens, who know how to astral travel and/or do remote viewing. The governmental powers have shields up to block ordinary people from astral traveling, or shamanic journeying to do remote viewing to see what the government forces are up to. It is believed they are up to some diabolical tricks. You have created some equipment that will break the shield. Naturally, stealth is involved.

Somehow, someone that you trusted and told what you were up to and who was supposedly going to help you, betrays you to the governmental powers. The two of you are executed publicly for leading this insurrection. Then, your own people hailed you as major heroes, martyrs to the cause. If your project had worked, things would have turned out very differently in the history of the human race. It would have worked, too, except for the actions of this one traitor. The traitor is somebody you now know, but I am not getting who that is. I am hearing that you do not really need to know. Not to risk starting up more karma, the information is not being revealed as to who this person was.

So what happened next was that eventually you two were taken to a place of public execution. You stand next to each other holding hands. Very suddenly a gigantic beam of light incinerates you both. Poof! It occurs in an instant, with all those people watching. Somebody swept up the ashes, and put them in the dustbin. That was your ultimate punishment—being relegated to the dustbin. But the ashes were swept together for the both of you. Your remains were conjoined

Have you any questions about that lifetime?

Candi: There is no way to know who the traitor was?

Lois: We are quite pointedly not being told who the traitor was.

Candi: So I am not supposed to know?

Lois: That is right.

Candi: And we were both friends, or were we lovers?

Lois: I do not think that you were lovers. I think you were intimately close friends, and the notion about a physical relationship would come and go, but you were both so focused on the task at hand, that neither of you wanted to risk failing at the project by becoming involved in that way. Wisely, you knew that it had the potential for distracting you from the more important goal. I think it was probably an unspoken thing, sort of an understanding between the two of you that this might happen once you got certain things accomplished, but then they were not accomplished.

Candi: Was I a young woman or an older one?

Lois: You were sort of middle aged, not young girls, but I would say the equivalent of what we are like in our thirties. You were not terribly young. You were old enough to know a lot about technology. It looks like you were scientists, or perhaps engineers.

Candi: And this occurred a long time ago?

Lois: Yes, and this would have been a long time ago, toward the end of the Atlantis era, whenever that was. Again, you suspected something funky was happening, and you were trying to find out what was going on, and the government just executed you for even trying to find out.

Candi: And what was the point of that lifetime?

Lois: The point of the lifetime....is your knowing more about past lives you have had with your friend, Bertha. You came in asking about her. That lifetime can totally explain some of the connection—the deep sense of connectedness you have with her. I am getting a strong confirmation of that. I am told that you go way back, both together and individually as Souls.

Candi: Yes, that explains a lot, if she were Bertha.

Lois: And also you needed to know that you two were crusaders together to change things, to try to make significant things happen in the world.

I am told there are no further lifetimes for you to hear at this time… except, I keep hearing this same sentence over and over. I am going to say it anyway even though it does not make any sense to me in this context, but I see you with a brush in one hand and you are brushing the ear of an animal. I cannot see the rest of the animal, and I am seeing what looks like a gigantic rabbit ear. But I am not sure what it is. The sentence is, "Trust in God, but tie up your camel." So maybe it is a camel's ear. (Laughs) I am feeling like it is symbolically referring to that last lifetime that we spoke of with you trying to create technology to eavesdrop on the government forces, and about trusting people who may betray you later.

Candi: In another past life reading I had, I lived in the desert. It might refer to that.

Lois: It might. But I hear it as a warning. Trust, but take precautions.

Candi: I am to be on alert? Is there someone I cannot trust?

Lois: Trust God, but tie up your camel means yes, trust in God, and at the same time, remember to take reasonable precautions. In other words, be careful. Lock your car. Wait until you have known someone a long time before giving him or her the "keys to the castle".

Candi: And I am brushing the camel's ear? What could that mean? Did they have brushes in Atlantis, do you suppose, where would the brush come from?

Lois: Well, I suspect universal tools like brushes go way back like knives and toothpicks do…

I then smile at Candi, and turn off the recorder.

Lois' Notes: Not too long after the reading, Candi reported that strange and mysterious things were indeed happening in her life. But this time she was being careful not to tell the wrong people—those who might tell her she was crazy, or just refuse to believe her perceptions. She said the past life regarding the drowning of the fine lady and her subsequent madness had been helpful in deciding to trust what she was perceiving without needing anyone else's belief or approval.

Candi was gratified to learn that her husband had been with her before, and knew why she felt so committed to him, even when things were not going smoothly between them. She knew they were Soul mates.

I later heard from Candi that there had been what she considered to be a terrible betrayal by her friend, Bertha, and Candi was deeply hurt. I wondered then if that was why she had been shown the past life where there was a betrayal before, and Bertha had been present, but it was not clear who had instigated the betrayal. I said nothing to Candi, though, fearing it might be even more upsetting to her. When we are ready for a realization, it comes to us.

Past Life Reading: Demi Jacobs: August 22, 2009

Sheila, the mother of teenaged twins, a male and a female, wrote me from another city that her daughter had experienced the spontaneous recall of a past life as Edith Piaf, the famous French singer who died in 1963. Edith was a tragic figure who had a very impoverished and difficult early life, and despite great success as a singer and mentor to other artists, made some bad choices later on in life. Sheila was concerned that Demi was being overly affected by the emotions and memories of Edith. I agreed to do the reading at a distance, although I normally would not do a full Akashic Records past life reading for anyone under the age of eighteen. If a lifetime comes up to be balanced in BodyTalk or EDINA sessions, that is different, in my view. The individual's innate wisdom has requested it in that instance. I made an exception in the case of Demi, only because she was having such powerful emotional "blowback" from a prior life, and suffering. Here is the transcription of that long-distance reading.

Lois: Demi, I normally would not do a past life reading for anyone under the age of eighteen. However, you are only a few days from your seventeenth birthday, and because you are having emotions that are bleeding over from a spontaneously recovered past life, I am doing this reading. It is hoped that by knowing more about a few of your other past lives, you will not be so overwhelmed by this one tragic past life. The main reason I am agreeing to do this reading is because these memories and emotions from your past life as a famous singer, who made a lot of mistakes, are interfering with your current lifetime. I am hoping that this will help you heal.

One of the reasons we do not usually remember our past lives is that we all deserve to come into each lifetime unencumbered by memories from the past such as sorrow, fear, pain, anger, resentment and so on. If we recalled all our past lives, many of us would spend the entire current one trying to "get even" with old enemies, or in dealing with other long-dead issues. The purpose of each lifetime is to achieve for ourselves certain goals our Souls set for themselves in the planning stage before each lifetime. We can learn our lessons more easily if we have a fresh start, free of the entirety of our past life baggage.

Once I had a dream, during a time of turmoil in my life, in which I was driving a bus. Someone had arisen from the back of the bus, walked to the front, and tried to take over as the driver. I told my teacher, William, about this dream, and he asked with alarm if I had allowed the other person to take over. I said that I was tempted, but had not. William said, "Don't let anybody get up from the back of the bus and take over and drive for you. Those are your past lives back there, and none of them have the right to take over and run this lifetime. They have had their turn, and now it is yours." I relay this story to you, Demi, because I believe it is quite relevant to you at this time. It is important that you create your life on your own terms, and that you not let any of your past lives take over and overshadow the person you now are, and that you may become as you mature. (I pause to view the first past life for Demi.)

The first thing I am seeing is you as a lieutenant in the American cavalry. You wore your blonde hair long, and you sported a handlebar mustache. I see you out in the prairie, riding on horseback; you and about seven hundred men are following the man who is your commanding officer, General George Armstrong Custer. Custer is definitely a headstrong and arrogant man. He is heading for the Battle of the Greasy Grass, as the Native Americans termed it. You were about twenty-four years of age at this time. The scouts are coming back, looking extremely worried, and warning everyone not to proceed, because the Lakota Sioux are more than ready for you. You and several others discussed turning away and leaving the procession. This would have been desertion, and the only reason any of you would even consider this was that you feared your imminent death. Yet you all so feared disgrace and hanging, that you were unable to make a decision to leave. All of you kept talking about it, but doing nothing, and you just followed along in the procession. The battle finally occurred, and you and all of your fellow soldiers died in that historic battle.

The thing you need to know about that life is an understanding as to what the lesson not learned was. Your Higher Self wants you to know that when someone else is leading, and you know they are wrong, step up and do something about it. You and all your fellow officers were supposed to "break out of the box" and leave. If you had, the entire battle might have been avoided.

All it takes is a few people to say, "This is madness; we will not do it," to change the course of history. Others will follow.

You drew the conclusion as you died that time and that life was pointless. This was the wrong conclusion. Life is not pointless. You felt that you had no choice but to die for no sane reason, but you did have a choice. It was just a difficult choice. That choice was to step into your power and walk away, or to die. You chose to die. (I pause as I look at the next lifetime.)

Now I am being given more information on the lifetime on the singer, Piaf. Your Guides want you to know that the reason she made the bad choices she made in her adult life was that she had been addicted to drugs. There was an automobile accident which deepened that addiction, so that others then learned about her addiction, but she had been an addict for a very long time. This is part of the reason she had such bad things happen to her. She made bad choices because her judgment was impaired by the intoxicants. Your Guides and the Guardians of the Records want you to know that you have had this weakness in your past, and for that reason, it is imperative that you avoid drugs and alcohol at all costs in this lifetime. Your Guides and Higher Self say that addictive substances are not something you can afford to experiment with this time around. In many peoples' lives, addiction brings on deep tragedy and Edith Piaf's life was no exception. (Pause)

Next, I am being shown an ancient civilization, which was in existence so long ago that it is prior to our recorded history, and no traces of it still exist. There are no writings about it; they were destroyed when the Library at Alexandria burned.

I am seeing you in some kind of flying contraption, which looks a lot like a motorcycle, but it flies. There is some kind of horizontal bar that goes across your back at your shoulders which has a luminous, flowing, ruffled fabric, which I can hear flapping in the breeze. The bar and the fabric helped with balance. It is also connected to the vehicle, at a spot down by your feet. You are leaning forward to cut down on wind drag. This is a purely recreational vehicle; you were not on any kind of spy mission or anything, just having fun during your time off from work. You are a young, strong, physically active, and highly-educated woman. You are all alone buzzing across the water, laughing and having fun. The shore is nearby, but you are flying all alone. I am pausing now to ask why The Guides are showing me this lifetime. (Pause)

Oh, how odd...Suddenly a gigantic animal, now long extinct, which was immense like a whale, but capable of jumping up out of the water, spied you and your vehicle. He took you for a strange bird, flew up out of the water, and swallowed you and your vehicle whole. (I begin to laugh.) It did not kill or wound you, but it appears rather comical, and your Guides are laughing, too.

The vehicle slammed into the back of the creature's throat/stomach which was largely hollow inside. The tissue at the back where the flying machine stuck was quite spongy, and allowed for a very soft landing. You plunged into the small lake that made up the stomach contents of the creature, and splashed about in that smelly stuff, quite angry. Everyone had been assured that these animals had not been spotted within many miles of shore for scores of years, so the animal's being there was infuriating.

You remained in the belly of this creature for two days, jabbing the creature with one of the horizontal bars from the craft, trying to get it to let you go. The vehicle remained stuck in the back of its throat. Because the animal was almost hollow inside, you could actually see out when it opened its mouth above water, and hoped to escape. It always had some air at the top of the stomach, to aid with its strange, slow digestion. So you could breathe, but the air was foul and gaseous.

At the end of the two days, the animal was sufficiently irritated by the vehicle stuck in its tissues, that it vomited you out near the shore of a far island. The vehicle, however, did not budge. The animal sees you, but runs the other way. (I laugh again.) You swim to the nearby island, mostly underwater to get clean from the goo inside that creature's belly.

Two days is a long time to travel, and this island was far from your home. When you arrived at the island, you stepped out of the sea wearing clothing very different than the inhabitants of the island. Your civilization's technology was so advanced over their technology that they could never have made such garments. So here you come, stepping up out of the ocean, wearing otherworldly garments. The people are in awe. Here you are; the answer to their prophecies of a gorgeous, strangely clad goddess stepping out of the ocean to bring them gifts and teach amazing things to advance their civilization. The prophecy said that she would be bringing them great prosperity; they hailed you as this goddess!

You were given lovely, yet simple, clean new garments, and a comfortable place to live with a breathtaking view of mountains and sea. You were waited upon hand and foot. Suddenly you went from being an ordinary woman with a regular job, to being someone that everyone else revered, and even worshiped. And so you decided to fulfill their prophecy. They were good people, and treated you well, and you decided to do the best you could to be what they needed you to be. You brought to them a good heart, filled with kindness and generosity. One of the things you taught them was how to weave more complicated fabrics. In the best interest of health, you taught them to always cook raw meat. They had been eating raw fish, and had horrible parasites as a result, so you improved their health by teaching them to cook their meats, including fish. Also you taught them how to create pottery from the soil and how to fire the pottery in fire pits in the ground. What seemed like simple things to you were totally amazing to them, like tattooing as a form of body art, which you also introduced. This island was somewhere around New Zealand.

You married and had children there, living a happy, fulfilled life. To this day in myth, they still talk about the goddess who came up out of the sea and brought a higher degree of civilized life to the people. At the end of your life you decided that it would be best if they did not see you die, since you were a goddess. So in the dark night of a new moon, you got on a raft with ample provisions, and decided to allow your raft to float out to sea to find a new island. What happened is that you were swept far out to sea by a current, and lost at sea in a storm. But that was okay with you, because your people could then maintain their myth about you. They never found out that you were not divine. They assumed you went back to the realm of the gods. Even in your own death, you honored the culture of these sweet, primitive people.

There was nothing dishonest in letting them believe you were the goddess in their myth. You had realized soon after arriving that you actually were the person in the prophecy! You realized that this is how prophecies are fulfilled; some ordinary human answers a divine, spiritual call. And this was what you had done. (I pause to see the next lifetime.)

I am seeing a life spent almost entirely in a convent. You were a nun in the 1400s in Italy. In that lifetime your assignment agreed to before incarnating, was to use your singing voice, and the ability to write music, as your spiritual tool to bring people closer to God. It was to this work that you were totally devoted. You have been a spiritual worker in many past lives. You went in to the nunnery at age fifteen, and mainly wrote music for your entire life. People were using the Solfeggio scale in those days, and your music sounded rather like the Gregorian chants, which were written in that scale. Many of the songs you wrote can be found in the archives of the Catholic Church. You only lived to be about thirty-three years of age, because disease was rampant in those days, and people did not live long.

The Guides want you to know that you have had some powerful, important spiritual lives so you get the bigger picture of who you are. (Pause)

Next what I am being shown is a lifetime in Nazi Germany, in which you were a guard in their army. You were sent to one of the concentration camps, when they first opened, and no one told any of the soldiers what the true purpose of these camps were. You were there at the trains watching the families being torn apart, men and boys sent to one section of the camp, and women and girls to another. Asking around for a few weeks, you began to realize that people were being murdered en masse, and buried in mass graves. Something welled up from deep inside your Soul, and you knew that you could not do this. You just could not be a part of that horror against humanity, and you told your superior officer, who just laughed in your face. He told you that you had better follow orders, or you would be hanged. After a few days, you woke in the middle of the night, knowing what you had to do which was to put on your civilian clothes and sneak out of the camp. You were apprehended in a town not far from there, and taken to jail as a deserter. Eventually you were executed. If you had not walked away, you would have died at the same time anyway, from some other cause.

This was the whole purpose of that lifetime, to not follow blindly any authority figures. From the vantage point of the Soul, this was an exemplary lifetime. You died as a hero! You stood up in the face of sure death, gave your life as a proof of the fact that there were, even in the middle of this horrific genocidal war, people who were honorable, moral people who would not stand aside and participate in monstrous things being done to innocent people. The story of your sacrifice filtered up to the higher reaches of the military, and was one of the inspirations for the attempt on Hitler's life.

This lifetime in Nazi Germany helped mostly to balance the one from General Custer's time, and yet your Soul wants you to be aware that never again must you follow authority blindly. This is one of the things you will be tested on in this lifetime again.

This concludes your past life reading for today. Email me if you have any questions.

Lois' Notes: When someone experiences what I call emotional "blowback" from another lifetime, it can be very powerful. The potential is there for it to overwhelm the person emotionally, as I have also experienced personally. This can happen when we either remember the lifetime spontaneously, or are regressed without the benefit of a capable therapist. It is important not to allow past lives to overwhelm the current one, as that person has had their turn at life, and now it is ours. We must "drive the bus," so to speak, and not allow the people in the back to take over. Otherwise, we run the risk of not accomplishing our Soul's purpose in this lifetime.

Demi's mom reported, and Demi confirmed, that the greater view of who she had been in other lifetimes took the edge off her preoccupation with the sad lifetime of Piaf. She returned to her normal teenaged life, but with attention to her spiritual development. Demi was able to continue her interest in a singing career without having the shadow of Edith's tragedy and her addictions looming over her.

Past Life Reading: Denise Brown: June 24, 2009

This is the transcription of a recorded long-distance past life session done for Denise Brown, who lives in Nevada. She sent me a photo of herself.

She wanted to know more about her late husband, who died early due to alcoholism, and her first husband, Ben, and who he was to her in past lives. She also wanted to know if she is on the right path spiritually at this time. That last question is not one that is often addressed by a past life reading, but I was open to clues to that showing up in her reading.

Lois: The first thing I want to do is to clarify why we do past life readings. One major reason is to help us remember things about ourselves that we have forgotten. A reading can explain a lot to us about our personalities, as well. The past lives can explain recurring patterns in the lifetime of a given individual, and they can also explain hidden talents, and inform us of heroic acts from past lives. Knowing these kinds of things can help us understand why we are with certain people, have certain interests, or aversions, and so on. One of the things the reading might also explain is experiences we had decided to have during this incarnation for the purpose of learning specific lessons—lessons we might have wanted to master in this lifetime. It may include all of those, or just one or two of them. The reason the reading only covers some of these is that the Guides/Higher Self are taking advantage of this rare opportunity to communicate regarding what it is that only they would know. For example, which things that one most needs to know at the time of any particular reading are covered first.

Now, if you were actually physically in my presence, what I would be doing is having you lie down on my treatment table, face up, and I would be putting my hands underneath your head with my palms on the back of your head. I would be doing this because that is where the portal to your Akashic Records is located; it is in the occipital region of the brain. The palms of our hands have mini-chakras in them, which function like eyes. If you have ever seen any of those Tibetan Thangka paintings you might have noticed that there are eyeballs in the palms of the hands and feet of the gods and goddesses. This is due to the fact that Tibetans also actually practice shamanism. Especially the Bon sect, they still practice shamanism in concert with Buddhism. These paintings show the eyes in the palms because these people have the memory and the understanding that the chakras in the palms of the hands and the palms of the feet function like eyes. We can put our palms onto people, and then see inside their bodies. (Pause)

So now I am doing that. Using a remote-viewing technique, I am placing my hands on the back of your head. I have you in my treatment room in the inner planes on my treatment table. Now, as I do this reading, in between the lifetimes there will be long pauses. I will cut those out. I will pause this digital recorder that I am holding. I do this so you do not have to listen to long silent pauses while I begin to view the next lifetime. (Pause)

In the first lifetime I am seeing, you are a man in the era of...in what looks like the 1300s or maybe the 1200s. You are a British soldier mounted on horseback and you are fighting, trying to quell an insurrection by the Scottish people who are under British rule at that time. You are fighting against the rag-tag army of William Wallace. You are emotionally torn about the war, as many soldiers are. You are quite conflicted because there is a deep place inside you that does not believe in war. What is more, this part of you especially does not believe in using superior wealth and military might to take away money and freedom from other human beings. You have a sense that people have a right to support their families and live in freedom and govern themselves. You were not actually raised that way, but deep down inside, you knew it was true.

So after killing a few people you just could not take it any longer, and you stopped fighting, announcing this to your fellow troops, hoping that others would stop as well. However, immediately you were knocked off your horse and run through with a sword. The man who killed you was extremely puzzled, because you put up no resistance. From your Soul's point of view, that was an act of heroism. So it is a bright and shining star in your crown as a Soul. The decision not to fight anymore and to allow it to end at a Soul level is viewed as heroic. This is because you were not a married man, and you were not leaving a wife and children behind. Your refusal to participate in fighting was the only way you could see to get out of this particular situation. You hoped to be an example, and that everyone would do the same, so it is not considered a suicide.

Having been conscripted into the military for a very long time, against your will, you saw no other honorable way out. The only way to avoid killing people you thought had a right to do what it was they were fighting for the opportunity to do, was to stop fighting. That is called doing the right thing from the higher perspective of the Soul. (Pause)

In the next lifetime I am seeing you are a female. You are located around what would now be the border between Italy and France. I am seeing a field of lavender, and this belongs to the family. Your family business was that you grew lavender for the purpose of distilling out the essential oil to be used as medicines and as perfumes. This is a vast, fragrant and lovely field of lavender.

I see you as a young woman loving the Earth, loving the flowers and walking along with your arms outstretched, breathing in the wonderful scent, looking up at the clouds almost in a mesmerized trance; a rapturous state.

Suddenly you stepped on a snake and it bit you, and you were all alone out there. Snakes were pretty rare there, but it was warm and one had come out to sun itself. Because you were alone and in a moment of intense joy, you suddenly shifted gears and were shocked into terror. Your heart beat much faster and the snake's venom killed you rather quickly. As you lay there dying you drew an incorrect conclusion. You decided that it is not safe to let go and get into a rapturous trance; it is not safe to let go and just be in the moment and enjoy yourself, it is not safe to experience joy or bliss. None of those things were seen as safe because at that moment, you could be attacked from out of nowhere. Therefore, on the Soul level, you have some resistance, whether it is conscious in this lifetime or not—you have a resistance to going off into a trance in meditation for example. There is a great deal of anxiety at the thought of just letting go. It might even translate to the intensity of orgasm might elude you, or there might be anxiety if you allow yourself to let go, like, "Uh-oh. What dire event is it that could happen if I just let loose and surrender in this moment?"

What you need to know, from the vantage point of what your Higher Self hopes that you learn from listening to this, is that it was just time for you to leave the Earth plane when the snake bit you. It simply was a quick way for you to leave. You had accomplished everything you intended to in that lifetime and your early demise as a teenage girl brought lessons to the family. This was an agreed upon event prior to incarnating, and it was in the timing that was agreed upon prior to incarnating. Yet at the moment it happened, your personality resisted. Consequently, this negative experience was imprinted on the Soul. What is hoped as you integrate this past life, whether it takes weeks or months to integrate all these past lives, is that you will gain the understanding that everything happens for a reason, whether we can see it in the moment or not. Many times things were agreed upon before we came to the Earth plane, and we cannot recall them at the time. It is hoped that you will come to see again that it is safe to go into a trance. It is safe to let go and feel intense, deep joy or complete abandon and pleasure. That is all we are to see and learn from this lifetime in the lavender fields. (Pause)

I am seeing the next lifetime now. I see you in Atlantis as a medium-build, muscular male with reddish hair, working in some kind of factory which manufactured metal parts that had to do with some sort of machines that make war. They do this through creating discordant vibration. This is a technology with which I am not familiar. We do not have anything similar to it. You were like a spy or mole of some kind. You were sent there by another organization and the organization you worked for had vetted you carefully, and thought you were on their side. And in fact, they would send you to spy on the other side. Yet you were really representing the other side. When you were manufacturing these metal parts, you were quite clever about changing the tolerance of the metal so when it gave off the vibration, it only disrupted people's thought patterns instead of driving them insane, which is what these vibrations were supposed to do. It was a form of warfare that attacked the minds of the enemy. You could not render these machines completely useless, but you could render them only slightly harmful instead of devastatingly harmful.

You spent many years undercover there working very hard behind the scenes on behalf of humanity, successfully undermining the efficacy of these machines of war. Eventually you were found out, and you were scheduled to be executed, but a woman posing as your girlfriend came into the compound where you were being held. She slipped to you an instrument that allowed you to escape. Again, the technology utilized vibrating metal in such a way that whatever was locking you in was released. You could create frequencies that opened locks. You did manage to escape, and you were just dumbfounded that this escape was actually pulled off successfully. You thought you were going to be executed. There you were prepared for death, and then you managed to get away. Your rescuers were waiting outside for you with a disguise, and you were whisked away to a very far off land.

You were taken to a place where there was a group of people taking crystals to a specific cave the United States, and they were hiding a lot of highly sophisticated crystal technology. In fact, they left some of their transport vehicles there. These transport vehicles could change in vibrational frequency and move through rock as though it were water. They are still inside that cave somewhere. So are all the crystals. Anyway, that is where you retreated, and no one could find you, because no one in the government in Atlantis knew about this secret location. Those who did were some of the priests who were trying to save part of the culture, because they knew there were serious problems, and that Atlantis was about to suffer a great loss.

Again, you exhibited a lifetime of heroism, but as a spy. Only this time you got to survive it, and you went on to do your work far into old age. You died of natural causes. Of course, the purpose of knowing about this lifetime is to know that you are capable of working on the side of the good no matter what the cost in personal terms, on the side of that which is right. You are able to sacrifice yourself if necessary. In that lifetime you were able to do that, and yet escape the clutches of the dark forces.

Just as I was prepared to look at the next lifetime, what I saw was the person who helped you escape from jail, who posed as your girlfriend, did go on to the secret cave with you. And in this current lifetime, this same Soul incarnated as your husband who passed over from alcohol. In the prior mentioned lifetime you eventually became a couple. You happily spent your old age together.

I got a little flash of several lifetimes that you had with your first husband, and that there has been a lot of conflict in those past lives. The general theme of most of them has been that he took advantage of you in some way. You loved him unconditionally, and he took advantage of you. He was not telling you the truth about everything. (Pause)

In this next lifetime I am seeing that you were in Egypt but there was a sort of tropical feel to it. This must have been a very long time ago in what is now Egypt. You worked as an attendant at a temple. There was a body of water in which lived some amphibious beings from the star system, Sirius. They are human from the waist up and fish from the waist down. You can see images of them in the ancient artworks; they are depicted in various ways like on pots and bas reliefs. There were many different races from Sirius, but this is the primary one that came to Egypt. And they lived in the water which surrounded the Sphinx back in those days. You were one of their attendants, and that was considered an enormous honor. These Sirians came to educate the people of Egypt, and they did transmit a lot of really important information before they all went back to Sirius.

In the next scene what I am seeing is a man, who was your first husband in this lifetime, who came from far away and was unusually handsome. This is one of his patterns. He comes in, and he is extremely attractive in some way either personality-wise, or physically amazing, or something like that. He doggedly pursued and seduced you in this Egyptian lifetime, and his purpose was to make contact with these Sirian beings you were serving. There were people from far away—and he was sent from far away—who wanted to destroy these beings from Sirius, because they thought the Sirians were giving your culture an unfair advantage over everybody else. They feared that you would be dominating them. They were projecting onto your culture what they would do if they were in the same position of power that these beings from another star system seemed to be giving you. Of course, it did not work because the Sirians were so much more advanced. They were telepathic, and knew exactly what was going on in the plot against them. They quietly observed the whole thing unfold, and saw to it that the man's plot was discovered. However, the experience for you was that you felt horribly betrayed. You did not lose your position, but you learned a very valuable lesson.

What I am hearing is that in this current lifetime, you have managed to finish your karma with him somehow, in the way that it ended this time. He no longer mesmerized you in the same way. You did not get betrayed to the level that you could have if things had continued. I am not sure how that relationship ended, but there was a positive reason it ended. And whether or not it ended with your conscious intention, or whether your Higher Self engineered it against your conscious will, I am not sure. It was a potential betrayal that may never have happened, but you had a little bit of karma to finish up with him, and it involved not having some sort of major disaster occur. What bits of karma you had left with him were resolved, and now you can be friends at all levels. At the Soul level you can be friends, and you do not have to incarnate together again.

In fact, it is often best if you do not reincarnate together again once you have completed your karma together. (Long pause)

I am seeing one more lifetime. Yes, I am being told there is one more you need to know about, and it is again as a man. You were living in the Urals, a mountain range in Russia. You were a gem cutter. People would dig gemstones out of the mountains and you would facet them. You were very gifted at that. You did not make jewelry, but you would draw jewelry designs and somebody else would execute your designs. You were the one who could do that most difficult part, faceting the gemstones. You had to know a lot about geometry in order to do that, and to be able to see things that were inherent within something. You could look at a rough piece of stone and see the possibility of the faceted gem within. That is one of your skills from the past into which you could tap if you wished. You need to know that you have the ability to see the possible in something that looks really rough, whether it is an object, or whether it is a person. You have this inherent ability, deep within your Soul, to visualize what is possible, and to bring it forth. You also would have an easy time learning about gemstones, both precious and semi-precious. So if you are attracted to those, there is a reason. You were, I am being told, especially attracted to the light as it came through the stones. You were fascinated with the different colors of light, and you had an ability to see a huge range of color in light. Some people do not see the subtle differences between colors, but you do.

I am told this is all you need to know about your past at this time, and if you have questions about this reading, email me and I will answer them to the best of my ability. If I told you more, you would have trouble assimilating it all.

Lois' Notes: I knew almost nothing about Denise prior to the reading, as she had contacted me via email after listening to one of my BlogTalk radio shows. After the reading she emailed me again to say that in many ways, the reading had been quite specifically on target, though she did not say in what way, except for two items. She said that she related a lot to what I had told her, "especially the second lifetime about not feeling safe to experience JOY… huge in my life. I have a hard time really letting go and having fun. Thank you so much for your time and this amazing reading."

She also stated that she uses aromatherapy in her work, and that she almost daily uses lavender, having a deep emotional connection to the scent, but never before knew why.

Sometimes this limited kind of report is all I get to hear, simply that the reading was on target and "explains a lot." The point of the reading is to help the client, however, not to benefit me, and so I am fine with this.

Past Life Reading: Hannah Chappel: June 23, 2006

I explain to Hannah the whys of past life readings, and then begin talking with Hannah about what she wants to get from the experience of opening the Akashic Records. Hannah wants to know what in the past might have contributed to the head injury that she sustained in college, and if a past life contributed to the inherited Meniere's Disease she has had to live with which is periodically so debilitating.

Lois: Do you have any particular questions about recurring patterns or certain persons in your life before I start?

Hannah: I notice that I am a very aggressive person. If that comes from somewhere else, I would like to know, because that trait does not always work to my benefit.

Lois: Okay. We will see if that comes up. So there is not a particular person in your lifetime right now that you would want to know about?

Hannah: Leah. Leah is about the only person. I have had a new man in my life very recently, but he is still new enough that I am… (her voice trails off)

Lois: So new you are not convinced it is worth checking into?

Hannah: Right. I would like to know about him, but I think I already know where it is going. I need to calm down and stop being quite so assertive.

Lois: Assertive is good. It is aggressive that is not good. Assertive is telling people what you want, and stepping back and allowing them decide what they are going to do about it.

Hannah: Yes, and I am definitely crossing the line into aggressive.

Lois: Aggressive is when you Karate chop them when they do not give you what you want.

Hannah: Yeah. I am not quite that aggressive, but I have crossed the line past being assertive, so I need to calm down and see what he wants to do.

Lois: …in his own good time.

Hannah: Exactly.

Lois: I am seeing you as a man. He is a miner. He works at a very large mining concern in North America, what is now the United States but the location was in one of the territories then. It was the early 1800s. Your job is to handle the dynamite and do the blasting, and you are training somebody to help you out. The job you did was to tamp things into a hole which had been drilled into rock. The tamping device was a metal pole. You are training this other man, and the charge accidentally goes off and the metal pole sticks him in the head. Instinctively, you pulled the pole out. He could function, but he was never quite the same again. His personality was utterly different, and not for the better, either.

This is something that really bothered you, and it was not your fault. He was not following instructions, but you still felt responsible. If you have a heavy-duty sense of responsibility for other people such as they must not get hurt, or if you are overly concerned about how other people are doing things, this could be part of why. This feeling dogged you the rest of your life. You never got over it, and you did not live much longer than that, maybe ten years, into your early forties maybe, but still, you never got over those feelings. You worried yourself sick that people were going to get injured because you did not tell them enough, or you did not watch them closely enough. It was something of a stark, sterile lifetime. I think the purpose of that lifetime was to learn some independence. Never finding time to get married, you just traveled around a lot blowing things up, which you actually enjoyed. You were a one-of-a kind guy who would take risks, and the purpose of that lifetime was to learn to be purely independent. And you did!

Yet the accident with your trainee cast a pall over everything else you might have gleaned in terms of positive experience. This was not so much because of the accident as much as your reaction to it. Taking responsibility for something that was not your fault was an inappropriate reaction. This was because it was just so horrific to look at the guy with the metal pole sticking in his head, and admit you had no control over anything. That was too scary, the realization that we do not control most of what happens.

Hannah: I do overcompensate. I do definitely try to protect people. I am extremely independent in this life so it is definitely a carry-over.

Lois: Well, you are finishing the task.

Hannah: I probably hurt myself in some areas because I am so independent. It took me a long time to understand, and to ask for help.

Lois: Well, the guy who was helping you knew what was going on. You were training him to be your helper, and that is why you are afraid to ask for help now. You have carried a fear that bad things will happen to those who help you.

Hannah: Any time anyone ever hurts themselves when they are trying to do something for me, I always feel horrible about it. Yeah. I can at least understand where it comes from now.

Lois: So you can let go of it now, if you choose, because it was not your fault. You can look at it from the perspective of this lifetime and say, "Well, he was not following directions. He got injured. It was not my fault. He was being careless and not listening." Your name was Harold in that lifetime. (Hannah murmurs "Okay.") Sometimes the names come up and sometimes they do not. (I pause waiting to see the next life.)

I am seeing you as a male, in your teens. You are riding a sled in a snowy, mountainous region; I think it is in what is now called Scandinavia. I think you raced sleds in the wintertime for money. People are betting on you. These are the types of sleds that you sit in and ride down the hill. It is kind of like skiing where, depending on your skill, you might go faster than somebody else. You may also know how to make the sled smoother on bottom, or aerodynamically in sync with speed. You have some straps attached to the front of the sled, and then going to your hands, and then wrapped around your wrists. This way, you can put pressure on the front of the sled with both feet. It is an interesting setup. The back is wide open. You are going amazingly fast down the hill, and nobody could beat you.

I see that you were winning all of this money, and it is not amateur racing. It is professional sledding. It looks like it happened about three or four hundred years ago. You were an inventor, and had developed a super-fast sled. I am being told that it is in a museum somewhere. The Guardians and your Guides want you to know you have some important experiences as an inventor in your background. You completely redesigned sleds, and changed sledding, which at the time was extremely significant. If you think about it, at the time, all they had were horses really, no cars, and if they had a good sled that went faster, it was far easier to transport things. They would use a sled drawn behind a horse in snowy weather. You also created a company that made sleds, so you had done quite a bit of blacksmith work.

You had four sons who also joined you in the business, and it became a really big business. This was successful for generations. You did some very important wealth-building things. Besides being an inventor, your Guides additionally want you to know you had some major accomplishments in being in business for yourself. Why you need to know that, I am not sure, but you have those abilities to draw on should you want to.

DO you have any questions about that lifetime?

Hannah: I think it is also trying to explain my personality as part of what is coming through. I get a pretty good visual that it possibly explains some of the aggressiveness, too.

Lois: You were not to be beaten no matter what it took.

Hannah: I can be extremely confident in my abilities, too. I think it is helping to explain some of my personality. Now I better understand why I am the way I am.

Lois: I think you have a few lifetimes that have to do with conquering the wind. I do not know if that means anything to you or not. The sledding lifetime was about conquering wind drag as much as anything. I am seeing another lifetime as a quite successful sailor. You were the captain of a big clipper ship, and you really knew how to trim the sails to make it go unusually fast. It totally amazed everybody who worked for you, and everybody who hired you to move their goods from one continent to another.

You just had a reputation for being able to outrun all the pirates. It looks like you were again into racing, only then you were carrying goods and made more money hauling materials. That was possible, because you went faster than other sea captains did, and it did not take you as long to get there. So you could make more runs, and more money.

Something caught fire in the hold of your ship one day, and you were maybe in your late forties when this happened. There was a wounded sailor caught underneath some wooden boxes, knocked over by a little explosion which happened right after the fire started. Nobody could get him out. Boldly claiming that you would not leave the ship until somebody got him out, you went down below and worked at freeing him yourself. Sending the others into the lifeboats, you stayed there toiling to free him. Eventually, you went down with the ship. The sad thing is you did not have to, because no one could get him out. He begged you to go and leave him there, but you would not do it.

So everybody got off the ship, and I guess they want you to see this because they want you to know that was not necessary. Sometimes discretion is the better part of valor. In other words, you thought it was being honorable to die because nobody could get the guy out from under the boxes, or crates. But it was not necessary. It was just wasteful of life. To think about it, there was no reason to die and leave all those men at sea in all those little dinghies without a leader. Your first mate took over, but you were over the top with being responsible. You were thinking, "If he cannot be pulled from out of there, I am going down with the ship." Questions about that lifetime?

Hannah: No, but again, I think it is totally in sync with who I am today. It explains a lot about my personality. I am still that guy.

Lois: But now you know there is a limit to that kind of "taking responsibility," right?

Hannah: Yes there is.

Lois: Those were quite a lot of lifetimes as men. Let us see what else is in here. (Pause)

I think you come from a Soul Group that really values independence. I am seeing you as a woman and you are from what is now called Russia. You adore dancing and are very athletic. You wear a lot of red and yellow together. Wearing ruffled skirts and a hat that was sort of cylindrical with tassels which dangle, you traveled around the countryside for many years in a wagon. Selling was your primary money-maker, and you sold or traded things like metal tools, and this was approximately five to six hundred years ago. You also loved to entertain children. You had children of your own, but did not want anything to do with a husband. Children and dogs, these were your family, and you completely ran the show. There were a few people working for you. Erecting a tent and a stage everywhere you went, you needed extra people and wagons. You lived in one of the wagons with your three kids and the dogs.

You had four live births, but one child died in infancy. This was a little boy who was run over by a wagon. You had asked one of the older girls to watch him, and she got distracted. A stinging bug flew into the wagon. The older girl was trying to get it out of the wagon. The baby got excited and fell out, and was crushed under the wagon's wheel. You did not have any more children after that. The pain was so horrific from that, you vowed never to have another child as long as you lived, because it made you too vulnerable. And I am wondering if some of that carried forward. Perhaps this is a vow that you might now consider releasing. You still had three other children, and you were a good mother.

So, again, you were independent, traveled around entertaining people, trading tools to help them in their work, while making them happy and giving relief to the drudgery of their lives. In addition to arranging the occasional dance, your people had a puppet show designed for the village children as part of the entertainment. All in all, it was a very pleasant lifetime, except for losing the child, which cast a cloud over everything thereafter. You never even started to get over it. You have trouble letting go, apparently, when bad things happen. It is important to accept the lesson of moving on and letting the past go. I am seeing you grieve far too long, and too strongly. You hung onto the grief in that life in a way that was not healthy for you or your other children. They needed you, and you were not emotionally available any longer.

Hannah: I need to learn to let go of grief?

Lois: Yes, grieve until it is gone, and go on with your life, do not stay stuck there. There is nothing glorious or honorable about wearing your losses on your sleeve.

Hannah: Yes, again an issue of mine.

Lois: What is the person's name you spoke of earlier? Laura?

Hannah: Leah.

Lois: (Pause) I am seeing one life in Egypt where you two were lovers, and she was a woman. Actually, she was a slave, and you were her owner, but you were also lovers. You were the male, and she the female. It was painfully difficult because you wanted to marry her and have children with her. As it turned out, you had children with her anyway, but you were unable to marry her. It broke your heart that she could not be treated like everybody else's wife was treated. In fact, your family forced you to take a legal wife. You have some real affection for her in this lifetime as Leah, and that is why you get to be buddies, and not have the stress of being lovers. So if you had some heartache about her, or have feelings that you really need to do right by her, it may be about that lifetime. I sense that you always make sure she is okay, and that you feel that you have to protect her and make sure nobody mistreats her. That is from the Egyptian lifetime. However, she is a big girl in this lifetime, and can take care of herself, okay?

Hannah: Okay, got it. Logically, I know I do not need to protect her. She is ten years older than I am, and has a good job. And what do I need to know about Drew? He is the guy I met three weeks ago, and it feels as if something definitely is going to happen, and I need to know...

Lois: I saw some flashes that let me know that you have been with this person before, but I am also hearing one of our Guides—I cannot tell if it is yours or mine, but I think it is yours—that the mystery must unfold. To know too much too soon is not good.

This is the end of Hannah's reading.

Lois' Notes: Immediately Hannah's old head injury began to heal and was significantly better after this reading. She found that she soon got the money to begin having regular energy medicine healing sessions with me. The money just showed up magically after Hannah "put it out there" that she wanted money for energy medicine sessions. She experienced even more healing of the side effects of the head injury, as well as her inherited central nervous system disorder of Meniere's disease. Her personality began to soften and she was much less aggressive in that masculine way. The relationship with Drew came and went quickly; there was karma to balance with him. She remains geographically distant from, but friends with, Leah.

A few months later, Hannah met the perfect man, who thinks she is the perfect woman, and as of this writing, they are still together.

Past Life Reading: James Green: June 4, 2009

James came in for a past life reading because he was facing both certain career and major personal life crossroads. He wanted to get a better idea of what factors might be at play from the past which would impact these decisions. He was hoping to gain insight so he could make a more informed decision; I was sincerely hoping he was not expecting the reading to make his decision for him, and yet I had a sense that this might be the case. He also was having difficulty leaving his work at work, and not bringing those issues home with him.

I told him what he could expect to happen during the reading, and then began...

Lois: I am seeing what I first thought was a camel, but this is actually an elephant. I am seeing that you are being carried along in a howdah, a type of saddle which they place on elephants' backs...you know, they have chairs in them. You and one other person are there, on the elephant's back. This occurs in what is now Pakistan. Those borders have moved many times over the years. I am hearing this is approximately five hundred years ago. You are a man comfortably slouching beside a woman on the back of this enormous elephant, taking a leisurely ride. This is the first time I have smelled an elephant in a reading. It is a pleasant, musty smell.

You are on a journey, not a long one, but you have gone from one town to another. There is somebody walking out in front of the elephant; it is an elephant handler carrying a staff. I am seeing that the Earth starts to shake, just as you are preparing to cross a stream. The Earth begins to shake harder. Rather than stop and dismount, you decide to get across that stream really fast. Why you decide that, I am not sure. But the decision was made to get across the stream quickly. It was not very deep, maybe three or four feet deep. Yet I am seeing that the Earth opens just slightly beneath this stream, as the Earth will do at times in an Earthquake, and it closes back up again. The elephant's foot gets caught in the crevice that was temporarily created during that brief opening of the Earth, and the animal gets stuck there. I do not understand why, but a big wall of water then comes down the river and seeing it, everybody freezes up in panic.

Nobody knows what to do, and the next thing happens very fast. And it was truly a freakish thing to happen. You both are swept off the elephant by the water. The elephant cannot go anywhere and drowns, of course, because she is stuck, but you tumble and tumble through this dirty water, this rapid flow of water convinced you would drown. The water's movement is the opposite of an undertow. There is this big tunnel of water which shoots the two of you upward. The woman, by the way, is Nita, your current wife. You have been with her before.

The water shoots the two of you up onto a bank, a muddy, steep slippery bank and you are holding onto a tree, surrounded by loose debris and bodies. There is a huge volume of water swirling very near to you, ready to reclaim you both if you lose your grip. Your wife is holding onto you. You have one arm clutching onto the tree, and the other arm gripping her, and she is clinging to you.

Eventually, it becomes clear that you cannot hold onto that tree with one arm any more. You tell her to hang tightly on to you, because it takes two arms for you to maintain your grip on the tree, due to the weight of both your bodies. So she does hang in there for a while. But there comes a point where you have to decide, when she starts to lose her grip and slip, are you going to let go of the tree and allow both of you to go back into the water where you will die? Are you going to grab hold of her and slide back into this horrible, violent torrent of water that is roiling and filled with vast amounts of debris? Still there are things being swept under and things being shot up by the violent action of the water.

This water activity is a direct result of the Earthquake. You decide there is no point in two people dying, that you are going to go on and live, so you hold onto the tree with your arms. Still you are trying to hold onto her with your legs and feet, and you know it is not working. Finally she looks at you and says, "Please let me go. I am tired. Just let me go. It is all right. You hold onto the tree." The two of you had children. Someone had to take care of them, so you needed to live.

You never got over that horror of losing her. You beat yourself up for the rest of your life, repeating possible alternate scenarios in which you could have somehow saved her. Daily you thought about it, and second-guessed yourself and tormented yourself. You lived twelve more years, and you tormented yourself each day of that time. There was no absolution for you.

What your Higher Self wants you to know about that situation is that sometimes, I am hearing the phrase, sometimes you just have to "cut your losses" and not feel bad about what you cannot control. She told you not to feel bad about it, and yet you did. This is not saying that you have to let go of her again, but this is saying that if you cannot do the impossible, do not beat yourself up. Do not torment yourself day in and day out for not being able to do something that no living human being could have done. You kept replaying the scenario, "If only we would have gotten off the elephant before we walked into the river." You do not know for sure if that would have saved everybody. Your Guides and Higher Self want to be sure you understand that you did the best you could at the time, and you did need to just let her go. You were supposed to let go of beating yourself up. Self-recrimination is not helpful. So do you have questions about that? Do you have a tendency to beat yourself up when you do not do things the way you think you should have?

James: In my professional life I cannot let go of what I have done. I think about it and even if it is regarding very small things, telling myself, "I should have done more..."

Lois: That is partially where that personality trait comes from. It can be expressed in a lot of different ways, and apparently it is expressing through work at this time.

James: How did you know it was Nita with me?

Lois: They tell me. The spirits who are called the Guardians of the Akashic Records tell me. They explain things to me. Are you ready for me to go to the next lifetime?

James: Yes, I am.

Lois: I am seeing you in Spain in the twelfth century. You are a Catholic priest and you are walking—you are doing a pilgrimage. You are leading people on a quest on a sacred road through the Pyrenees Mountains. This takes many weeks, and it is exhausting, but you are a dedicated leader, and you are taking these people on a sacred journey. They are people who have actually paid a lot of money—not to you personally, but to the church—to go on this exquisite pilgrimage. There are really just the most beautiful, inspiring views, and there are not any big cities along this road, just little villages. In the midst of this splendor you become ill. Everyone encourages you to stop the procession for a day or two and rest, but—and here is the thing—you are on foot, and I am not sure why, but you felt strongly that you had to remain out in front of the procession on foot. I feel that perhaps it was the tradition that the priest should be out in front, leading the way. Given the terrain, on foot was the only option in this particular era.

Therefore, you will not stop and rest. You feel like you have this sacred, holy duty to get to a certain point by a Holy Day, and you keep thinking you will get better. This is why you will not stop and rest. You actually become feverish and delirious, and still adamantly refuse to stop to rest. Eventually, you just collapse and the group is forced to stop. Still, you are not getting better so you tell your assistant to take the group and move on. You take refuge in a private home in one of these little towns, and are cared for by a local resident. They do not really have any healers nearby, and you just keep going from bad to worse. You had developed some infection that would have been difficult to combat anywhere. That kind of thing killed people in those days pretty easily, and you took about three days to die. While you were there you kept coming in and out of consciousness thinking this was insane. What am I doing here dying? It is so crazy. It is so pointless! And you were just so confused.

It seems amazing to me that you could not put two and two together. You had difficulty in drawing conclusions based upon the effects of your actions. You kept saying, "I do not understand." It was simply that you were too driven. The lesson lies in the fact that you did not stop to rest when you were sick. I am seeing the theme here, which is you need to know when to lay down your burdens and rest. Learn to take care of yourself, because if you do not, there will not be any self left. But you did not figure that out at the moment. In the moments before you died you were just confused. "I do not get it. What happened?" You did not ever admit to yourself that your actions might have been flawed. There seemed to be a lack of the normal ability to see the relationship between cause and effect.

Do you have questions about that lifetime?

James: No.

<u>Lois:</u> One of the things I'm being told is that you have a spiritual tendency to begin with, coming from past lives. At least, there is an interest in this.

<u>James:</u> I have a question, on that past life, with the spiritual aspect, is that something that is a theme for me? Have I had a lot of past lives as a priest or some other religious figure?

<u>Lois:</u> I only see one lifetime at a time, and I wait. Your Guides are showing me a spiritually oriented trend here; sometimes Guides will do that. I am not being shown a trend for choices of careers in your past lives. Not at this time, but as things unfold we might. (I pause as the image of the next lifetime forms.)

I am seeing you as a musician and again, a lifetime in Spain where your family had immigrated, and you are Jewish. The Jewish people were starting to have difficulty in Spain by the time you became a man, so a whole lot of them masked their practices, and only practiced at home in secret.

Then a vast number of them began immigrating to Mexico. I am next seeing you in Mexico, playing a guitar in a group, and honest to goodness I am seeing people dance around a big hat, just as we are accustomed to seeing in movies from the 1950s. That is what you did for a living. You traveled with a group of entertainers. There was one woman and four men. I think you are all brothers and sisters. No. One of the men was not your brother, but two of you are brothers, and then the one woman was your sister.

So, you did your spiritual practices in secret there as well. You celebrated your holidays and spiritual practices in private. The types of prayers you sang, and your ritual objects, all that you kept secreted away, out of fear of death. That is just the way it was back then. Many followers of various religions have been in this situation, much like the Christians in the catacombs of Rome.

For a long time Spain was tolerant of Jews, then they stopped being so. That is when Jews started to obscure their practice. Apparently you were the equivalent of a Rabbi in that life. You settled squabbles, and you taught from the Torah, but again, it was all undercover and secret. That is how you spent your life. You were a musician in the daytime, and you would travel around to other groups of Jews who were looking forward to your showing up very much. Rabbis were rare. Camouflaged as a traveling minstrel, you were really traveling Rabbi who brought light into a whole lot of people's lives. You helped them with their spiritual work, and were assuredly well known in underground circles. It was a very successful lifetime. Your sister was, by the way, Nita again. The same Soul incarnated as your sister that time. So, I am not seeing that you need to know anything else except that you were a very helpful, successful, loving, preeminent Rabbi who settled disputes and taught from the Torah. Do you have any questions about that?

<u>James:</u> No. I guess that is just the second example of spiritual…

Lois: Why yes, that is the second instance of a spiritual leaning, although it is also an instance of creative, musical propensities, too.

James: Any messages about Nita in that life?

Lois: She was your sister. That is all I am hearing. You and your brothers and sister got along really well. You worked together every day and seemed to never have very much in the way of discord.

Are you ready for me to go on to the next lifetime?

James: Yes, please do.

Lois: I am seeing another lifetime as a male. You were a short, muscular man who wore glasses and had tattoos and curly, light brown hair. You are in the U.S. Navy during WWII, and are an airplane mechanic. More than anything you wanted to be a pilot—it was an anguished longing. You would dream of flying, but you never got to do it. You did your absolute dead-level best to make sure those planes were in perfect condition, though. Everything you did was positively to the best quality you could do, because you were keenly aware that other people's lives depended on the quality of your work. The other sailors called you "Chaplin" even though you were not a Chaplin. You were a mechanic. Yet you were always circulating among the crew with your Bible, and talking to people and counseling them, and earnestly working to keep their spirits up. You read to everybody from the Bible every night.

One day there was a fight with the Japanese. Your ship was kept in the South Pacific. The Japanese aircraft, called the Zeros, came flying overhead and strafed the deck, hitting your people. For some reason you were above decks that day, not down in the belly of the ship. You were shot and killed that day in WWII. From a Soul level, you were very pleased with that lifetime, because you did your ultimate best, and you were only twenty-two years old. Yet in spite of your youth, you did an excellent job. You counseled and supported other people spiritually to the best that you knew how as a lay Chaplin. Actually, you threw something out in front of another crew member, which knocked him down, when that Japanese Zero came overhead shooting. You did it to force him to take cover, and you threw yourself on top of him. That guy lived, and went on to have a big family, so that is a massive gold star on your crown, so to speak, as a Soul. Your Higher Self wanted you to know about that; your family in spirit is very proud of that lifetime. Have you any questions?

James: Other than that, was I supposed to learn anything from that? Did I make any mistakes?

Lois: No, this is being shown to you to make you are aware of this really powerful, successful lifetime; and once again you had spiritual leanings. No, you just needed to know what a great job you did, so you can pat yourself on the back. You were truly a hero. Your spiritual family is proud of that, and wanted you to be aware of your achievements. Any other questions?

James: No.

Lois: Okay, I am told those are the lifetimes you needed to know about today. I suggest that integrating those may take up to three months. Some people come regularly for these readings every three months. Other people spread it out a lot farther than that, but I am going to recommend that you listen to the recording a couple of times, as you feel guided, to help you integrate this.

The reading is complete.

Lois' Notes: That day, after the reading is over, it is clear that James wants to discuss the material with me to help him decide what he is going to do next in his life. He seemed to be hoping that the reading would tell him exactly what to do. I tell him before the tape is turned back on, that one of the things he could conclude from that last lifetime is that you can do your spiritual work and have a day job, too. That is what the shamans do in indigenous cultures. They work the fields, plant the plantains, cultivate the tobacco, raise babies, cook food, build huts or whatever the job is, but when somebody is sick, they will make a ceremony in the evening, and heal them. They get paid for that—whatever people can afford. But they also have a day job, so it does not have to be either/or. It can be a combination of the two. In fact, I think that is probably going to be a trend in the future. We have a lot of people who are part-time healers now. In this way, no one is financially dependent upon there being sickness in their neighborhood.

Plus, that is really hard on the healer's body, to do psychic or energy healing work all the time. It is really better if the shaman/healer has a day job, and just does some healing work part of the time. He/she will live longer, and will not get emotionally burned out. It does not look to the uninitiated like this kind of work takes that much energy, because the healer is mostly just sitting in a chair, but it is actually exhausting! Psychic energy takes a lot out of the practitioner. (I turn the recorder back on.)

James: I do not know how these lives apply to my current life, though, except I have been spiritual.

Lois: Well, yes, one of the things you now know is that you have had several lifetimes where you did spiritual work like a priest or Chaplain, and that you also have been a mechanic. What do you do now?

James: I am a structural engineer and I work for Halliburton. But you knew where I work, right?

Lois: Yes, but you could have been an accountant, a manager, a salesman, or a variety of other jobs at a company like Halliburton. But you are not doing any of those other jobs; you are a structural engineer. And so, are not a mechanic and an engineer a little bit alike?

James: Yes. I guess they are.

<u>Lois:</u> So, that shows you have a history or habit of working with machines, which explains abilities you have in the current life. This is significant information, and some people would see this as something of a confirmation of the validity of the reading. And that young sailor did both of those, his spiritual work and a day job working with machines. But you would have to be able to leave work at the office when you return home, in order to be able to do two different things. The sailor and the rabbi both could do that. You could consciously draw upon their strengths in that area. You said in the beginning today that you were having trouble with creating this separation between work and home life, so that would be why that issue came up in this past life reading, I feel. It came up to let you know you already know how to do that, if you just draw upon their strengths. It is not a recurring lesson, but a past strength.

<u>James:</u> Oh, then I could do that, if they could. That is what you are saying?

<u>Lois:</u> Yes, you could "mine" those abilities, or draw upon them. The famous writer Lee Carroll, who channels Kryon of Magnetic Service, says that this is something we are coming into as a race of beings, the ability to "mine the Akash". This means that we will increasingly be able to draw upon our past life strengths.

<u>James:</u> You have mentioned about the traumatic lives, and yet my lives were not that traumatic, you know? The first one there is the separation portion of it, but in the second one, there was not anything about my dying and the last one there was the shooting...

<u>Lois:</u> Well, in the priest lifetime, the second one, you did die because you refused to slow down and rest when ill.

<u>James:</u> Oh, yes, that is right! I forgot about that...

<u>Lois:</u> And you got shot dead in one of them. Some people would think that was violent, the one where you died in war. And there is the fellow who is in the earthquake, followed by the horrible flood and near drowning, and because he fails, and cannot hold on, his wife dies. He never gets over the loss. Some people would think that was violent or traumatic, but you are not interpreting it that way, so that is kind of...(and he is shaking his head, no). I am wondering what your idea of trauma is, James. (He laughs softly.) A lot of this has to do with interpretation, and I do try not to re-traumatize people. I try to tell about the past lives in such a way that my clients are not going home having nightmares and screaming.

<u>James:</u> So going forward, what would you suggest I do with this material?

<u>Lois:</u> Well, listen again to the recording of the session, which I will email to you. Allow it to gradually sink in to a deeper level of your psyche. Remember it is not all supposed to be about trauma. In the lifetime as a rabbi, for example,

you needed to know about your spiritual leanings and heroism. In that job as well, you had a dual function. You had a day job and still were a spiritual leader. This dual purpose is true of the lifetime on board the aircraft carrier as both mechanic and lay-chaplain. Past life readings are not exclusively about trauma, they can also be to help you understand who you are in many contexts.

My opinion is that it takes up to three months to fully integrate all the knowledge and lessons. For some people it takes considerably less. You have heard some new information today. Allow yourself time to integrate whatever it is you need to integrate. You can remember it again at your own pace. You know now what happened in a few of your past lives. Listen to the tape whenever you feel guided to do so.

James: Yes. I will. Thank you very much for this, Lois.

Past Life Reading: Jessica Hipplewhite: November 6, 2008

At Jessica's request, we are asking to see past lives relating to issues she is currently agonizing over having to do with a male co-worker for whom she has deep, inexplicable feelings. This man is much younger than she, and thinks of her solely as a confidant. Jessica is also hoping to heal her long-term unresolved bad feelings and resentments about the father of the only child she has ever had. They had a relationship which resulted in pregnancy when she was twenty-six years old.

After explaining the reasons that we do past life readings, what we can gain from them if we choose, and giving instructions to Jessica about what will be happening during the reading, I begin Jessica's reading.

Lois: (Long pause) I see you dressed in all your finery, wearing a stunning white hat with a large ostrich feather sticking out the side, and a lacy yellow dress as well as white gloves. You are aboard a train. There is a small child, about three years of age with you. It is probably in the mid to late 1800s, somewhere in the eastern half of the United States. I am not sure I can tell exactly where. I keep hearing Ohio, although I am not quite clear if that is where you were from, or where the train was passing through. A strong, big man with a blue bandana over his face, wearing a large, black hat and sitting on an Appaloosa, rides up beside the train, and then climbs onboard to rob everyone. Because of the bandana covering his face, all you can really see are his eyes, which look frightened.

When he comes to you, he tells you he wants your watch and your wedding ring. You tell him he can have your watch, which is one of those round gold kind which is on a broach pinned to your dress, but he cannot have your wedding ring. He behaves as if he were quite nervous, and screams that he is going to kill you if you do not hand over everything, but you do not believe him. You tell him you are sorry, but you will not give up your wedding ring. Sweetly explaining that your late husband gave that to you, you beg to keep it since it is all you have left of him. Not wanting to be made to look a fool by a mere woman, or have others think he is weak, or that they do not have to comply with his demands, he shoots you right through the heart. You slump over dead almost instantly, with your child sitting right next to you. Thick, dark red blood gushing out all over your pale yellow lacy dress was the last thing you saw. That is the man...Jim (is that his name?)...who fathered your child in this current life. Now, he had his reasons for robbing that train—he was desperate, but his reasons do not matter in your context.

In the present life, Jim was given a chance to pay back the crime committed during the train robbery. He was supposed to step up and take care of you and your child, but he did not do so. It was an opportunity for him to balance bad behaviors from the past, and he did not do that. He offered to marry you, but after he had already beaten you in this lifetime, you did not feel safe marrying him. This was a wise choice, I believe. I know of no sane person who recommends that a woman marry anyone who has ever beaten them. I am getting that on a Soul level you are resentful about it, because there you were, raising a child by yourself. And because in fact, he was supposed to be there paying off his karma from prior bad actions. He could at least have helped with raising her while living in a different house, or paid child support or something, but ducked those duties entirely, and after a couple of years, he just disappeared.

A lot of times incidents like that cause us to have karma in one direction or another with somebody, and he has definitely a huge karmic debt which is greater now than it was before. The only way for you to get clear of the karma is to reach deeply within yourself to develop compassion for him, and some affection.

Do you have questions about that lifetime?

Jessica: Can I really get over this resentment?

Lois: It sincerely is up to you. The reason I give past life readings is so the client can get enough insight into why they have the feelings they have, so they can heal and let go. It is like this. If you have a buried memory, it can cause problems, because it has not been brought to conscious light. This is true of childhood memories in this lifetime, and true of many memories from past lives. When you remember the past lives and assimilate the memories, it can help you to heal so that you are not constantly running up against something painful of which you are not consciously aware. But it is up to you to choose to forgive. Whether or not you decide to get over the resentment is solely up to you, ultimately. You are the one it harms. Does that make sense?

Jessica: Yes.

Lois: So I do not know if learning about this today will be enough all by itself, but it will help if you make a conscious choice to allow that forgiveness to occur. Okay, we are going on to the next past life. (Long pause)

Sorry, these are not easy to look. I am seeing you in a jail—a prison-type situation. You are a female and Jim is your jailor. This is a concentration camp style of prison, not any ordinary prison. There is brutal stuff going on here—not just things like beatings, but there are people being fed rotten food and a lot diarrhea and vomiting and people dying. This jailor was raping several of the women, and you got pregnant. Prior to your delivering the baby, he saw to it that you died. Again, this poor Soul has some serious, negative karma to clean up. If you can release this, if you can have compassion for your own past lives, forgive the past, and know that you do not have to continue to be at the mercy of these memories at the Soul level, then you can clean up the karma with him. Then it will not matter what he does. You do this forgiving so that you do not ever have to incarnate with him again.

Jessica: How can I make sure that I never have to incarnate with him again?

Lois: Again, by forgiving him and finding a way to develop compassion for him. Find a way to see things from his point of view—or have compassion for all the terrible things he has to make up for, all the suffering due in his next lives. Accept these past lives with him, and have compassion for yourself, too, and understand why, at a Soul level, you have these resentments. It's in your best interest to make a decision for your own benefit that you're going to forgive him. Not for him, but for you—so that you don't carry forward the karma and the pain and the need to reincarnate and be harmed again by this Soul or some other. View it as a lesson for you, not him. It means that you have to say that you are letting go of it for your own good; this is what we refer to as forgiveness. It is not that what he did was all right with you, or that it is acceptable in any way, but just that you are not going to be eaten from the inside by this poison called resentment. I have come to understand that unforgiveness is an acid which devours from within the vessel which contains it.

Another way to look at this is to ask yourself, "What lessons have I learned from this man? If this Soul came into my life teach me a lesson, what was it?" There is a really good book and it is for use in this lifetime, but you can apply it to your past lives, as well. The title is *Radical Forgiveness* by Colin Tipping. I suggest you purchase that book and do the exercises in it. Your inability to forgive is not hurting him. It is not affecting him at all. It is only harming you and those around you; this acid of unforgiveness harms the people we love. It spills over from time to time. Harboring continued resentment over his actions is also a way of giving him power over you.

Now we will move on to the next lifetime. (Another lengthy pause)

It is not easy to tell what the time period is on this by looking at the clothing, but you are in South America, pretty far south. There are horses. You are wearing a hand-woven, colorful poncho, pants and a wide-brimmed hat with a colorful hat band. In this particular lifetime you are a woman again, and I am seeing you riding on horseback. It seems that the situation feels desperate. You are riding a great distance all alone, up into the mountains to take provisions—food, water, blankets—to someone who is hiding in a cave. (His name in your current lifetime is Steve, your co-worker.) But in the past life that we are now viewing, he lives on a neighboring ranch. Your family created this joyous match, and you have been engaged to him since you were a child. Without intending to, he has run afoul of the law. The situation is supremely unjust, someone in power wants his possessions, and you are taking him provisions so he can make it through the winter. Winter seems to be coming on early, hence your urgency. You are the only one who knows where he is hiding at this time. Unfortunately, you are being followed by three men, but you are unaware of that fact.

Arriving at the cave, you two carry in all the provisions, and there is actually a place to tie the horse up inside the cave. It is beginning to snow so you decide to remain there with your lover and rest up, visiting with him for a while. You are sleeping together, having made love, when the people who were following you stealthily move to the middle of the cave, and set it a pile of brush on fire. The two of you have fallen asleep, and when the smoke gets to you, you die in your sleep, entwined in each other's embrace. That is one reason you found each other in this current lifetime. You two had a Soul agreement to reunite later, and decided to come back together one day. But you had not specified exactly how you would come back to be together. This vow was on a Soul level. As you were leaving your body you looked down, and said that you would find each other again in another life. Do you have any questions about this particular lifetime, Jessica?

<u>Jessica:</u> No. But I knew when you said I was being followed, that we would both die.

<u>Lois:</u> (Long pause) There is another lifetime with horses. It looks rather like England. Yet it is difficult to tell where it is. You are riding sidesaddle, wearing an elegant pale green ruffled dress and a lovely, matching ruffled hat to protect your face from the sun, as well as white lace gloves. The picture you present is of an elegant, wealthy lady. You are being taught to jump on

horseback—sidesaddle! You are an advanced equestrian, but you are a very young woman, maybe seventeen years old. The man who is teaching you is Steve from your current lifetime again, and he is a riding teacher who instructs people how to do fancy, complicated things on horseback. He is not in the same social class as you, and yet you fell in love with him. He touches you respectfully to correct your posture, and to show you where to put your hands and knees, feet and such, and you have never before been touched except by a nanny—and those touches were rare. You are an only child until you were about eleven or twelve, so you never had siblings who might have touched you, either. The man's musky smell and firm, gentle touch were overwhelming, making your heart race every time he came near.

This man was about ten years older, married, and not of your social class, yet you fell desperately in love with him, to the point that you thought you might faint when he touched you. Your face would turn red, and you would begin to breathe heavily, and of course, he knew the effect he had on you. The strange thing was that he was in love with you, too. This painful situation went on for a very long time, because he needed the work. He could not give up teaching and training you, and you had never had to worry about work or money in your life, so you had no clue what a difficult situation he was in. You also did not understand what a risk his expressing his feelings would be to his family and his career. But he never could let you know, except in the way he looked at you. You could see the love in his eyes, but he never showed it in any other way. It would have cost him entirely too much. He could have lost what little financial security he had, his children, his job, and he could have ended up in debtor's prison. It would have truly been bad for him, because your father was very powerful and rather vindictive. Your father could be terribly unbending once he made up his mind about someone, reacting in a way that was quite unmerciful to people who crossed him.

So this went on for about ten years, and finally your mother noticed one day that something was wrong. She decided that a nice vacation in France would be good for everyone. She took you to the coast of France where you took up with a man your own age. One day while out riding with him, you had the realization that nothing was ever going to happen with the older man from the riding stables. It did not matter if he loved you with his eyes—nothing was ever going to happen. You married the gentleman you met in France. There was a grand, elaborate wedding in your gardens at home, and the man who had been training you to ride horses could see it from his house. Shortly thereafter he had a heart attack and died. Essentially, he died of a broken heart. Do you have questions about that lifetime?

Jessica: It is just like this lifetime, in a way.

Lois: Yes, it is something of a reversal. You care for him and cannot express it because you are much older. He still has the same fears he had before. Often even though we do not remember the past lives, yet the identical feelings come through with the person we have had the past life with. It can be quite confusing to everyone concerned. It can also cause us to avoid someone with whom we could have been happy. (Pause)

There is yet another lifetime with Steve. This is Egypt right after the fall of Atlantis. Certain Atlanteans had come to Egypt right after the fall of Atlantis to re-establish civilization. You are sitting in some kind of jungle (the weather was quite different all over the planet at that time) with other people in a ceremony or a group meditation, using your minds to build pyramids. These Atlanteans built what we call the early Egyptian pyramids with their minds. You and he were in a circle together. You were fraternal twin brothers, and were very connected. But you did not look exactly alike. There is between you, however, a deep closeness that goes very far back.

The group you were associated with spent a long time establishing civilization in Egypt, and you lived to be very old. You two were very close the whole time. You both married and had children, but were still inseparable. Both families lived in the same oversized house, because the two of you were so close. This kind of arrangement was not unusual in those days. The children were confused as to whether they were brother and sister or cousins. I just wanted to let you know about the closeness and relatedness about this being an essential part of you.

Jessica: So we have been together for a long time?

Lois: Yes. There truly is a very deep connection there. I am not seeing another lifetime.

There appears that there are others, but this is enough for one person to try to assimilate at one time. You have heard some pretty heavy duty information about your past just now, so not to overburden you in the ensuing weeks, as you assimilate these past lives, we are going to stop there. If you want to do some more, I suggest you wait at least three months. Do you have any questions about that lifetime?

Jessica: No. Did we ever have a happy lifetime?

Lois: Yes, I think there were other happy ones, yet knowing about these we have covered is more helpful when you are trying to figure out why you are having the bad feelings.

Jessica: I am just trying to figure out where to go from here.

Lois: As you begin assimilate what we have covered it will begin to be obvious where to go from here. Listen to the recording a few times. Give yourself time. What will come to you is not necessarily something that is immediately apparent, but you will gradually integrate all this information.

Jessica: Okay.

Lois' Notes: After the recorder was off, Jessica mentioned that the past life in the prison setting explained why every time she thought about the father of her child, the first few years after she rejected him, she would begin to vomit. She had dated this man when young and got pregnant by him. One day he became enraged, and very violently threw her up against a wall during a minor disagreement. He offered to marry her when she told him she was pregnant, but she refused, knowing him to be violent. He never actually stepped up to the plate and came to visit his daughter, or paid any child support, although he did talk about visiting a few times. He would set a date, but never showed up when he arranged to visit his child. Jessica has no idea where he is now.

Though the man at work, Steve, is quite a bit younger than Jessica, she still has vivid sexual dreams about this man. However, he seems to see her only as a friend, and she feels almost tortured about it. They work together, and they carpool to and from work daily with a third man. Steve seems to see her as a friend and confidant, but nothing more. He even tells her all about his girlfriend. She thinks if she told him how she feels, it would have dire consequences, as she would be rejected and humiliated, and yet still have to see him every day at work.

A few months after the reading Jessica reported that her feelings for Steve had abated somewhat, and she had accepted that there were deep, valid reasons for her feelings, but that it was just not meant to be in this lifetime. Steve was just not ready to accept things like past lives, so she never told him about them. Jessica gradually let go of the feelings, and was able to be more comfortable in a simple, warm friendship with Steve.

Unfortunately, this happens to people occasionally. Two people are meant to get together, or there exists the possibility, anyway. One of them wants the relationship, and the other just cannot or will not fully engage. We cannot manipulate others into loving us, so it is better to let go of that painful dream. Understanding our past lives together can often facilitate that ability to let go, and help us to move on.

Past Life Reading: Karen Thompson: December 4, 2008

Karen received her gift of a past life reading from a good friend. This reading was done at a distance; and Karen emailed me a photo of herself. Karen, who was a kindly-looking woman in her late fifties, had no particular information she was interested in receiving, just whatever her Guides wanted her to know.

Karen almost single-handedly runs a cat rescue program in a small town. It is very difficult, demanding and all-consuming work, and she has been doing it for many years. Funding is hard to come by, which makes the work even more trying. Karen works incessantly, is not married, and dedicates her life to the rescue of cats.

Lois: The first thing I am seeing is a temple in Egypt. You are a male in this lifetime, a very large, brown-haired, strong man with kind features and strong hands. You are a Priest who is a keeper of sacred lions. There was a temple where lions were revered and even considered sacred. In service to this temple, there was a whole group of Priests and Priestesses who tended the lions, and the image I am getting is that you all communicated with them telepathically. In that lifetime you took a vow to protect them as well as all other species of cats. What was going on in your mind at the time was you vowed to protect all species of wild cats. However, the way you worded it, the vow included domestic cats as well, which were also revered, but to a lesser extent, in that time. But the large cats were particularly considered sacred in the temple to which you had devoted your life.

There was an accident. A female lion became ill, and it was from some sort of infection that invaded her brain. These animals were relatively tame. They were in the temple and allowed to walk loose among humans for the most part during certain times of the day. This illness affected her brain. There was a fever which came on suddenly, and nobody realized that she was as sick as she was. Consequently, as you walked by this lioness, for some reason you were attacked by her and killed. In the moment you that were dying and looked down at your body, you reinforced your vow to devote yourself to the feline kingdom. And for that reason, it is a Soul level promise. In other words, you forgave the cat, understanding that the cat did not know what she was doing, and renewed the vow to protect the feline kingdom. This is a vow that you may or may not wish to continue. People decide to release vows of celibacy and poverty taken in prior lives. They do so because those vows belong to the other lifetime, and are not appropriate to continue indefinitely, from life to life. In other words, you can rescind a vow once you realize it has outlived its purpose to your Soul. One might question the necessity to you as an eternal being, a Soul, the same way that a nun or priest might take a vow of chastity or poverty or silence and in some later lifetime, decide it was not meant for all time, and for all eternity. Any vow that continues to express itself in later lifetimes might be considered an appropriate one to release from the Soul's field of energy.

Therefore, a promise to protect the felines of the world might be something you want to reconsider as being the main or primary focus of your incarnations. Not that what you are doing is meaningless, but how many lifetimes is it necessary to keep doing the same thing over and over? Does that repetition help you to grow as a Soul? I think not. Most Souls want to experience a variety of learning experiences, and doing the same thing over and over might not be in your best interest as a spiritual being having a physical experience. There will always be someone who is there to rescue the animals if you choose to do something else. If you release yourself from the vow about cats, in each lifetime it would be an option, not a Soul vow. I will just put that out there for you to consider. That is complete for this lifetime in Egypt. (I pause, while I look for the next lifetime.)

Lois: I am seeing in the 1930s a traveling circus and again, in this lifetime you are a male. You are a lion tamer, which is what they were called back then. It was a very difficult time in the 1930s in the United States. Traveling with the rest of the circus was your wife and one child. Of course, there were also the lions. Things had become extremely difficult. To get people to come in you had to lower your prices. People were not able to come to visit the circus, otherwise. It was not a huge circus, and there were two lions. It became harder and harder to feed everyone until it got to the point that you knew you had to choose between feeding the family and feeding the lions, and lions ate a lot. Everyone was getting skinny including the lions. Your wife threatened to leave you if you did not just quit the circus, and sell the lions. She actually wanted you to slay the lions because she knew it would take forever to find a buyer, however, she knew you could not do this. But she desperately wanted you to quit the circus, settle down on the family's farm, which was producing enough food. If only your family had been settled down, helping her father and brothers, you would have had plenty of food as well.

The family farm was in Iowa, and you were very torn because you had a way of treating the lions that was extremely humane. You were very concerned that there was not anyone who understood lions the way that you did. And because of this vow, you decided to let your wife and child go ahead to the family farm, and you said you would catch up with them later. What happened was that you decided to feed the lions rather than to feed yourself. You were not eating enough and eventually fell ill and died. At the moment of death you were asking yourself, "How could I make such a silly mistake? The lions still are not going to be taken care of properly, and here I am dying before my time." You were in your early thirties. And so that has been something you have had to continue to deal with, the question of how do I keep it all in balance? How do I take care of the cats and take care of my other obligations?

There has been a lot of confusion in various lifetimes about how to continue to honor your vow and also accomplish what you agreed to accomplish in that particular lifetime—things you decided to learn at a Soul level. So you may be feeling confusion about the cats even now, is what I am saying. That is all I am getting for that particular lifetime. (Long pause)

Lois: The next one I am seeing is a lifetime as an Asian woman and living in an interesting situation. Your Soul decided you needed some experiences where there were simply no cats to rescue or care for of any shape or size, so you have this lifetime as an Asian female with three children, a husband and an extended family and they all live on boats. They are boat people. They live in a community where everybody is on the water all the time. This is about five hundred years ago. You earned your living by fishing, and by gathering certain kinds of seaweed and weaving things out of them like baskets and hats, and creating nets for fish. You did not use fishing poles; you used nets, lots of different types of nets. You used an incredible variety of creativity with net-making. You would experiment with one type of net, and make changes. As you caught more fish than you needed, you would go into different small ports, and trade excess fish for vegetables and other articles you needed. This was a little flotilla of boats that had all your family in it.

And this one was a very peaceful, tranquil life and as you may well imagine, since there were no cats there. That was a lifetime in which you actually kept birds as pets. You were very fond of them. They were very colorful, small birds. I do not know what kind they were, but I am seeing them in a little cage. You had three children. One of them died when he was three years old, because he caught some kind of disease that no one was familiar with. You named him "Lionhearted" or something like that. The name made reference to a large, wild cat like a lion or a panther. You are hearing about this lifetime because you need to know there were ways your Soul worked around that vow you took. It was done in order that you could have some learning experiences, because one of the things you wanted to do was to be a good wife and mother, and you were. In fact, the only tragedy of that lifetime was the loss of that little boy when he was three, which was not anybody's fault. He just got sick. He actually had a parasite from eating undercooked fish which your mother-in-law prepared, but nobody ever knew what had made him ill. He just had a high fever as far as anyone knew. We are going to move onto the next lifetime. (Pause.)

Lois: This is a lifetime spent——I do not see very many of these for some reason——a lifetime spent on another planet; Venus. I am seeing a culture of ascended beings called the Hathors. They are masters of sound. As a Hathor, in the early kingdom of Egypt, you worked with the Egyptians, who came to Egypt from Atlantis. You and a group of other Hathors came to work with the Priests and Priestesses in different temples and mainly worked with helping spirits cross over when people died. Another group of Hathors helped with births. But you worked with helping their spiritual bodies make the transition from the physical world to the next level of learning. You were also teaching people in several of the various temples about initiatory processes which would speed up spiritual evolution so that when people do eventually transition out of the physical body, they end up at a higher level of what is called "Heaven" for lack of a better word—the place where we all go in between incarnations.

I am being told you need to know about this because due to your past life as a Hathor, your Soul origin is not the Earth, it is someplace far away. It is wherever the Hathors came from, and they did not originally come from this universe at all. They came to Venus at the request of Sanat Kumara, through the Sirian portal into our universe. You are asked to do some research on the Hathors, and to learn more about them. There is something you are going to learn from that, something important you need to learn in this lifetime to move you to the next level of what you are supposed to be doing with this lifetime. The reading for this particular lifetime is complete. (I pause again to see the next life.)

Lois: There is one more lifetime your Guides want you to know about. This is as a mountain climber. On looking at this mountain climber, at first I thought it was a male, but it is not. This is a female. She is German, or lives in that region, whether it is called Germany yet, I cannot tell. Actually she trained in mountain climbing in Nepal or Tibet region, then brought back some of those skills and tools, and so on, to what is now called the German Alps. This was quite a long time ago. Usually I can tell what the time period is by the costume, but I cannot from this. It is so unusual. This is a lifetime where you chose to focus on your body, and on athleticism. Having a strong body and experiencing on a Soul level what it is like to have a very powerful, strong, athletic body was one of the goals of that life. You spent your entire lifetime from about the age of twelve on until your early forties which in those days was very old just climbing mountains, and teaching other people how to climb. You heard that in this far away land of Nepal they had special mountain climbing techniques. So you studied them and brought that information back to your region.

I see you were totally devoted to that. You did not marry. You did not have children, but you did train a lot of children how to climb mountains and taught survival techniques, such as how to survive if a storm blows up, and which way to point the tent when you set up camp so that the wind does not blow the tent over, and so forth. This is interesting. You tried to import a certain type of animal whose fur was denser so that the hoods could be lined with this fur, and so could the jackets and the pants and the hats and whatever it was, but it did not work. The animals never adjusted to the food choices. But you were quite a pioneer in that lifetime.

The way it ended was that found yourself in a cave when a heavy snowstorm came along. Snow gradually covered the mouth of the small cave, blocking off your air supply, but it was dark and you did not notice that. You became quite sleepy, then sleepier and finally the oxygen ran out in the cave.

You passed over in your sleep. It was a gentle death. You had a very joyous lifetime, enjoying almost every minute of it.

Okay. You let me know if you have questions about any of these lifetimes.

Lois' Notes: Karen later emailed me with questions that were not directly about the reading itself, but about the Hathors, and questions about some dreams she had. I referred her to Tom Kenyon's website about the Hathors. She had dreamed prior to my having done the reading that she could heal others and move things with the power of the mind. I did not feel this had anything to do with the reading, and so told her she should do some research on the internet about dreams. That is a deep subject.

And then several months later I emailed her to find if she had experienced any changes in her life as a result of the reading. I had definitely drawn conclusions from the reading about the implications for the direction of her life, but I did not know if she had experienced the same insights. And I would not impose my insights on her. I wrote her, wondering if she had seen what I had seen. I remind myself that I am not in control of or responsible for how others interpret their past life readings. I deliver the message, and the rest is up to the client.

Here is Karen's reply:

Dear Lois,

I think about the reading and discuss it with friends often. I am grateful to my friend, Elise, for the gift of the reading.

As far as my vow to care for the cats both in this life and past lives, I am still deeply involved. It is a daily struggle, still demanding much of my time and energy. It is a difficult choice I have made. There is much sadness and many disappointments. There are joys and causes for celebration, but most days it seems that the lows outweigh the highs. I wish that getting the reading had changed things but it has not.

I continue to fight the fight and continue to wonder about my choice to do so. There is so much to wonder about. Am I making any difference? Am I doing the right thing? Am I really meant to do this? Can I ever stop? How can I achieve more balance in my life? Am I "called" to do this? Do the animals know what I am doing for them? What am I to learn from this calling? What is the purpose of this work? Is it for the animals or for the people in my life that I do this?

In short, my answer is that the seeds of thought that your reading planted continue to grow. I have not seen all of the results yet. There is so much to think about.
Karen

Past Life Reading: Kacey Oliver: April 1, 2009

Kacey is a sweet-faced, heavyset woman in her mid-fifties with a high-pitched, baby-doll voice, and extraordinary, silvery-blue eyes. She has naturally curly black hair sprinkled with the occasional thread of silvery grey. Kacey has not married and has no children; her cats are her companions and her babies. She has not expressed any desire to marry or to have children, either. There is no unfulfilled longing there.

Kacey was raised in a very small town in an extremely dysfunctional family. Her mother tried to keep her children inside the home all the time, and Kacey felt this attitude of her mother's has stunted her growth. It made her afraid of everything, just as her mother had been terrified of the world, and transmitted it to all the children. Having moved to the big city over twenty years earlier, because there was no work in her small town, has not helped Kacey grow away from being a small town girl much at all; she is still very shy and fearful of the world. She talks often about her family, and how strangely she was raised, as if to say that this is why she cannot function as well as she would like. She has always wanted to travel, even if it is only to climb into the car and drive to a neighboring town, just to see what is there. But she cannot manage this because of her fears.

Kacey works for the government and also holds down a part-time job at a local historical museum, where the catty infighting among the women deflates her spirit. She is not a woman who can hold her own in a verbal cat fight.

Another thing Kacey mentioned was that at some point in her early life she had experienced a severe burn to her belly and genital region. She referred to herself as a "burn victim." She wondered why this had happened to her.

After giving Kacey the explanation about why we look at our past lives, I begin to narrate the session.

Lois: I am seeing you first of all living in medieval times. This is in what is now called Eastern Europe. Each lifetime is chosen by the Soul for the particular set of experiences, so that the Soul can grow and learn. Sometimes it is for the purpose of teaching others, too. We call this planet the Earth School for those reasons. In this lifetime you were a person who worked in a dungeon, and you are a guard of sorts. You are also responsible for extracting the truth from prisoners—which involved torture, and also you were responsible for handling some of the executions. This was just a job. Nobody thought it was a bad thing to do, but there were some things that after you had gone over to the other side, after you passed from that lifetime, you decided that you needed to experience, so that you could understand what it was like to be on the receiving end of torture.

It was for this reason that you got the burn. It was a karmic balancing from that lifetime as a torturer, because there was some boiling water, and that use of hot water or hot oil was used as part of the torture. You had applied this form of torture as part of your job. You had balanced a lot of the karma already in different lifetimes since then, but this was the one last thing that you needed to do, to experience up close and personal what it felt like to be burned with hot water. Again, this was for your own karmic balancing. Do you have any questions about that lifetime? You were also very muscular and hairy in that lifetime, by the way. You were definitely a manly man, a big burly guy with thick, muscular hands. Do you have any questions about this life?

Kacey: No, no questions yet. (I pause as I view the next life.)

Lois: The next lifetime I am seeing is as a Chinese man who came to the United States. There was not much money back home in China. So you came to the United States because you had heard there was a fortune to be made working at building this railroad. You did this because there was not very much money where you lived, and you sent home a whole lot of money to your family compared to what you were able to make in China. You did a lot of digging and blasting in this job. You were going through mountainous regions part of the time—in other words blasting with dynamite—and chipping away at rocks. You and the crew built that railroad for years and years.

You all took a great deal of pride in the work, though, and in the fact that you could send home so much money to the family. The work was far beneath your intelligence level, someone with a lot less snap could have done this work, but you chose that job, that work, that lifetime, to experience being part of something big and magnificent. And the building of the railroad just fit the bill. There was nothing else going on at the time like the railroad which had such a huge impact on the entire nation, and subsequently upon the world. You wanted to have that experience of being part of something greater, being part of a team that accomplished something lasting, meaningful, and worthwhile in the world. You were there, by the way, when they drove that last spike in the railroad, the golden spike. You were there. That was a big honor, you know? The men, especially the laborers, who were present at that ceremony sobbed with pride at the magnificence of the accomplishment, and you were no exception. Do you have any questions about that lifetime?

Kacey: Um, no, I guess not.

Lois: I think the Guardians of the Records wanted you to know about that so you know that you had such a major accomplishment. That was considered a really big deal particularly on the other side, where the angels are, for everybody who participated in it. Joining the east coast and the west coast of the United States was a major accomplishment. (Long pause)

I am seeing another lifetime, again, as a man. This time a very powerful, tall man who was a member of a tribe of nomads in Northern Africa. You had a huge harem. I am seeing twenty-eight wives, yes, twenty-eight is the number. You traveled a lot and these were a harsh, tough people. You were strong, powerful, feared by your neighbors and able to survive in extreme desert circumstances where other people cannot even begin to survive. These people are known for their fierceness, and you were a leader in that culture. This is maybe about 700 years ago. You lived a long life and had sixty or so children who survived into adulthood, which is a fairly profound feat for people who were nomadic, desert people—even with twenty-eight wives. Life was extremely harsh.

What your Guides are telling me is that you have had very few lifetimes as a woman at all. One of the major things you wanted to experience in this lifetime was just the experience of having a woman's feelings and a woman's sensitivities, and to experience what it felt like to live inside a woman's body. They are telling me that it would have been overwhelming to you to get married and have children. You just needed to be inside a woman's body, to have menstrual periods and emotional swings to know what it feels like to have soft muscles and skin, and so on. I am also being told you are doing a really good job of being female, as you are most feminine, and that was the main purpose of this lifetime. Also your Soul wanted for you to learn what it is like for a woman to be on her own and independent, and how difficult and demanding that actually is, so that you could appreciate women more. It was very important for your Soul to gain balance by having exactly this female lifetime. Do you have any questions?

Kacey: (She shakes her head no.)

Lois: I am seeing another lifetime you had as an Egyptian. This was in early, ancient Egypt, in what we call the Old Kingdom, which is not that far in time from the Atlantean times. When Atlantis came apart, people splintered and went to different places. Egypt is one of those places. You were a female ruler. You were a powerful, wealthy figure, and a beautiful woman. You never did find any man who could handle you, and you did not marry in that lifetime, either, yet you had children. Other people raised the children. You just gave birth to them: two sons and a daughter. You were a highly respected member of the aristocracy, a clever, gifted ruler actually, and you lived to be fairly old. You functioned like a man more than a woman in that lifetime. So your Soul felt that it was not a good experience of being female, since you lived life like a man anyway. Do you have questions about that lifetime?

Kacey: No, but I think that is funny. (She giggles.)

Lois: (I pause to see the next life.) I am seeing a life as a Catholic priest in one of those orders where they do not talk. You were not a very tall man, and you had brown hair and went bald very early in life, but you had warm, friendly eyes with soft eyebrows, not the big bushy kind. I think this man is more of a monk, actually. He is a very gentle Soul, and came from a noisy, rough neighborhood and violent family, where he did not fit in. He took a vow of silence. Twenty-eight must be an important number for you, because you went twenty-eight years without speaking, even when you were alone, you did not speak. You never broke your vow for twenty-eight years. He spent almost all of his time working in the vegetable gardens and in meditation.

You were also an illustrator of manuscripts—a scribe. Mankind did not have the printing press yet, so people wrote or copied out all the books by hand, and consequently, books were very rare, valuable things. It took a lot of man-hours to produce just one of these books, but they were works of art. Actually, there is still one in a library in a Catholic University somewhere in which you did most of the work. You also did some of those exquisite illuminations of the first letter—the beautiful colored drawings around the first letter on the page of the new chapter. You did a lot of that. You were extremely gifted as a scribe and as an illuminator. This was a very peaceful and happy lifetime, but of course you had absolutely no physical contact with anyone. You wanted one lifetime that was quiet and peaceful, and you had this one to fulfill that need. So, please note that you have certain inherent artistic abilities from a lifetime as an illuminator, if you want to tap into them. Do you have any questions about that lifetime?

Kacey: No.

Lois: Here is one more lifetime as a woman. This one is so different from the others. This one was as a dancer and you were with a roving troupe. This was in Europe in the 1400s. You had a nicely appointed, decorated wooden wagon, and your group would go from town to town setting up shop, like in a tent, entertaining people with minstrel-type storytelling and bringing things from other towns, merchandise to trade. Everyone had a great deal of fun. You moved constantly, so you never really got to know anybody except your group, but that was like a family. You were very partial to feminine garments. That was a very positive lifetime for you, and it was a very happy lifetime. I think you only lived to be but about forty, but that was old enough for those days. Again, you had no children. Have you questions about that lifetime?

Kacey: It appears there have been many lifetimes without children. Am I right?

Lois: Well, as a woman that is true. You had more lifetimes as males. Actually you had plenty of children when you were a male, but in your few lifetimes as a woman, the only one in which you had children that I have been allowed to see, at least, is the one in Egypt, and somebody else raised them.

So this might be something you will work on in subsequent lives. (Pause) I am being told that is all you need to know about for now. This will be enough for your tender sensibilities to assimilate at this time. Do you have any questions?

Kacey: Well, not right now. But I will think about this, and maybe email you or something if I do have a question.

Lois: Okay, good.

Lois' Notes: Prior to this reading Kacey had been restricting herself to going to work and coming home. She had no other activities in her life. Going to work and coming home to her cats was her whole life. Kacey did not talk of this prior to the reading, but for many years, she had secretly dreamed of doing something she thought was really wild! She had dreamed of just getting into her car some weekend, and driving out of the big city she lived in, to the small town a couple of hours' drive away where she had spent her childhood. She had not seen her home town in at least fifteen years, maybe twenty. She was so quiet and shy that she did not have really close friends, and was definitely too shy to ask anyone if they would drive out to this tiny hamlet with her.

A few months later Kacey came in for a session and reported that she had done this wild, exotic, risky thing! She prepared herself with ample snacks and plenty of water and juice to drink, climbed into her car, and drove all the way to the tiny speck of a town where she had spent her painful childhood, to see what it would feel like to be there now. Kacey bravely roamed the streets all by herself, looking at how things had changed, and what had not. It was a thrilling experience for her. She felt so daring, and she related the entire trip excitedly when she next came in for her energy medicine session. This seemed like a pretty big shift for her. She directly attributed it to having had the reading, and knowing about the past lives where she traveled.

She also said that she had decided to call a woman acquaintance who had come to Texas from Poland, and ask her if she would like to take a longer car trip with her sometime. To her surprise, the lady agreed, since she loved to travel, too. Again, this seems like a huge, positive change for Kacey.

Past Life Reading: Kayla Noriej: March 24, 2007

Kayla, a sad, confused young woman in her early twenties, comes in requesting a past life reading regarding a married man, Sayed, with whom she is powerfully and intimately involved. She is desperately in love with this man, and had felt she deeply recognized him in the very moment she met him. She gasped when she saw him for the first time, and he could not take his eyes off her, either. He obviously loves her, too, but cannot seem to leave his wife.

Kayla wants to know why all this is happening; it seems to her the obvious thing for Sayed to do is to leave his wife and be with her. She does not understand why it is all so difficult and painful, or why she cannot walk away. She clearly hopes that knowing about any past lives they may have had together might help her make a decision. It also appeared that she wanted to be told what to do, but when someone is working out karma, the person whose karma it is must choose what to do. The past life therapist cannot in good conscience make decisions for other people. The clients are the ones who then must live with the consequences of their own decisions and so from a moral standpoint, they must be the one to make the choices. A past life therapist who makes the decision for the client by telling them what to do may very well incur karma to that person for having interfered in the client's choices.

After explaining to Kayla the details about why we do Akashic Records readings, the reading begins:

Lois: (There is a long pause as I watch the first lifetime for a bit in the mind's eye.) The first thing I am seeing is a dust storm. I am seeing you and two other people, a man and a child. You are a woman in this lifetime. You are walking very slowly struggling and leaning hard against the wind in a dust storm that is not quite heavy enough that you feel you must take shelter, but very unpleasant and blowing in your face. The fine, powdery sand is coming in through your mouth and there is a fine grit between your teeth, though your lips are clenched tightly together. Although you are wearing ankle length robes, and have a soft, woven cloth around your head and the lower part of your face, still the sand gets everywhere. It is in your armpits, the creases of your elbows, under your finger and toe nails, and inside your nostrils as well. The sand coats your eyelashes at the base. There is fine sand trapped around the edges of your hairline, too. Even though you are accustomed to sand, this is an unusually heavy sandstorm.

Under normal circumstances you would be indoors somewhere, in a tent closed off from the storm. Yet this night, you are walking, leaning into the wind. You have with you a child, but the child is older like twelve, thirteen or fourteen years of age, and you have two strong, shiny dark brown horses with you as well. It looks like perhaps you are from an Arab country. You are married to this man—and this is the same man you came in here asking about. The situation in this particular life on the day that we are seeing is that the child is feverish, very sick, which is why you are moving around in this potentially dangerous storm. Together, you are really struggling to get where the healer is located.

The healer is the only one who can take care of your ill son, your one single beloved child. You and your husband are both becoming exhausted. The boy is riding upon one of the horses, slouched on a colorful tribal-looking woven blanket with tiny bells hanging off the fringe, and on the other horse are carrying the supplies; the food and the stores of water in large, ocher-colored Earthen pots are tied onto the horse's back with crude sisal-looking ropes. Due to the impossibility of these harsh conditions, the two of you are moving too slowly through the desert, and you know it. It is quite dark, and walking is difficult. Finally, you have become lost due to the darkness and the impossibility of seeing where you are going, but you are both desperate, and very determined to save your son, so you plod on against all hope. After a few more hours, the storm gets so heavy that you are simply forced to stop or die, and you drape the blankets over the horses which are now lying down on the sand, and place yourselves with the child in the middle, between the horses, under the makeshift tent made by using the blankets. It is impossible to proceed further as the storm has become too intense.

This sandstorm rages on for hours during the dark of the night. The three of you huddle together between the warmth of the horses, clinging to each other, and briefly drift off to sleep. By the time the storm finally stops just before dawn, your son, who is cradled in your arms, has become entirely too still. Realizing that he has stopped breathing, you begin to wail. The tears and sobs are out of control, and this wakes your husband. He knows from your grieving sounds what has happened. The resulting feeling for both of you is simply unbearable, crushing grief.

Both of you feel that you are unforgivable failures as parents, and as human beings, in that even together, striving desperately, you could not save your only child. You only ever had this one, long awaited and deeply-loved child. This was a deep, heart-breaking sorrow you both carried for the rest of your days. Neither of you ever spoke of it, and neither ever healed from the pain. To make matters worse, every time you looked at each other you were reminded of the absence of your son. You were living in a culture where people stayed married, no matter what, until one of them died. They were not allowed to give up or quit, but for the rest of both of your lives there was this heavy, unspeakable pain that hung between you. The result was when your husband passed over to the other side—and he did go first—he thought, "It was a mistake to have married her. There must be a bad curse upon us."

So at the end of this lifetime together as husband and wife, apparently, he decided he would never be with you again, because unbearably painful things happened when you were together. You had only been able to conceive the one child, and the two of you, even with combined forces, could not save him when he got sick. As your husband lay dying, he thought of the relationship with you as damned from the beginning. At the moment of death he was thinking this, and whatever you are thinking at the time of death, is imprinted on your eternal

Soul. The birth moments and the moments of death have a powerful impact. And he fervently vowed as he took his last breaths that he would never be with you again. This was not a logical conclusion to draw at all, but it is the one he drew. The Souls pre-arrange certain experiences, hoping they will learn a particular set of lessons from the experiences.

Yet after he incarnated in that life, he drew the wrong conclusion from his lesson. His lesson was even if you cannot have what you want you can find joy in what you do have. If you choose to look for the joy in the situation you can find it. The lesson was one of gratitude for what is. We are to focus on what we have, not on what we do not have. Self-forgiveness was another part of this lesson, yet he never considered forgiving himself for not doing the impossible and saving his son in the face of that storm and the intensity of the boy's sudden illness. And even though he loved you dearly, after the death of your son he never really took joy in your company as he might have. So this is a lesson for him, too, coming back together with you making one choice or another choice. He gets to make a choice. Will he choose to experience the joy of being with you? In this situation you really do not have a choice unless it is just to walk away. Or you could choose to feel the joy of being with him when you are able, waiting patiently, and fully living your own life until he "wakes up" or the karma is cleared.

Do you have questions about that lifetime before I move to another one?

Kayla: So, you are saying right now he does not have a choice?

Lois: No, I am saying that where his making a commitment to you is concerned, it is you who have no choice. He does. He has a choice. He could walk away from the situation he is in and leave his wife, but he is not doing it. He is the one with a choice because he is already married. You do not have one because he is not coming toward you, right? Your only choice is whether to walk away and start over with someone else, or look around, date, yet keep the door open for him.

Kayla: What do you think that reason is?

Lois: Well, because his Soul swore he would never be with you again, because he believed that with you, unavoidable, bad things happen. He drew that conclusion from that lifetime which I just described, right? So, in this lifetime, he gets to make a choice about whether or not to be with you. Being with you brings him joy. So the question for him is, does he choose joy or does he stick with the wrong conclusion? The wrong conclusion was that being with you makes bad things happen. It may take him a while to work through it. And he may work through it one day, or he may not. Sometimes it takes several lifetimes working on the same thing to work through the karmic issue. The question is, will he choose joy? Or will he remain in fear, stuck with the wrong conclusion, which at a Soul level, was drawn from another lifetime: that uncontrollable, bad things happen when you two get together? Your only choices are either to move on, or wait for him to figure out what he's going to do.

Kayla: How would I cope with that?

Lois: You have to choose to either let go and move on, or you have to choose to be patient and wait for him. Those are only the possibilities I can see. Perhaps you see another? Is there one that I am missing?

Kayla: What is in my best interest? I would like to move forward but it is hard for me. I am a very strong-minded person. There is not anything I set my mind to it that I cannot do. This one particular thing I cannot—no matter how hard I try, it just seems to—my heart has basically taken over.

Lois: Well, again, this is your karmic lesson and your choice. But this is what I believe. The heart is what will not lie to you. Your brain/ego will lie to you, but the heart will not. Your Soul speaks to you from the neck down. Your body tells the truth. The ego resides in the brain and that is what can lie to us. Ego is fearful. Every lifetime is a struggle between the ego and Soul. Ego will fib to us for its own physical self-preservation and to maintain control over everything, even the decisions that the Soul should be making, like whom do we marry, do we have children, or what career do we choose?

Soul/spirit has our best interest at heart, and speaks to us through the body like the chills on your arms you sometimes get when you (or someone else) say something deeply true. Or perhaps you feel the sensations of excitement, joy or danger signals in your heart or your gut. That is where the truth is, from the neck down. I call this "Body Truth." So you get to choose if you want to give up on this karmic lesson, which for you sounds like it may be a lesson in patience and really hanging in there for another person, and being reliable.

If you have tried to move on and are unable, it sounds as if that is what the lesson may be. But you always get to choose. Contemplate for yourself if there is another lesson inherent in this. Every single day when you wake up you either are waiting for him or you are out looking for someone else. It sounds to me that you are saying that in your heart, you are still waiting, at least for now.

Kayla: I have been out on two dates with other men, and it just does not feel right.

Lois: I know that this lesson is difficult and painful for you, and I am sorry it is so hard on you. We choose these lessons before we incarnate, and we are feeling so strong, so invincible, telling ourselves that we really can get the lesson this time, and then we get down here in a body, forgetting what we once knew, and it can be really quite hard. Even though we agreed before we came here to the Earth School, to the scenario's unfolding, it can seem just so painful, even impossible at times. Yet pain is a powerful teacher. We can choose to learn through joy and pleasure, but many of us do not really get the lesson until we feel some pain. (Kayla is silent on this point.)

Shall we look at another lifetime with him, and see if we can get some more clues here? (Kayla nods in the affirmative.) (Long pause)

Lois: I am seeing two men on a sailing ship—two friends—and this would be the two of you in a lifetime where you were both men. You happened to be best friends. It looks like a great sailing ship, so this was probably over 100 years ago. You are sailing on the same ship for years and years and years. So the crew in a situation like that becomes a close-knit family. They are not really genetically related, of course, but they know one another well enough because they work day and night for months at a time, and so they feel like family. You are very close with this man, almost like brothers. There is a storm one very dark, moonless night and you are steering the ship—at the helm, or maybe it was just a rudder, but you are steering the ship, but I think I am seeing a large wheel with spokes.

That night it is also his turn to be on watch on the deck. It is raining hard and everyone is tired, but apparently you fell asleep at the steering position. He notices this, and he is trying to wake you up and watch guard at the same time. It is raining sheets of water, and rather too late he sees that there is another ship approaching to the starboard, and your vessel is moving really close to the other ship. He cannot seem to get you awake as you are heavily draped over the steering mechanism. He needs to take over the steerage, and make one of those maneuvers that must happen quickly. Struggling with all his might, he still cannot get your sleeping form to budge at all. So there then is a loud crunch, as wooden hull smashes against wooden hull, a sickening crashing sound. Finally you wake up as the boat sinks, and you are half awake, wondering what has just happened. Your friend hits his head on debris falling onto your ship from the other ship, and he drowns. Eventually, so do you; the water is too cold for anyone to survive for long. He dies very upset with you, because he feels that you betrayed him. You did not do your job, which was to stay awake and steer the ship. And so once again, he dies upset with you.

Now, if you wish to overcome that particular karma, that particular belief he has that you are somehow bad luck, or unreliable, you really have to hang in there until the karma is all balanced. That means that you might have to hang in there a long time. It might be three to five years, or even longer, I do not know for sure. You might find that even though you date other people, you never can seem to get serious with anyone because on some level you have an agreement to hang in there for a certain period of time, to demonstrate to him at a Soul level that you will be there for him. Perhaps you are here to prove that you will never give up. I do not know, you will have to determine this.

Hopefully, one day he will wake up, in a sense, and consciously or not, realize the karma is now over, and then at that same time, you will find at that exact same point, because the karma is completed, you can then easily get involved with somebody else. Or perhaps one day he may wake up because the karma is over since you waited long enough, and leave his wife. I am not being allowed to see which will happen. You cannot work out the karmic past if you already know in advance how it is going to turn out. Does that make sense?

Kayla: Yes, it does.

Lois: Okay. Do you have any more questions about that lifetime?

Kayla: No, I do not believe I have more questions.

Lois: Let me see if there is another lifetime that you need to know about at this time with the same person. (Long pause)

Ah, yes, I see another one. In this one, I am seeing that you two are a little boy and a little girl out innocently picking wildflowers. You are playing out in a valley or a field, in what is now called Italy. This was right around 79 CE, because this was the time of the eruption of Mt. Vesuvius. This is what is happening on the day I am seeing. Pompeii was the name of the city, and Herculaneum was nearby. You were living in Herculaneum, but your families were visiting someone who lived very near the sea. You began frantically running from the ash. So to be clear, in this lifetime, the man you have been asking about was your neighbor friend, a little boy who was slightly younger. When you felt the Earth rumble and ash began raining down, the two of you began running hard until you reached the sea.

Splashing on into the water, you and he join in with thousands of people trying to get into the water to save their lives, hoping the water will stop the lava. A boat comes along and dips the two of you out of the water. This is a family's boat, and they are just rescuing dozens of small people, thinking they can rescue more children than they can adults. They are plucking total strangers' children out of the water—if the children seem to be alone as you were, they rescued them because there was nowhere for them to go but the water. They knew that the children left there without adults would eventually drown, it was such a melee. Many thousands of people drowned that day, and even more were suffocated, covered in ash, or burned alive in the lava flow. It was a terrible day, filled with fear and death, yet filled also with heroes.

Once out in the water, when you see the boat coming nearby you push your smaller friend up into the boat first. In doing this, you saved his life, and became an eight year old heroine that day. You are both taken away to another place, to a different city and neither of you ever saw your parents again. All those rescued children were farmed out to different families, and some of them got to see each other occasionally, but after that day, the pair of you did not see much of each other. It may have only been every few years, and by accident at that. What is truly significant and important that happened in that lifetime, is that he was able to realize you were trustworthy since you saved his life. This was a major event in the lives of your Souls.

So there is something he knows, on a deeper level; he knows that on that day, you were there for him. This is one of those positive lifetimes where the experience, the karmic "gold stars," or whatever you want to call them, were earned by you. In other words, there was a positive outcome to your relationship in that lifetime by your pushing him up onto the boat ahead of yourself, because he could not really swim well. So you saved his life. At a Soul level, he does have that to look back upon. You were only eight, but had learned how to swim already. Your father was adamant that children must know how to swim—so he taught you when you were about three years old.

Now the thing I have to tell you about past lives is that they are not linear. They happen simultaneously. There is no such thing as time and space; they are just illusions. They are an illusion that we have because we are on a spinning planet. Einstein explained this about a hundred years ago, but most people still do not know it. Just because I mention a lifetime first, does not mean that it occurred first chronologically. Do you have any questions about the lifetime in Herculaneum the day that Vesuvius erupted?

Kayla: Not a question for the lifetime but the way it ended. How does that factor into this lifetime? The past lives?

Lois: Well, if you think of it this way...these are all experiences the same Soul has had with you. It is not like you are a different Soul than you were in those other lifetimes. At the Soul level, it is all the same "person" having different experiences. It is rather like before incarnating the Soul says, "Okay, I am going to try on this "Earthsuit," meaning a body, and then I am going to have these experiences." It is the same Soul having all these different experiences, and each set of experiences has an impact on you as a Soul. It is somewhat like playing a role in a theater drama, but you believe it is real. You have to forget what came before and believe it is real, or you cannot clear your karma. You simply forget that you are anything more than the person playing the part, and believe that the illusion is real. This is so you can learn from the drama as it unfolds. Do you understand?

Kayla: So this is the same person in every lifetime you are talking about?

Lois: Yes. This is the person you came in asking about, Sayed.

Kayla: And he has had the most amount of influence in my lives?

Lois: No, not necessarily, it is just that you came in asking about this man, which is why we are looking at those lifetimes with him. He is not necessarily the most important Soul you interact with in all your lifetimes, just the person you came in asking about. And it is clear why you want to know, I mean, you have had several lifetimes with him. I would say he is most likely a Karmic Soulmate of yours.

Do you have any questions before we look at the next lifetime? Oh...wait... there is more to this lifetime where you were plucked from the sea by the strangers in boats. You were taken into someone's home. You were adopted on another island, and he was sent to a different house. All those rescued children were sent to any family that would take them, and you really did not see him much after that, because the people who took him, the people who wanted a little boy, were far away from the people who took you. Now this is important. The family that took you, the mother in that family is your mother in this lifetime. She took you in when you had lost everything. Your parents were killed. Your parents had frantically gone looking around in the wrong direction, desperately searching for their children; they did not run toward the sea. They were trapped and then killed by the lava flow.

The woman who took you in on another island nearby—is it an island or a town on the coast, I cannot tell for sure—anyway, this woman who took you in is your mother in this lifetime and she truly, deeply loves you. There are all kinds of degrees of love from a mother, but this woman has been with you in more lifetimes than any other person in any lifetime with you, whether as your teacher—she really is a teacher—whether she comes exactly as a teacher in a school or as a spiritual teacher or as a mother or a father. She is slightly more evolved spiritually than you are, an older Soul, and often comes in with you to teach you. This woman, if you have ever had have any doubts at all, this woman loves you a lot more than most people ever love another person and has had more influence on you than anybody else in many other lifetimes. She has incarnated with you more than anyone else. Sometimes her teaching may seem harsh, but it is because of how much she loves you and she believes that she has to be tough, or you do not seem to get it. Do you have questions about that? She raised you in that lifetime, and then you helped take care of her when she got too old to take care of herself.

Kayla: So me and that boy never met again after that?

Lois: I think you may have passed in the streets and not recognized each other, except at a Soul level. The important part of that relationship happened when you saved his life. That was what was supposed to happen in that lifetime. There was no reason for further contact from the perspective of your Souls. He went on to marry somebody else and so did you. You were both most content. The most important thing in that lifetime happened when he was six and you were eight years old. Strange, is it not? Here we have six and eight year olds clearing the biggest karma of their lives. Okay, I am going to check and see if there is another lifetime with him. (Long pause)

Yes, here it is. I see you in a terribly cold landscape, and you are sliding down a snowy hill, sitting on something that looks like a rolled out metal garbage can lid with no handle. It was round and metallic and curved, but a rough metal. It looks like a shield of some kind. There are many other children. Here is another lifetime where you were just partners and great friends and playmates. You knew each other from about the ages of three to about eleven, when his family had to move away because the father died, and they did not have any money. They had to go live in a really bad neighborhood. You did not see him after that, but in childhood, he was your closest friend, and you thought about him often after he moved away. However, you never consciously bumped into each other again because at a Soul level, you were trying to create the balance of having a close relationship that did not incur the kind of karma that can be created within a sexual relationship—just a loving, trusting, sweet innocent friendship. So what your Guides now are telling me is that if you can be patient, there is a good chance that he may choose to be with you in this lifetime. You have a lot of good karma between you even though there has been a lot of misunderstanding in other lives. There is a distinct possibility that you could have a happy life together later on, after he has figured a few things out, and after you have exhibited your patience. In the meantime, "Have fun," they are saying, "Have fun and see a lot of other people, so that you will have a treasure chest of other experiences to tell your grandchildren about, and you will not just be sitting around in your rocking chair knitting at much too young an age." Does that make sense?

Kayla: Nods in assent.

Lois: That is all for today, I am being told.

Kayla: Okay, thank you. (The recorder is turned off.)

Lois' Notes: Here is my note to Kayla when I forwarded the recording of the session via email:

Hi Kayla,

I would like to remind you that at the end, after we turned off the recording device, you did comment that Sayed had said in the very beginning in this lifetime, when he first met you that he did not want to have children with you. As young as you two are, that is a strange statement for him to make. The first lifetime I saw, where your only son died, had already explained the reason for that comment of his. I feel certain that as you think over some of the things you have remembered in your relationship with Sayed since we did this reading, you may find other things that the reading will help you to understand about your relationship with him.

Often we have these major or even minor Aha! moments later on, when we listen to the recording a second, third or subsequent time and ponder the other lifetimes. So be sure and listen to the recording many times. It will help you deepen your understanding and broaden the benefit derived from the reading."

Blessings to you,
Lois

(There was no further contact from Kayla. It is unknown if she reaped the benefit from the reading which was inherent within it, or if she and Sayed ever got together.)

Past Life Reading: Kelly Cramer: October 10, 2007

Kelly is an attractive, energetic, highly-educated, well-dressed and successful, dark-skinned woman in her early thirties who has come in for an Akashic Records reading primarily to find out about a long-term relationship. She has been in an intimate relationship with Frank for years, but she is feeling rather frustrated and confused. She truly wants to marry him and he is desperate to marry her, but she just cannot bring herself to actually go ahead with the ceremony. They will set a date for the wedding, and then break up, and then get back together. This happens over and over. There is deep conflict about the wedding itself, not really about the relationship. She repeats several times that he is "driving her crazy."

Kelly is also interested in hearing about any talents she has that she might be able to tap into from past lives. I explain a bit about the need for Kelly to keep her eyes closed during the reading and to wait until the end of each lifetime to ask questions. And then I begin.

<u>Lois:</u> The first thing I am seeing a vast army of sword-bearing soldiers approaching an area where people actually lived inside of a group of interconnected caves. These caves extended deep into the Earth. It is a small community of people. I am not really sure where this is. What I am seeing—I see enormous trees with huge canopies everywhere, and entrances to caves with springs inside where they get their water. This group of people is fairly evolved in terms of a civilization, but it does not look at all like the invaders' civilization. These soldiers were extremely arrogant because they assumed that their military might made them superior in every way, and that everyone on the planet knew and feared them. This belief of their own superiority was

out of their ignorance of spiritual or cultural advancements beyond their own. The soldiers approached these people who they think are primitive, and you are the leader of this "inferior" group who lives inside the Earth. The foreigners have their swords drawn and are yelling at you, but nobody in your group is acting afraid. You do not understand their words. These fierce soldiers, who are accustomed to people running and screaming in terror as they approach, cannot comprehend why nobody in your group is behaving as if they are afraid. Your civilization did not know what swords were; there were not any swords because you did not have metal. The soldiers were expecting fear because that is what they normally saw.

As the leader, you very calmly approached them to speak to them, to explain that you were welcoming them as visitors. You were interested in offering them some food and a place to sleep, as they passed through your territory. They had just told you in their language to shut up and kneel down or they were going to kill you, so when you walked forward with your arms open and your palms turned up which to you was saying "We do not want any trouble." They got really upset. One of the younger soldiers whacked you with the sword and knocked your head off. When you realized what was happening, but too late to do anything about it, you thought you should have kept your mouth shut because now your people had no leader.

What this means for your life is this: there was nothing different you could have done. You were acting out of what you knew and you did not know what a sword was. You knew these strangers were upset because they were being very noisy and making angry faces, but you did not know why, because your people never had war with anybody. No one had harmed these newcomers. Everybody was friendly in that vicinity. It was rather where France is now—there are a lot of caves and large numbers of people lived in them back then.

What you need to know is you had no experience with the Roman culture, and there was not anything you could have done any better. How could you have known to keep your mouth shut? Nobody else was around with greater experience to advise you on how to behave around an invading army with swords.

The soldiers never asked anything about your background. They did not care about such things, did they? The lesson was for your people. They got to see what happens if you do not cower in the presence of a fierce army of foreigners. There was a lesson there for the invaders, too. The soldier who did decapitate you went away feeling horribly about it. He was young and inexperienced, and he was trying to look tough to his friends, but the other soldiers were not impressed. They thought he was an inexperienced jerk, and everyone was shocked, and felt the man (you) did not deserve to have his head cut off. What you need to take away from this lifetime is, you were doing the best you could, given what you knew at the time. Do you have any questions about that lifetime?

Kelly: No, I think it is pretty clear. And I do have a strong tendency to keep my mouth shut in new situations and size everything up. I have real communication issues, which I did not mention to you, but I really do struggle with what to communicate and when.

Lois: Well, that life would help to explain this tendency. (Pause)

Are you familiar with Lemuria? (No) It was a world-wide culture prior to Atlantis and existed for a very long time, longer than the Ancient Egyptian culture, which spanned over three thousand years. Lemuria was quite sophisticated and had spread all over the planet. It ultimately ended from some cataclysmic natural event, part of the cycle of the planet, when the landmass went under the water. It left the original Lemuria with only parts of the landmass left above the sea—which we now call the Hawaiian Islands. These islands had previously been the Lemurian mountain tops. A couple other islands were still above water, but the rest of it all went under water. In Lemuria things were totally different than our way of life. Not in the beginning, but in later centuries, women ruled and men were not allowed to speak. Men were kept for pleasuring women and for procreation and treated like slaves, and never taught to speak. That civilization knew the power of the spoken word.

The women feared the men. Men were not educated, and even not told they were necessary for procreation. They were intentionally kept in the dark, and not taught to speak. And when babies were born, they did not allow most of the male children to live...only a few of them, so there were not very many males, and those who were kept alive, were treated like slaves. The pendulum moved in the opposite direction eventually, but at that time, if a male tried to learn to speak or try to communicate with another male, they would get into harsh trouble. The women viewed men as inherently vicious, capable of destroying the planet via warfare. The females were afraid the men would take over because they believed that males were naturally controlling and competitive, caring nothing for creation, but only for destruction so they could have power. Women feared that men would destroy all life on Earth if not carefully controlled.

In this lifetime, you owned some male slaves who worked out a form of communication, and you managed to discover this fact. Since this was a severe violation of your laws, you took a whip to them and beat them up pretty badly. One of them actually died of an infection he got from the deep whip marks on his back. That is probably the earliest experience you have with communication issues. Sometimes what we do is—it is not like they were stupid, but these men were seriously uneducated and lonely for companionship which communication confers. They were trying to create a form of communication so their lives would be enriched, as they were really bored to death when they were not working. They had their own little restricted area where they stayed.

One of the things that happened during this lifetime includes finishing off the karma of having been over-reactive then. You did not overreact given the culture at the time, but did overreact in terms of human kindness. You could have just separated them, sold off a couple of them and made sure that nobody lived together who attempted to communicate, but you lost your temper and hurt them.

One way to balance the karma we have works like this; you harm someone you come back to be harmed in the same way so that you can experience what it is like at both ends of the experience. There are other ways you can balance this karma. You could also come back as a healer who takes care of people who have been beaten or someone who frees slaves. This is the Earth School, and we are here to experience both sides of any given equation. So if you create karma in one area, you are going to decide to come back and experience a different aspect of it. So you had created karma by losing your temper and beating up slaves. You are being told about this primarily so you may know this aspect about yourself and learn not to judge others who might lose their tempers and beat people. We have all been slaves and slave-holders, beaters and their victims. A majority of the karma has been balanced in this incident for you already, with lifetimes that you have lived as a healer.

Kelly: Was I a violent person?

Lois: No, not necessarily. You just lost your temper that day. You were teaching all the men they had better not talk. They all had to watch. One of them tried to speak their own little language while he was being whipped, and you whipped him so hard for that defiance, that he ended up dying.

Kelly: Really?

Lois: Yes, the cuts were so deep from the whip that he ended up getting an infection and dying. You are not the only one who has done anything rough in a past life. We have all played many roles in various lifetimes; sometimes we kill or get killed, are warriors or their victims. This is just how we have learned over the millennia. You are to take away from this knowledge of the lifetime I just described not judging others who beat people. We must have compassion and forgiveness for them as well. (Long pause)

The next lifetime I am seeing is that you are living in a sandy area and you are pulling a really big, um, what is that I am seeing...you are drawing gigantic symbols in the sand, pulling a great big rake-like tool behind you. It was literally maybe fifteen feet wide. You are walking along, creating patterns for a religious ceremony. You are a male shaman/priest, a healer, medicine man and the leader of the spiritual community. Part of your job is creating beautiful patterns in the sand utilizing sacred geometry. This is created for people to stand within so that they can find their quiet and peace of mind within the geometric shape, and receive the benefit of the spiritual energy which is naturally emitted by sacred geometric forms.

While you are dragging this rake along, you accidently discover a body. This person was buried quite a long time ago in this dry sand, which is a marvelous preservative. The body was just pristine. It was preserved in its nearly original condition because it was covered in this fine, dry sand. The corpse is wearing lovely jewelry, which had ritual magic significance to your people. Because of the jewelry, you realize that this person is someone important from another tribe who had disappeared about fifty years earlier. You had heard stories from your grandfathers regarding how particularly important man had mysteriously disappeared, and it was rumored he and his powerful jewelry had gone elsewhere. He was not killed for the jewelry, however when you uncovered him he was still wearing it. It turned out instead that this was a political assassination. Your discovery had the potential to change the current political balance.

It was quite obvious who had killed him, since there was an axe still embedded in his skull. This was an unusual axe which had markings on the handle that indicated a particular tribe or clan. There had been a truce between the clans for the fifty years since that powerful man had disappeared. You considered seriously whether or not to keep this discovery to yourself or to tell everyone. It had long been a mystery which no one could fathom, and you thought it would be better for the mystery to be solved. Truth seemed more important than anything. You decided that it would do no harm, because there had been peace for fifty years. Instead of re-burying the body, which you considered, you determined to bring the body back to camp and return it to the man's family, or to the tribal leaders of that particular family. In so doing, you revealed that a famous, revered leader of theirs had been murdered by another group, a rival tribe.

Unfortunately, and you had no idea you were going to set off such a conflict, but your revelation of the truth caused a horrible war in which an enormous number of people were killed. You felt utterly responsible again, because you did not keep your mouth shut. You thought later that you should have hidden the body, and berated yourself because you did not correctly discern the outcome. You thought, "I should have hidden this body. I should never have brought this to the light of day. It should have remained a secret. I am such a fool. What was I thinking? Look at the irreparable damage I have caused."

The reason your Guides want you to know this is once again, you communicated something without realizing what the far-ranging implications were. You were moaning and repentant and wearing rags the rest of your lifetime because you had caused a war resulting in severe loss of life and property. Does that make sense?

Kelly: Yes. Maybe I should tell the truth at all costs, or maybe I should be thinking about....?

Lois: Well, what the Guardians are telling me is this: Weigh your words carefully when you do speak, and then do not take undue responsibility for how others respond to the truth, when you do decide to speak. We cannot know, nor can we control, how everything will turn out. Control is an illusion.

You spent a great deal of time studying this issue between lifetimes, and one of your gifts in this lifetime is that you have come to help other people see alternatives of the different, possible outcomes to their actions. It is a gift. You came to make a gift to the world in that area, and that is one of the tasks you are here to do on Earth this time. Have you ever thought of being a counseling minister?

Kelly: My mom always told me that in my later years I would be a minister. And I do counsel my friends all the time. I am the one they come to when they have an issue.

Lois: Sometimes ministers just do counseling. They do not necessarily get behind the pulpit and do the sermon, they are counselors. That might be one possibility for you to consider. (I pause to see the next life.)

I am seeing American Indians, and I am seeing you as a very young, pretty Indian girl with a sweet smile. You are preparing for your wedding day. You and your family have spent months preparing the ceremonial wedding garment and all the ritual objects you need to create a wedding properly. I am seeing something flying through the air. It is like a condor or vulture or something, coming down and picking at the bones of the groom. He has apparently been killed far, far away by a bear. He had gone to do some fishing a few days before the wedding, and a bear got him. Subsequently, vultures have come down and are picking at his flesh. You cannot figure out why he has not shown up for the wedding day, because he really wanted to marry you. There are people present who actually do know he is dead, and they are not telling you, because they did not want to make you sad. They wanted you to think that maybe he will be back later, or he just got lost, or he got sidetracked, and he will be back, but nobody wanted to tell you on your wedding day that your groom is dead.

Why his companions left his body out there I am not sure. I am getting a feeling that there were so many bears in the region they were just trying to get out of there to a safe place. They jumped into their canoe, and went back down the stream. They left the body and thought they would come back later and when they did come back, there was not much left.

But because nobody ever told you what happened it was emotional torture. Perhaps his friends just thought it best if you did not know. It was considered a very bad omen in that time for a woman's groom to be killed on her wedding day. What you surmised was that he just ran away. You concluded that he realized that he did not want to be with you, and that he simply deserted you. This notion made you go into a deep grief, because you really loved this person, and you were definitely supposed to be together.

You went into such a pit of despair, and so deeply grieved, that you reached a point where you eventually lost your mind. You wandered away from the others, and were crouching inside a cave all day long on your haunches, rocking to and fro. Other people loved you, so they were bringing you food and water, but because you were not making any sense when you talked, and you did things that were insane, no one could get near you. You started scratching yourself and pulling your hair out—and it was all from grief. It was because people did not tell you the truth.

In several lifetimes, you have had issues with people needing to know the truth and not getting it, or getting too late it when it would not be helpful any longer. This is why you have made such a study of this topic in various lives. You had problems on either side of the question, do you tell somebody or do you not? On a Soul-level, this philosophical issue is huge for you.

So let me tell you who the groom was now. It is your fiancé Frank in this lifetime, and I think the reason you two are not setting the wedding date is because you are afraid something bad will happen to both of you. So maybe you need to tell him about this reading. That kind of tragedy is not going to happen again in this lifetime. You came to see me because it is time to remember this, and to heal it. You two can get married and live as happily ever after as anyone. There is no reason to recreate that prior trauma, but that may be the fear you have, even though you cannot remember it happened at all, you just have that fear working against you, in the subconscious mind.

Kelly: Something always happens and we break up. Then we fix things and cannot pick a date.

Lois: Why do you not spontaneously go away together and elope? Sometimes that is the best solution.

Kelly: Yeah!

Lois: You can go to Sedona and get married in one day or you can go to Las Vegas and get married in one day. There are a lot of places you can go to get married in one day. (I can see the wheels turning in Kelly's mind.)

Kelly: Oh, wait! That is why...??? (The light of understanding is beginning to turn on in Kelly's face.)

Lois: That is why you say he is "driving you crazy." No wonder you are scared to get married.

Kelly: (Gasp!) Suddenly I can feel it! I remember! Oh, it is him! Oh, my god...

Lois' Notes: (Kelly is overwhelmed and agitated at feeling the past life at a gut level, and knowing that she really was with the same man again.)

Kelly lies on the treatment table for about a half an hour, crying. This crying is a form of soul-level "release work." When she feels like talking later, Kelly says that she feels that an enormous weight has been lifted from her heart and Soul. Finally she knows, while in an incarnate state, what had happened to her beloved groom! Just as she had believed, he did love and want to marry her! Gradually, she regains composure. This was clearly a most powerful session for her. She expresses deep gratitude that this has happened, and knows that this is the reason she was never able to make it to a wedding ceremony without breaking up with Frank.

It has been my experience that frequently when we finally realize something important, something we had not known in that lifetime, we will have a powerful emotional reaction. Somehow, it is different from knowing about this kind of thing between lives. If we need to, we can feel all the emotions that go along with the revelation if we realize this while we are in another human incarnation. We will feel all the feelings that the other person in the previous incarnation would have felt if they found out about it while still living, if necessary. Somehow having this kind of understanding while in human form confers a healing that just knowing about it between lives, in spirit form, does not.

Past Life Reading: Lynette James: February 2, 2009

Lynette was not a regular client, in fact, I had never met her before. She had called to say that she wanted to see what she might be able to learn from a past life reading. She was open to whatever her Guides and Higher Self wanted her to know. She was one of the least talkative clients whom I had met thus far. After explaining what kinds of things we can learn from past life readings, and what Lynette could expect to happen during the reading, I started the reading.

Lois: This first life which I am being shown is from Atlantis. I have seen something like this before. They had some sort of machines that flew that were partially powered by mechanical means, and partly by mental or psychic energy, or whatever you want to call it, of the person who was driving the machine. This craft was about the size of a motorcycle; only one person could fit on there comfortably. Therefore, there is but one driver. You were not sitting inside this machine, you were standing up. It flies through the air and is partially directed by a contraption which looks something like handlebars. The sides of this small aircraft were mounted with guns.

Now I am seeing an aerial gunfight between two groups. You were a male in this lifetime, by the way. I am seeing you winning this particular aerial gunfight, even though you were significantly outnumbered. There were two of you—you and one other man—fighting fourteen of the opposition. The reason that you won this and other fights was because you were very competitive, aggressive, very powerful, quick and determined. You had an unusually intense sense of needing to be top dog, to win, to be the one person who was superior to all the others. And you very much were that, in that lifetime. You won numerous awards for your military service, and you were fairly well known in that particular era, especially in their military history texts. You were also known as a hothead. The need to win was a bit too prominent in the personality—I will just put it that way. (Laughing)

I am being told you need to know this about your past, because it gives you some very pertinent background about yourself in the present. You need to understand some of the past lives you have had, in order to fully understand who you are now. Questions?

Lynette: Not yet.

Lois: This man was really driven, he never married; he just had a lot of women. He considered them to be conquests, which goes along with his competitive spirit, and although he had some feelings of affection toward certain of them over the course of his life, he never felt it was wise for him to distract himself by settling down.

Lynette: Where was he when he died?

Lois: The Guardians of the Records did not think that was important, and that is why it was not mentioned, but let me see if I can find out. (Pause) He was in a hangar, sort of, where they repair those machines that fly, and somebody was fixing another one of them. He lost control of it, and it got loose and hit you from the back. You did not see it coming at all. This then broke your back, and you died rather quickly. You were a bit of an older person by then. (Another pause while I search the archives for the next past life)

Lois: I am seeing very clearly a rough-looking sea captain, with a weathered face and long, stringy brownish hair. He wore black all the time, this was his trademark. This lifetime that I am seeing occurred during the days when there were great sailing ships. This man was a Norwegian (at least, from what is labeled Norway now) sea captain who never put into port for very long. He was very much in love with the sea, and in love with battling the elements. He deeply drew pleasure from the feeling he got pitting himself against the challenge of leading a large group—a crew of people—and winning against the sea. He loved the adrenalin high of not being destroyed by the sea and the winds. He lived to outsmart nature, in a way. The money meant nothing to him, and the cargo meant nothing to him. He was just in love with the challenge. This man really wanted to break speed records, and did not pay as much attention to the comfort of his crew as he could have.

Once near the end of his career, there was nearly a mutiny, and he began to realize that in order to win at this game he had to pay some attention to the crew. He did learn a tiny bit about human relations in that instance. He was so goal-oriented, and so focused on the task of getting from one port to another as quickly as possible with as little damage to the cargo, that he neglected his men. He never lost a ship. Never. He never lost any cargo. Sometimes a man would get washed overboard in a storm, but that was something he never took as his responsibility, because there was nothing he could do about the storm, at least that is what he told himself. He died onboard ship of a brief and sudden illness in his early forties and was buried at sea. He never settled down, did not care to, occasionally he would spend a little entertainment time with a woman in port, a prostitute or barmaid or someone like that. But women were viewed as just entertainment, nothing more.

We are seeing a repeating pattern. Are there any questions?

Lynette: I do not know if this can be answered, but two men, both of them quite driven, never settled down, and did not seem to put much stock in women? Would this explain why I am so resentful of men who dismiss women now? I am just curious.

Lois: Well, yes. That is a great question. Certainly it would totally explain your anger at sexism. Many times there will be a repeating pattern like that, or perhaps a series of lives as women who are dismissive of men because they are insensitive, or lack social skills, and so on. And then, at some point between lifetimes, the Soul says, okay, we are out of balance here. We are going to have to experience life as the kind of person we have been mistreating or resenting, so we can get some perspective on what it is like to walk in their shoes. So then if you do reincarnate as a woman, you might easily become infuriated about superior-acting males, because their behavior is such a perfect mirror for you.

Lynette: Yes, and I do. I become really infuriated when men treat me like that, much more than I see other women getting upset over the same degree of mistreatment. (Pause)

Lois: I am seeing a lifetime in Portugal. It appears to be in about the early to mid-1800s. This time you have come in as a relatively small boned, fragile woman with long, curly brownish red hair. She was a saucy little thing, who easily rebelled against her family's wishes for her, which was that she become a dressmaker. Not a seamstress, but a woman who designed clothing, as the family had a little shop. This family was very well known for their artistic achievements in the field of couture. The mother, her sisters and the grandmother before them were very well known as dressmakers. I guess you would call them couture artisans. You totally rebelled against that as a lifestyle for yourself, with the corsets and erect posture, and the prim and proper lives like your relatives had. You wanted to go wild, to go off on your own, be your own person, and as soon as you were old enough to get away with it, you got a job far away. You moved perhaps seventy-five to a hundred miles away on the seacoast. You got a job in a pub as a barmaid.

You did this because you wanted to see the world, and you knew you never would be able to do that if you were constantly pinning garments on people, and the whole thing seemed awfully prissy and frou-frou, and you were just not interested. It seemed to you like a wasted life.

You also had a really hot temper. One time in the middle of a party in the pub, where men were drinking in a group, rather like a bachelor party, some fellow who had a bit too much to drink, grabbed your backside. Your rage at being diminished in that way flared out of control. You suddenly spun around and not only threw the drink in his face, but hit him in the face with the heavy metal cup the drink was in. A fight broke out that you lost, and that is how you died. You were really very young. This enraged drunk whom you humiliated in front of his friends just hit you a little too hard, and killed you. And so here is at least one situation where you were a female.

Lynette: That did not last very long, did it?

Lois: No, because some drunk grabbed your ass, and you just would not have it. You reacted as a man in a woman's body might. Women usually know when to back down due to their lesser size and relative strength compared to men. You did not. It was an important lesson: you got to experience firsthand how powerless it can feel to be a woman denigrated by a man. This was important because of your tendency in past lives to do the same kind of thing to women. (Pause)

Next I am seeing a World War I experience as a Canadian male. Again, flying aircraft and this time, very frustrated at how slow and vulnerable they were, and how much the wind always had its way with those flimsy, lightweight aircraft back then. You were doing some shooting and primitive bomb dropping, and there were two of you to a plane. You did survive that war experience and you did, actually, become—you did a good job in this lifetime—you became a shoemaker after that and you got married. You had one child, a son, of whom you were very demanding. He tried very hard to please you, and it was not easy for him, so you may have to work through some things with this Soul in this lifetime. You did soften a bit in your old age, but you also had this longing like, "You know, this is not where I am supposed to be or what I am supposed to be doing. I need some excitement." You were always fairly grumpy about things, because it did not seem like there was not enough, that you were not offered enough high-adrenaline experiences. It was a radical shift from the usual lifetime for you. You died of food poisoning in your early fifties, which was pretty young for those days, actually. You were very attached to your wife, showing her a great deal of respect. That was an incredibly positive experience from the viewpoint of your Soul in attempting to get some balance of experiences. You hunkered down and took care of the family and actually respected your wife. You stayed close to hearth and home, fulfilling familial obligations, even though it was sometimes tedious and boring to you. (Pause for next lifetime)

Lois: I am seeing you in ancient Egypt, during the Middle Kingdom, as some kind of priest who worked with their version of alchemy, and it was for the "resurrection of the dead." So it looks like you were tweaking the formula for the chemicals and herbs you embalmed people with, and you were experimenting on animals to see if you could get the results you wanted before you tried them on human corpses. You were very successful at that, actually sometimes getting these animals to move again after they were dead using some sort of alchemical process. People were afraid of you because you were working on this odd experiment, and you were very much a mysterious loner. Yet you did have some friends that nobody knew about.

These friends did not even know your real name or what you did. You would sneak off in disguise to visit them. They did not run in the same social circles as you. But there was a deep caring on your part about these friends, both men and women. Interestingly, they were studying some kind of religion; it feels as if they were a religious order of some sort. I do not think that we know of anything about this group, their written records did not survive, if they kept any. It was most secretive. This was your real life, the one that mattered, and the Egyptian priest thing felt like just a job.

As a priest, you were a chemist doing experimental alchemical processes. However, due to your secret group of friends there was danger. Had they known down at the jobsite what you were up to with these friends, you would have lost your job. In that little group of friends you became very open, warm and tenderhearted not just with the men, but the women, too. It was an unusual group relationship, almost like a communal living kind of group—there was a real commitment to each other, rather like a group marriage, and you all discussed everything together. I think one of the children might have been your offspring. Paternity was not clear, as there was group sex. But the sex was not a big deal to them. They treated the children with a great deal of care and respect. This is very strange. I never knew anything like that group existed. You lived to a pretty ripe old age then and when you passed, it was in the company of those friends of yours with the strange religion, and the priesthood never knew what happened to you. They just thought you disappeared. Do you have questions about that lifetime?

Lynette: Who did they worship?

Lois: It was not who, actually. (I pause momentarily, waiting for the answer.) They were in contact with beings from other star systems, and they worshiped nature. It was more like a form of shamanism.

Lynette: Anything he wants to tell me?

Lois: Well, that is not how it works, but your Guides and Higher Self have told you everything you need to know about this particular individual's life. (I check again, and am unable to get more about this lifetime.) What I am seeing is that the religion went against everything his logical mind believed in, but he followed his heart and his gut which is...that is how you follow your spirit. Listen to the heart, not the brain. The brain is where ego resides; signals from the heart come directly from Soul.

So to summarize, this was a very successful lifetime for you. You followed spirit and your heart, even though it went against the grain of your social background and your career interests and your intellectual training.

I am being told these are all the lifetimes you need to hear about at this point in time. Your task is to assimilate these lifetimes, and you will notice over the next few months things are going to change in your personality and in your life as you assimilate these memories.

Lois' Notes: In speaking later with Lynette, I was told that the primary effect of the past life readings for her was to relax and become more accepting of herself as a human being working through certain issues on behalf of the Soul's learning and balance. She used the familiar phrase for the readings, "It explained a lot..." Lynette had never understood why she was so energetic and intense, or why she possessed so much of the so-called "male" energy, even though she was a heterosexual female. Nor had she understood why she was so competitive and aggressive. Additionally, prior to the reading, she had not grasped why she became so enraged at men's condescension or dismissive behaviors. She found herself starting to be more patient with men, seeing them as misguided when they behaved this way, having been that way herself in other lives.

The greatest benefit of Lynette's having the reading was in knowing herself more fully, which led to greater self-acceptance, and to relaxing about her feelings of not being "womanly" enough. It allowed her to become more patient with herself as she gradually became more soft and feminine, knowing that it was something that was relatively new and difficult for her particular Soul. Since she was not measuring herself against others as much anymore; she decided to release her iron grip on being competitive.

Past Life Reading: Paula England: June 8, 2009

Paula came for a past life reading so she could understand why she is finding herself trapped in a dead marriage with Greg, who acts like a baby and demands that she mother him. He even manipulates situations so that she has to support him financially, even though he is older. She has been married to him for fourteen years at this point, and wants out. At the same time, she has been having a long-term love affair with a married man named Donald, about whom she cares deeply. He seems to play games, though, telling her she is the one he loves, but cannot leave his wife and lose his one young child by this marriage. He sets up meetings with Paula for sex, as he is living in a sexless marriage just as Paula does, but cancels and backs out of the meetings frequently. He "yo-yos" back and forth between his wife and Paula. Paula feels a bit confused about it all, and wants to understand the situation better. She says Donald is her best friend.

Additionally, Paula wanted greater clarity about her relationship with her adult daughter, who seems angry with her much of the time. Paula cannot seem to stop angering her, but does not know what she is doing to set her daughter off on her rages. Paula does not like the son-in-law, and has made her disdain for him clear. While Paula assists her daughter financially, she does not seem to approve of her daughter's choices in life, being fairly critical and non-accepting.

After explaining why I do past life readings, I begin the reading.

Lois: I am seeing you riding on a donkey, bouncing along—oh, I see, you are in what we are now calling Northern Mexico. You are an adult male and very small in stature. You have bags hanging off the back of the donkey on either side. The land here is extremely dusty and dry. The plants are mostly the arid type, cacti and such. On the day I am seeing, you are going home, having been gone for rather a long while. You have been mining, actually, and it looks like you have found some bits of silver and gold. You have some huge specimens of rock with the metal inside them that you are taking home. Arriving home, you discover that your wife is in bed with another man. You have suspected that this has been ongoing for a long time. Your wife back in that lifetime is your lover Donald in this lifetime, and his lover in that lifetime is the woman Donald is married to in the current lifetime. We often go back and forth having both male and female lifetimes.

Realizing that your wife (who is now Donald) was having a long-term thing with this other person, in a rage you picked up one of the sacks filled with rocks that had metal ore in it, and before you had time to think it through, you swung it and hit the lover on the head. He was injured enough that he died in a couple of days. That is one of the lifetimes you have had with Donald and the woman to whom he is currently married. One way of balancing the karma was for him to be married to that person in this lifetime, and you to be in relationship with him without anybody getting killed.

You two were living in a real hovel, by the way, but I do not think you were distressed about it, because everybody else was living like that. You had one of those cactus fences all the way around the house and yard. Have you ever seen this in Northern Mexico? They have fences made of tall, skinny live cacti that grow to be about ten to fifteen feet tall, and they create a fence-like enclosure. They plant the cacti close together in a row all the way around the house, on the outside the edge of the yard, just like you would a fence only it is a living cactus wall. There is one very mangy dog; the kids are grown and not living at home by the time this happens. However, there is one tiny grandchild, a baby, asleep in another corner of the house.

That seems fairly straightforward. You three came together in this current lifetime to relate to each other however you decide to relate, and not to kill each other. I am going to move on to the next lifetime if you have no questions. Paula is silent. (Long Pause)

Lois: I am seeing another lifetime in which you are in the United States, and it seems to be fairly recent. The time period is the 1930s and (Donald) is male, and the eldest sibling in this lifetime; you and his current wife are his younger sisters. You two are constantly vying for his attention, competing intensely with each other. In other words, this pattern has been going on for a while between the three of you. You are wearing your hair in one of those really short, bob hairdos, and so is she. You have lighter hair, and hers is darker. You are living in Kansas; it is very rural where you are. On the one hand he (Donald) thinks that the situation is rather flattering although he may not consciously know that he rather enjoys it. You two are constantly competing for him, but it is also driving him nuts at the same time. You are a year older than she is in this lifetime, by the way.

One day you all decide to go down to the pond. It is one of those man-made ponds they put fish in. I think they call them "tanks" around here. While you are out there, it begins to rain. You have all been swimming, and he gets out of the water. He insists that you two need to get out of the water, too. Ignoring him, you stay in the water. It begins raining harder, and then the lightning strikes begin. At that point you and she start to get out of the pond. While standing right next to each other, practically touching about half-way out of the water, lightning strikes and knocks both of you unconscious and backward several feet, down into the deep water. Suddenly it is up to him to save you. The water is murky, and because it is so dark outside from the black clouds covering the sky, he can barely see anything underwater. He comes to realize he can only save one of you.

With his typical pattern of indecision, he keeps going back and forth between you. Trying to pull you both out at the same time is not working. Finally when he does get you both out, it is too late. You are both dead, because he could not choose. He could not decide whom to save, and he knew he could save just one person. He doggedly kept trying to save both of you so that he would not feel as though he made a choice, and thereby intentionally killed one of you. This, of course, would have bothered him until his death, and possibly beyond. By the way he died of cholera in an epidemic. He was not very old; maybe fourteen years of age, which was not long after the swimming accident. I am not seeing parents anywhere. This is strange. I am just not seeing them. It is almost like you live in a vacuum with nobody else around. That is all I am seeing of that lifetime. Do you have any questions about that lifetime?

Paula: (She shakes her head no.)

Lois: In the next lifetime I am seeing you as a mother with one small child. Apparently you do not have much money for food or medicines, and you are really sick most of the time. Your husband has a serious drinking problem. He spends the food money on alcohol and gambling, which is why you are ill so frequently. The one child is very sickly as well. I cannot tell what the time era is on this. Looks like France in the late 1700s, early 1800s maybe. So here is another relatively recent lifetime. On the day I am seeing, you are cold, and your addict-husband is off squandering what little money he has. You did not have the strength to stand up to him, or go behind his back to his wealthy family for help.

It is bitterly cold the day I am seeing, and the two of you, you and your five-year-old son, are huddling in the cold in the bed. You are trying to keep warm because it is so cold, and there is no firewood or food. You are so malnourished! Lying there holding each other in the bed, you freeze to death together. The child is your husband, Greg, in your current lifetime. It looks like the two of you have come back together in this lifetime for Greg finally to get some nurturing and for you to give it, as well as to work through the not-enough-money issues in a different way this time. The Soul you were married to in that lifetime is not in the picture currently. He is not incarnate at this time. This definitely looks like something you and Greg came to work on: money issues and mother/son thing on some level, to help him "grow up" in your care. This often happens when something ends and is incomplete. You did not get to see him grow up the last time; he died as a small child. You decided to help him mature in this one. Does that make sense?

Paula: (She nods and murmurs yes.)

Lois: Now I am seeing a very long ago lifetime. It is hard to say when or where this was. This particular culture is one in which people travel a great deal by air, and they have one and two-person vehicles just like we have cars and motorcycles. They also have a type of vehicle that has a similar shape to our stealth bombers. They are V-shaped and gold in color, and comprised mostly of wing. You and your daughter from the current lifetime are men in this lifetime I am seeing. The two of you are having a "playful dogfight." It seems to be friendly competition, just trying to best one another, like in a tennis game. Something goes very wrong, and it is not clear whose fault it is, but the two of you crash and burn. The craft suddenly spiral down to the ground. Hitting the ground, they both explode. When you crashed, it was in a rural area so you did not hit any buildings or people. But it sent up a massive cloud of smoke and fire that could be seen for many miles. You had known each other since childhood, always having this competition going on, and you both felt strongly that you had to win. As you were dying in this lifetime you said, "Uh, oh. Maybe I do not have to win every time. Let us get back together in another lifetime and get it right."

While on the other side, between lives, you reviewed that lifetime. It was then that you decided to experience another lifetime with her and not be so competitive. So you came here to learn how to work cooperatively with this Soul who is your daughter now. That is why you came in as women and as family members, so that you could be close and cooperate. Formerly you experienced fatal competition. This is one of those things you wanted to clear up with her, to stop competing and to support one another in a cooperative relationship.

Do you have questions about that lifetime?

Paula: (She shakes her head no.)

Lois: Now I am seeing a lifetime where you were a Roman charioteer. You raced chariots, and were reputed to be quite good at it. This is in the countryside somewhere, or perhaps prior to the coliseum, because I am not seeing the coliseum. However, I am seeing a competition which looks similar to drag racing with chariots. You have an assistant, and that assistant is your daughter in this current lifetime. In the lifetime I am seeing you are both males. This time he is quite younger than you are, and he is turning himself inside-out to please you. Unfortunately, you are a rather demanding and exacting person who knows precisely how things need to be done. Your major concern is doing things correctly. You are oblivious that this young person idealizes you, and wants desperately to please you. Trying to teach this person, and teach him to do it right, is the only focus for you. You are using the techniques which seem like the best way you know to transfer information, which is okay, but you disregarded the feeling side of things. Your attitude was, "This is how it is done and you are going to be corrected when you screw up," with no consideration at all for this fatherless young man's feelings.

This goes on for a number of years, until he finally gives up on ever getting your approval and goes away. He decides he is not going to become a charioteer; he is going to go do something else entirely. It causes him to lose a lot of time from his career-building efforts. And you are puzzled. You could not figure out what went wrong because you were oblivious to his deep desire to get that pat on the head from you. He needed this desperately in that lifetime. You were not noticing that this young man did not have a father, or that he was looking up to you. It eluded you that you needed to give him some approval occasionally. Frequently losing your cool, you criticized the way he did things. It sometimes even had to do with his personal life. Sometimes it had to do with the people he was hanging out with, and he finally just realized he was never, ever going to get what he needed from you emotionally, so he quietly left one day. He left with no explanation. Deeply disappointed, he went away and started studying to become a person who prepared food, like a baker, or a baker's apprentice. He did very well at that, by the way. So again, in that lifetime, there was a missed connection between the two of you. Have you any questions about that lifetime?

Paula: Does he have a mother or other family around?

Lois: No, there are no parents or family anywhere around... Well, now I am seeing that he had a mother who lived quite some distance away, and they had a good relationship. But he was old enough that he needed to start working— he is maybe thirteen or fourteen years old, so he becomes your apprentice, to learn a trade in exchange for room and board and a bit of spending money. The widowed mother was not financially in a position to support the boy. Children in those days were considered ready to go to work by the age of thirteen. However, you were a grown man, certainly old enough to be his dad. So in any lifetime, all I will be shown are the relationships that are pertinent to you, which is why she did not show up until you asked. His mother did not play into the situation in any significant manner. She could not help him and culturally would not have been expected to do so.

In this current lifetime you incarnated with the intention to turn that relationship with this Soul around, by giving this person some approval, and to not criticize her friends or her choice of husband. You intended to be there for her, patting her on the back telling her you approve of her, and that you are proud of her, no matter what she is doing. Your job in this lifetime is primarily to build her self-esteem. That is one of the things that the two of you came to do together. It was for her to win your approval, and for you to give it without her having to reach a really high bar. Do you know what I am saying? (Paula nods yes.)

When they are small, we can correct our children's behaviors without criticizing them as people. We might say for example, "I love you, but I do not approve of your shooting birds with your BB gun. I wish you would change that behavior." We are not attacking their character, just disapproving of the behavior while assuring the child that we love him her as a person, no matter what. So again, with her, you are here to bestow self-esteem upon her and give approval because she craves it so much from you. At a Soul level, she still deeply craves your approval. That is one of the major issues you two came to work out in this lifetime. This thing I am suggesting you give, the famous psychologist Carl Rogers calls it "unconditional positive regard." He says that this is what the child is innately owed by his parents, and he is absolutely right. It is every parent's duty to just love and approve of that child unconditionally because he or she exists and is their son or daughter. It is never too late to give that to our offspring. We owe them that, just because they are alive. And it is our duty to give it. (Long pause)

I am seeing one more lifetime as a man. You owned and operated an apothecary in Wales. You are the equivalent of what today we would call a pharmacist. Additionally, you were a gifted gardener, and quite good at growing most of the herbs yourself in a garden out behind your shop, which was also located at your home. You would process the plants by making tinctures, or drying them, or making teas or poultices. You functioned very much like a healer. People would come and tell you their problems, and you then would give them the appropriate herbs. It appears that you are being told about this lifetime because you have certain definite talents in that area. What I mean is, if you wanted to grow healing plants, you would do well at that. In fact, that might be a fun way to make some extra money on the side. Get some rare, healing plants or heritage seeds, and grow them, make tinctures or dry them and sell them on the internet or to stores. If you have any interest in all in gardening, that might be something you could do...learning about healing herbs and just selling (retail or wholesale), or prescribing herbs to people, actually. You could learn (or remember) all about the field of herbology quite easily. Do you have questions about that?

Paula: No.

Lois: I am being told that we are complete for today, and now you will begin to integrate those lifetimes.

Lois' Notes: A few months later I interviewed Paula about her past lives and asked what, if anything, had changed since the reading. She was still with Greg, but making concrete plans to leave him, although she still wavered occasionally. She had been with and mothering him, for fourteen years, the same amount of time that would have been needed for that four-year-old who froze to death in her arms in the 1700s to grow up. Paula felt she had fulfilled her obligation to him. Additionally, she wondered if having had a child die of illness was part of the reason she had chosen to have a healing profession working with children in this current lifetime.

She still occasionally saw Donald, but viewed the entire relationship differently. She decided that he met certain needs she had at this time, and she was not giving him up just yet. She feels more comfortable and safe knowing that she can see him occasionally. She also realized that no one belongs to anyone else, we are Souls who take on human form to experience life, and the roles switch all the time from life to life.

As for her daughter, Paula seemed to still be having trouble approving of her lifestyle and giving her the positive "strokes" the daughter needs so badly. Hopefully, this will turn around given enough time. It takes time for people to integrate their past lives; it does not always happen overnight, though sometimes it does. There is no blame our judgment for this. The Soul has lessons simply because whatever the issue being worked out, it is difficult for that Soul. If it were not difficult, it would have been resolved long ago. It is wise of us to be patient with ourselves and with others.

Past Life Reading: Sallie Hopkins: January 5, 2006

Sallie is a relatively lively and happy, attractive golden-haired young married woman with a pre-school aged daughter. She has come for a reading to learn more about her husband, Ted, and their daughter, Megan. She is also curious about any ties with an old boyfriend she inexplicably cannot get out of her head, Mack. She is wondering about the context of their past lives together. This is primarily out of a kind of spiritual curiosity. She is really not having any problems, except for the annoying tendency to think about Mack.

After the explanation of how past life readings can assist in the spiritual growth process, the session begins.

Lois: I am seeing you as a young man who is a member of a tribe we would now call Arabs; these people were the precursors of the Bedouins, and this was hundreds of years ago. Your tribe lived in the desert, and they were nomadic.

At some point, a different group of nomads, marauders actually, come into your camp and steal a vast quantity of your belongings and most importantly, your food. You and another group of men return to camp to find that this has happened and give chase. Mack is one of the men in the group; he is a close friend of yours, and a relative, perhaps a cousin. He and you grew up together, having known each other since infancy.

This group you are chasing came from far away. You followed them out of the desert and onto solid land. This rocky territory was quite alien to you, as you were accustomed to the cushiony feeling of sand under the horses' hooves. The feeling of solid ground, with huge rocks that did not move at all the way that sand moved around, was totally alien to you and your cohorts, and quite disorienting. It was almost like a sailor stepping onto dry land for the first time. The sensation of the solid, hard vibration suddenly began to shake you as the horses' hooves hit solid, rocky ground. This sent shock waves through your bodies. The odd sensation affected your ability to focus on your surroundings. You all felt like you were being beaten up. The horses did not like it, either.

The raiders you were chasing had superior weaponry, and were accustomed to this terrain. They easily ambushed your group. You personally were gravely wounded, and the group knew you were going to die, and for that matter, you knew as well. Lying there bleeding, you urged them to leave without you, as you knew that they would not survive if they tried to carry you in your wounded state. Everyone clearly understood that you were dying in either case. And so they did leave.

Even though you knew that this was the right thing for them to do, you died feeling horribly abandoned, and sobbing with an indescribably intense longing for your cousin (who is your ex-boyfriend, Mack, in this lifetime) to come back and get you. Your cousin was slightly older and had always protected you. Since you died with this horrible longing and the feelings of abandonment, even though you knew it was not logical, you have an imprint on your Soul where Mack is concerned. I would be quite surprised if you do not currently experience an illogical fear of abandonment and longing where he is concerned. Do you have questions about this lifetime?

Sallie: No, but that totally explains how I feel about Mack. I feel like I cannot live without him.

Lois: Well, as you integrate this past life, now that you know about it, you will begin to see those feelings and fears about him begin to dissipate. Would you like for me to continue to the next lifetime?

Sallie: Yes.

Lois: I am seeing a dazzling, glorious and enormous field of flowers which extends for miles. You are blissfully walking along among these fragrant spikes of blossoms, eyes closed, inhaling the fragrance, and reveling in the sun on your face. You are beaming, and your face radiates peace and joy. These flowers are planted in curving rows, and some of the plants come up as high as the middle of your chest. It is a daily experience of intense sensuality, the wind, the flowers, the sun, and the warm Earth beneath your bare feet. When it comes time to harvest, you and your companions grab the stalks down by the Earth and cut them off. Then you beat the top ends, where the flowers are, onto a tarp. You collect seeds like that, or at different times of the year, in different fields, you might collect their oils, or dry the flowers for use as herbs in medicinal applications. You would also create perfumes and lotions with the oils from the flowers, and sell or trade these. There are several varieties of flowers in different fields, so you were surrounded by vibrant color. This was a very pleasant lifetime. You were all highly contented.

The next scene takes everyone completely by surprise. One day along comes an army, just out of the blue. This was absolutely not expected. No one had heard they were advancing in your direction. No scouts from towns that had been conquered came to warn you. The only precursor was the vibration coming through the Earth as they rhythmically marched toward you. They literally shook the Earth as they approached. This was fearsome.

This was a vast army spread out as far as the eye could see, to the horizon. They continued marching in your direction, and you were just stunned. Everyone was. You almost could not comprehend what was happening and just froze up. This was the Roman army, and they marched straight at you. They trampled the entire place; the enormous fields of flowers were smashed underfoot, releasing waves of fragrance, as this massive army made their way across the land on their way to conquering the country where you lived. Your way of life was gone forever, from that day forward.

This Roman army took up residence and completely took over, turning everyone you knew into slaves. Eventually the smarter members of the population in an occupied country will befriend the conquerors, so this is what you did. And in spite of yourself, you were drawn to one particular solider. You fell for him, and the two of you become lovers. There is a child produced of this union. Then your lover is called back to Rome, and you are left with the child. This man was younger than you by a few years, and you have this handsome male child as your only memory of him. You raise the child alone, and your neighbors are initially furious with you for having his child and lovingly raising him. Yet there are a lot of other women your age doing the same thing. It becomes more accepted later on, but at first it was difficult. You never saw the Roman soldier again, and the child looked just like him, so you were constantly reminded.

Living to be an old lady, you think about the soldier on a daily basis but he is never able to return to you. He was killed in another military campaign not long after he left your side. But there was no way for you to know that and you were left wondering. That Roman soldier has reincarnated in this lifetime as your daughter. You have come together in this particular life to have a very long, loving relationship, which you were unable to have in that prior lifetime. Now this is very important, Sallie. There will come a time when Megan needs to travel, to leave and go far away, but you need to know that this time she will come back. It is very important that you know that. She needs to go a far distance from you, and then come back. This is part of your Soul agreement with her. You may want to prevent her leaving, but it would be unwise. The Guardians of the Records are saying that she simply must go away and come back. Just let her go. The experience will be very healing for you both....Questions? (Sallie shakes her head no.) (Long pause.)

   Lois: I see you rowing a tiny white rowboat on a calm, turquoise sea. This sweet little boat with highly polished oars is maybe big enough for three people, no more than that. I am hearing clearly that you are off the west coast of Italy, and you are from a fishing village. You are dropping a string overboard with a hook and bait on the end. There are no nets on board. You eventually catch some little fish. You are about eleven years old, and this fishing expedition is only for amusement. You are alone, and under strict orders not to go far from shore. And you do not. Yet as you are relaxing on the water, casually dipping your fishing string into the sea, a large animal comes underneath the boat, and knocks it over. You hit your head as the boat tips over and you are unconscious just long enough to drown....I am trying to understand why I am seeing this lifetime. What is the point? (Pause.)

   Oh, I see. You needed to remember this so that you know that even though some unexpected things can happen suddenly like that, we cannot predict or control them. They are rare. So if you worry a lot that something is going to come like, boom, out of the clear sky, and ruin everything completely, without warning, this is why. The Guardians want you to know that this was one of your pre-arranged possible "checkout points" in that lifetime. For every lifetime, in the planning stages prior to reincarnation, each Soul plans multiple "checkout points" where it can choose to honorably leave that lifetime, depending upon how things are coming along. It is like a safety valve on a pressure cooker, a way to get out safely and without penalty.

   And so, in the childhood in Italy where you drowned, the Soul had decided to go ahead and check out of that lifetime. There is no reason to fear sudden accidents, since there was nothing you could have done to prevent it. On one level you wanted it. Your Soul "checked out" because of external circumstances which were about to unfold in the village where you lived. It was so severe that your Soul did not think you could handle it. The personality was not strong enough, and it would have gone on through your teen years, and the Soul wisely took you out of harm's way.

Sallie: Is this just about me? Or as a general rule is this about my family, my worrying about them?

Lois: Generally, worrying about everyone you love and yourself. Because as you were passing over to the other side, you were thinking, "Gee, this could happen to anybody! Sudden deadly accidents can happen to anyone! I was powerless to prevent this." This was fear was imprinted on the Soul level.

Sallie: So, it was just too hard, and I decided to leave?

Lois: At the pre-birth planning stage, you set this event up as a possible Soul lesson. There was an event that was about to occur in your village and continue for about eight years. But when the Soul took stock of the situation at this designated "checkout point," it said, "Oh, no, this kid just cannot take it. I am out of here." It would have taken too many lifetimes to heal, due to the spiritual scar you would have incurred had you lived through the horror that was about to unfold in your village. And then the fishing accident occurred, you just get bonked on the head and boom! You were gone.

Sallie: Laughs. (There is a pause—to begin to view the next life.)

Lois: Okay. Yes, I am willing to go here. This is a future life, and I usually do not want to go there, but I am giving my permission to see this. The Guardians are asking if I am willing. Future lives are not as cast in stone as the "past" ones, which sounds odd, since they are actually all happening simultaneously. But anyway, I am seeing this one now. They are telling me you need to know about this so you can be prepared when it happens.

You are a female crew member on a space craft somewhere in deep space. There is an explosion and you get to an escape pod, but before you get on, there is something on the ground in the loading dock near the pod. You think about grabbing it up, and a lot depends upon whether or not you pick this thing up. It is a lurid, bright yellow color, and if it held fluid, it would hold about a half a gallon. So when this happens, you only have a split second to make up your mind. But you must grab it. Do you understand? It is crucial that you do this. So please stop and grab that thing, and take it with you. Otherwise you will not make it. Something will fail in that pod, and you will need the yellow thing to generate heat. I feel the cold right now, and my body feels almost frozen. Out among the stars it is very, very cold.

The next thing I see is that you are in the pod, hurtling through space, and the stars are a mind-boggling, magnificent sight. Looking at them puts you into an altered state of consciousness, feeling a piercing joy in your heart. The pod has a homing device, and you will be directed to safety. The only thing that could prevent your making it back home is if you do not have that yellow device. It will prevent your freezing to death. And it is important for you to survive, because you are carrying a baby whom your civilization needs desperately to be born. The future turning out correctly depends, in a major way, upon your having that baby, and you do not even know that you are pregnant when you get into the pod. So do not hesitate, grab that yellow device before you get into the pod. Okay?

<u>Sallie:</u> Okay, I will!

<u>Lois:</u> I am being told that this is all for today. This is all you need to know about at this time. I have not seen any lifetimes with your current husband, probably because you have no huge karma to balance with him. That relationship looks pretty safe and healthy. The Guardians of the Akashic Records tell me what you most need to see at the time you come to me.

<u>Lois' Notes:</u> After the reading, Sallie wanted to know if dying in the desert from blood loss was the only lifetime she had with her friend Mack, and the only one that caused this deep longing she experienced for him all the time. She did agree that the overwhelming sense of longing for him was a huge factor for her, even though she was quite happily married to someone else. I told her that this was not the only lifetime, but it was the seed lifetime, the one that planted the seed of that longing that had continued through every lifetime she had ever had with Mack. This caused her sense of not being able to live without him. Had he stayed, I saw after the reading, he would have died and left the group leaderless. The group all would have been killed and these were all the young, strong men of the tribe. The tribe would not have survived without them. So the choice was either him (Sallie) or the whole tribe.

The other thing Sallie said was that she had felt this enormous wave of relief sweep over her at the point when I told her that while fishing the boat had been overturned, bumped her on the head, and the boy died. She asked if that relief was due to the fact that something horrible was about to happen in her village. I replied that, yes, I feel certain that it was the Soul's relief she was feeling, knowing they would not have to experience that impending horror. As we discussed this, I was able to see that the intolerable event was an invading Army which came into the village and were going to capture this teenaged boy and torture him and others. They would torture him mostly, as his family seemingly had money, which is why he had the luxury of fishing for pleasure at the age of eleven or so. They would choose him to torture, thinking his family had hidden money that they would produce to stop his suffering. They had none hidden, so the suffering would have been prolonged and great.

What they were finally going to do after months of torture was genital mutilation followed by suffocation. This was a common thing for the more barbaric armies to do back in those days. The thoughts that would have gone through the boy's head in the minutes before death would have been too horrific, as well. Judging that this would have been too traumatic for this particular child, and no lessons would be learned, the Soul chose the fishing accident as a safety net for the Soul. So when Sallie heard me tell her about this accident, she was surprised to feel relief. But upon hearing that it was because of impending torture, the relief made perfect sense.

Months later I spoke with her, and Sallie volunteered that her longing for Mack had dissipated. She seldom thought about him any longer. This was a significant relief for her. She was noticing that she did not worry about horrible things happening suddenly to family members, not that she was careless, just that she did not have this nervous undercurrent inside her all the time. Overall, she felt more relaxed. She noted that since she found out that she was hit on the head in the childhood in Italy, she had fewer headaches when out in the sun. Before that the glare of the sun on shiny surfaces (like water?) had given her a powerful headache on the left side of her head. Sallie said the reading of past lives from the Akashic Records had healed her in many ways, some of them quite unexpected.

Past Life Reading: Sonia Preston: June 2, 2009

Sonia, a regular energy medicine client of mine, is a trim, beautiful woman in her early thirties with shiny, long black hair and tailored clothing. She comes in for a reading at my Houston office because she is distraught. This is uncharacteristic for her, as she is normally distinctly reserved, formal and businesslike. Sonia had been involved with a man named Agustin years ago, and the relationship never really went anywhere. She believed that it was his fear of the intensity of his feelings for her that stopped the relationship from further developing. She has always believed that eventually the two of them would be together one day. Sonia has had some news about him recently, and cannot seem to get control of her feelings and emotions. She is unable to sleep or function properly at work. She is crying frequently and feeling sick to her stomach. She needs to know as much as she can about her past lives, if any, with this man, Agustin, and hopes that this knowledge will help her cope with this painful and shocking turn of events.

Lois: So you have a nervous stomach, and this started after you heard news of Agustin?

Sonia: Yes. Really casually, over an email I got the news. A friend, Federico, and I were emailing regarding another friend of his who was all over this "new" girl at a wedding. I said, "You saw him at a wedding?" I was surprised, because they all live in different cities, and he said, "Yeah. I saw pictures of this on Facebook. He was at Agustin's wedding in Mexico City." This news just hit me like a bomb.

Lois: You really thought you had been over him for at least a year, as I recall. How long has it been since you have seen him?

Sonia: Eight years. Can you believe it? The last time he called me, he left a voice mail in the middle of the night. It was six years ago, and we really did not communicate after that. It is been eight years since we first met. We had a class together in college, but he had a girlfriend. The end of the semester arrives, and one weekend I have this dream that he and I are shopping for groceries, lying on the couch, just kind of snuggling. It was the strangest thing. I think we were in Mexico in the dream.

Why would I dream something like that? I had a boyfriend then that I had been dating for five or six years at that time. I went to class on Monday, The second he walked in and I saw him again, and boom! It was like something hit me. Ever since then there has been this powerful thing between us.

Lois: Did you ever date him?

Sonia: After that I felt, "Well, I must get to know this guy." Did we officially date? No. Did we have something going on? Yes. Within a few months, we started seeing each other. His girlfriend left for the summer, so he hung around with me. The second she came back, he dropped me like a fly. Then I started seeing one of his friends, who turned out to be his roommate, and that was uncomfortable. I think that was when Agustin realized how he felt, but he did not say it.

Lois: It bothered him that you were seeing his roommate.

Sonia: It bothered him. I could see that it did.

Lois: It was as if he was attracted to you, but remained at a distance.

Sonia: He definitely was attracted to me. You know, you can feel that kind of thing.

Lois: But he never really connected with you, for whatever reason.

Sonia: A few other things happened which told me he did care about me. He became quite upset seeing me out at a club, and leaving with a woman friend. He wanted me to leave with him.

I had this dream two or three months ago, and I knew it was a wedding. I am talking to this man thinking, "Oh, he has everything I want. He is like a live poodle." (It was not Agustin, though.) We were talking and then the man started crying, because he was very sad. It was about his career, and we were in a stadium, even though it was clearly a wedding. It was odd because I never dream of weddings. Then I later found out that at about that same time Agustin was getting married. I did not know about his wedding until much later. But my dream knew.

Lois: So, then later, when you found out that Agustin had married, you had an over-the-top, upset reaction.

Sonia: The blood just left my face. I felt sick. I wanted to run outside the office building—I should not feel like this after eight years. It makes no sense at all. I should be thinking, okay, well, so he found someone to marry. That is how it goes. But I am not feeling casual about it at all. I wonder if it is just my ego.

Lois: My experience has been that this level of reaction to somebody with whom you did not have any more of a relationship than you did with him usually has to do with past lives. So let us take a look at why you are having this really intense reaction to his marriage.

Sonia: This reaction is not normal. I cannot even listen to poems or songs or anything. It is like putting salt on a wound.

Lois: So songs remind you of him.

Sonia: Yeah, it seems that even happy love songs make me sad.

Lois: Are you having trouble sleeping?

Sonia: Kind of. Yeah.

Lois: You said your stomach is upset and...

Sonia: Yes, and I am just so very distracted. It is difficult to focus, and a lot of impulsive thinking—while doing laundry this weekend I was thinking, "Oh... she is doing laundry." What do I care? Why does that matter to me?

Lois: So when you were doing laundry you were thinking well, she is doing his laundry?

Sonia: (tears up) Yes. Just random, stupid thoughts like that. I thought about him proposing, and wondered if he got down on one knee.

Lois: Well, it might have been romantic like that, but on the other hand, she may have said, "You marry me right now, or I am out of here," and so he gave her a wedding band, and so he went ahead and married her. Quite a few men get married due to arm-twisting like that. That is not a good way to start a marriage—not for either party.

Sonia: You are right. I do not know how it all happened. One of my friends said that honestly, you do not know the circumstances. You do not know how it is at all between them. You do not know that.

Lois: She is right. You do not. She may be desperately unhappy because he had his arm twisted and reminds her of it all the time. I am going to pause here...and then tell you what I see in the first past life. (Long silence)

I am seeing you, and you are with one other man. Both of you are men. You are moving across a glacier, all dressed in heavy furs and woolen things, and the wind is picking up. There is snow and ice in your beards. Now, glaciers are very, very dangerous. For no discernible reason they sometimes crack open. At one point as you were trekking along, this glacier cracked and he fell in. You were somewhat prepared for this sort of thing because you lived in or near that area. You are European-looking people. You do not look like natives of the region. I am thinking you are German, but I am not really clear about that. You are European-looking, anyway. He falls in and you have with you some way of anchoring ropes up on top. You had pitons, so you lowered yourself down to try to pull him out because he was injured. You needed to wrap a rope around him, and help him out. The fall left him trapped, wedged tightly, and injured. You needed to pull the two of you out, which demanded a great deal of physical strength.

It is not clear to me what you are doing on this glacier. That does not seem to be the point, though, that is what my Guides are telling me. Why you were there is not really the point. Here is the point of knowing about this past life. You were both men, and wound up down in this crack in the glacier, and knew that you would run out of food and water. After you got down there, you discovered that you did not have enough physical strength to pull both of you out. It is becoming clear that you were refugees of some kind, trying to escape civil unrest or war or something of that nature. The two of you were kind of stuck down there, and you realized that you were going to die, and you gave in to something. Because you were so close to death, you gave into something that you had been resisting, and probably would have resisted the rest of your lives. And it was this: there was a sexual attraction between you.

You started kissing, and ended up having sex down in this glacier crevice. This action sped up your demise. Since it was bitterly cold, and you had removed parts of your clothing to make love, you died faster. But you knew you were dying anyway, and that sort of pushed both of you to admit the truth of the attraction between you. But at the same time because you were both men, it was really an extremely forbidden thing. It was very satisfying and exciting, and yet horribly shameful. Both of you sobbed out of shame, and that is how you were feeling as you both died. You were holding each other, in each other's arms, and at the same time, feeling disgust and shame. It was really a mixed bag. Both of you thinking your own thoughts, but your thoughts were, "I really need to stay away from this person and not get close to him ever again, because what a horrible, shameful end this turned out to be." He was thinking along the same lines, only he felt it was somehow his fault. If he had not fallen in this crevice, none of this would have happened. He felt that he had pulled you down into this humiliation and shame, and caused your death, and he must never allow such a thing to happen to either of you again. For him, the guilt and shame was even more intense. Do you have any questions about that lifetime?

Sonia: No. (Long pause)

Lois: I am seeing the two of you as members of a crew on a spaceship, and you are humanoid, but not exactly human beings. You landed on this planet, and were doing some exploration. I think you were mining, or collecting raw materials. The entire crew was warned before they came to Earth that it was a planet of karma, and furthermore that they could get trapped here. They were warned because off-world Souls can and have become entangled here. They then begin reincarnating over and over and over again, stuck on the wheel of karma. He is male in that lifetime, and you are a female. Again, the two of you have a very strong Soul-level spiritual and sexual attraction to each other. Yet it was strictly against the rules for crew members to participate in sexual relationships.

You found yourselves in some sort of cabin, or shelter, near the site where you were mining, or getting some material out of the Earth. You were supervising the removal of whatever substance your project was interested in collecting. This material was gray and luminescent. I see it, but have no idea what the material is, and I am familiar with most of the minerals on this planet. One day you walked outside this little shack, looked around and thought, "Gosh, nobody would ever know. We could have sex out here and nobody would ever know. When we get back to the ship, everything will go back to normal." And so you did. You both yielded to the desire, and had this wild, passionate love affair. You did not get much mining done after that, because you were in the throes of lovemaking so frequently. One day a man showed up to do an unscheduled audit of the amount of material being mined. He just happened to walk in on you two in the act.

It was a grievously wrong thing to have done from the point of view of the commanders of the spacecraft. You had broken a major rule, and when you were questioned separately, you both said, "Well, it was not really my fault." You claimed to be seduced by him, and he said you were the instigator. When you each betrayed one another, in that moment, karma was incurred. That is when you two set the stage to begin incarnating over and over on this planet. In so doing, of course, you inevitably created even more karma, with each other and with other Souls as well. That is what happens to many beings from other star systems or planets. They come down here for some purpose of their own, and do something which incurs karma. You had been warned about this aspect of landing on Earth. You both regretted the sexual experience because of the consequences. The ship left, and you were left behind. You were both deeply upset. Each blamed the other. Consequently, you went your separate ways, and did not have the mutual support and cooperation needed to survive in the foreign environment. Together you might have made it.

Soon after the ship left, you both died. And you both entered the reincarnation cycle of Earth. You have come back together many times since then to finish that karma. Your Guides want you to know that things are going well, and you are very close to completion. When you forgive and have compassion and affection for the person with whom you have had karma, it is cleared. That is how you know it is done.

There is something else you need to know. It would appear that in that other system where you two were together, you were family members originally. Not brother and sister but like distant cousins. Definitely you were members of the same tribe, and this affected your tribe back home, the fact that you two got trapped down here. That is still having an effect on them, actually. So, are there questions about that lifetime?

Sonia: No.

Lois: Is this starting to make sense?

Sonia: A little.

(There is a long pause as the next lifetime comes into focus.)

Lois: I am seeing another lifetime in which you were in the Middle Ages together. Agustin was a priest and you were a nun. Again, the male/female thing is the factor here. In that lifetime you worked really hard, and did manage to clear a great deal of the karma that was between you two by being supportive, platonic friends. You spent many years just being lovingly friends to each other, and not becoming sexually involved. Of course, sex was against the rules in this situation, too. You chose this setting so you could complete the task of being close friends and co-workers, and hopefully not break the rules about sex. This has been the pattern for you two. You make contact with each other, and then release each other so you will not have this sexual experience, because that is what got you into trouble in the first place. It will go on until it is finally completely balanced. Do you have any questions about that particular lifetime?

Sonia: No.

Lois: (Pause) I am seeing a different lifetime. This one does not involve the person you are asking about. You were in what is now China, many hundreds of years ago. You were growing silkworms, weaving silk, and making beautiful long fabrics that they would later roll up into a big roll when dry. Your job was drying the silks in such a way that they were safe, and the damp fabrics and their wet dyes did not touch one another, thereby keeping the colors from bleeding together. You were keeping sufficient space between the fabrics. I am seeing just so many acres of brilliantly hued, billowing silk dancing softly in the wind. It is visually stunning! These silks are also protected from the sun by canopies, so that their luminous color would not fade.

I am seeing a fire under a pot of dye; part of your job was to tend the pot, and to see that the fire remained contained. You became sleepy one afternoon, and dozed off under a tree. You would have never allowed the fire to get out of control otherwise. Also, and this is rather interesting, part of your job was to keep the birds away. You had a big palm frond, or something like a broom. This was used to swat the birds, so they would not leave bird droppings on the silks. You were also responsible for taking the fabrics down when they got dry. This was slow work and out of sheer boredom you fell asleep, and there was a fire. Eventually all of the silks caught fire and people were killed, and you were directly responsible. This weighed very heavily upon you.

You were not punished, however, because you were so clearly anguished over what happened. At the time, you were quite young. A council meeting of elders was called. These authorities decided that they had given you too much responsibility at too young an age. They took responsibility for what had happened. Nevertheless, it financially ruined many families, and you felt responsible for that as you watched people go hungry. Unfortunately, this was a very tenuous economy, and all it took was something like that—nobody had insurance policies, of course—to wipe out everybody's savings. Not just their money, but also what they had to trade for food was destroyed. You felt wretched about their plight.

By the end of your life you had still not resolved the feelings of guilt and shame for simply having fallen asleep when you were too young to bear that kind of responsibility. So what your Guides want you to know is that it is okay to make mistakes. Everybody does from time to time. You do not have to feel responsible for things that are beyond the level of what you should be expected shoulder. Does that make sense? Do you find that you have an exaggerated sense of responsibility inside yourself?

Sonia: Oh, yes, I think I am very hard on myself. I wonder how long I have been that way.

Lois: Yes, well, you certainly were that way in that lifetime. You were so much harder on yourself than was anybody else, which is why you were not punished. The Guides are saying it is not necessary for you to be so hard on yourself. They really hope you would lighten up and play. Have you any questions about that lifetime, Sonia?

Sonia: No, no questions...but... play? What is that? (She laughs a little.) (There is a pause as the next lifetime comes into focus.)

Lois: I am seeing you now as a precious little girl with long, curly hair, and wearing festive clothes. You are in a ceremonial procession in Central America. I am told that this occurs in what we are now calling Nicaragua. It would seem to be a religious procession. It was one where they are carrying a statue of one of the saints. It is hard to tell from the clothing exactly when it was. I am seeing again that you have been given responsibility at a level that is far beyond what is appropriate for your age. This is done because you seem like such a mature, responsible child, and older than your years. You tripped in this solemn procession, and dropped something and broke it. This was an important artifact, and was not supposed to ever be broken. It had to do with a float that had a saint on it. Your tripping messed everything up, in the prevailing view, and you were punished in that lifetime. The priest was livid, and your whole family was punished, as a matter of fact. Certain things that the church was able to do for people...your family did not get those perks for about ten years, all because an eight year old girl tripped. Now most people would say that this is pretty ridiculous, but you felt responsible and again, you were hard on yourself. So here is another example of people giving you too much responsibility, and you beating yourself up about failing at it. Again, your Higher Self is saying there is a reason you did this to yourself. Yet you need to let go of it, because as I am sure you can tell looking at that lifetime from the vantage point of being the age you are now, that it was totally unreasonable that people should punish a whole family for an eight-year-old tripping. Do you have questions about that lifetime?

Sonia: No. It seems fairly straightforward. But I still do that. I feel heavy responsibility on myself for too much. I bring it on myself.

Lois: I am being told that these are all the lifetimes that you need to hear about at this time. Also I am hearing that the lifetimes you subsequently had with Agustin have created a certain kind of karma where, in fact, the perfect relationship for the two of you would be this: Be an emotional support to each other, or friends, but at this time, not to have a sexual relationship or be married. But those lifetimes, where you had the "forbidden" sexual relationship, explain why you have these intense feelings toward him, because the two of you go way back and have loved deeply. And there is more, Sonia. This is very important. Here is what I am hearing. You were destined to marry after you went back to your own home and completed your tour of duty on the starship. If you had not had the mutual betrayal experience here on Earth, you probably would have ended up together. That was one of the more likely ways that this particular lifetime could have worked out. It is this for which you are still longing. Do you have any questions? (She shakes her head no.)

This ended the reading.

Lois' Notes: I felt that Sonia clearly did not want to hear these particular past lives about Agustin. She seemed quite sad that no hints of later reconciliation and a life spent happily ever after with him were in the offing. But knowing of these past lives with him did help explain why she felt as she did, and why it had not worked out between them this time. Getting married was not why they had come together in the current life. They met to further balance the karma. She could do this more thoroughly if she were his friend, but it seems doubtful that she could do that, as her love and her pain were so strong at this time. But who knows what the long-term future may hold? They may end up as neighbors or good friends one day, in this life or the next.

It was also important for her to hear that her Guides want her to lighten up, and not judge herself so harshly or take on more responsibility than she is reasonably able to handle. Sonia needs to play more, and not be so serious or so hard on herself. She also needed to hear about how burdened she had been as a child in past lives, due to the adults not protecting her from excessive responsibility. Hopefully she will heed these clues she was given in the reading. However, it is always up to the client.

As Sonia left that day, she remarked that she really was most grateful that she had found me, and that the work we did together was always of enormous benefit to her spiritual growth. She said that today was no exception. This was fairly effusive for such a reserved person, and I must admit, I was quite taken aback—both surprised and pleased at her comment.

Past Life Reading: Stephanie Siang: May 3, 2007

Stephanie is a dark-haired Muslim woman in her early twenties, and not a native English speaker. Not a regular client, she came solely for a past life reading. I asked if there were anything in particular she wanted to know about—people, places, or recurring patterns in her life. Stephanie says that she has an interest in astral travel, and wants to know if she had past lives where she did this. She wants to be able to do it again, especially to help her parents, and also her friends, and people she sees on the television. This is her primary reason for getting a past life reading. I am seeing a red flag, since astral travel can be dangerous, and people who are overly eager to "help" others sometimes have questionable motives.

Lois: That concerns me. Explain to me more fully why you want to do astral projection.

Stephanie: Because I want to see other places and to learn something if I can do that, I can help other people with some issues, some problems they are having. I just want to help.

Lois: So why would you want to take it upon yourself to "fix" other people? (This is always a red flag to me, people who think they know what others need to be "fixed" or to be the way they think others should be.)

<u>Stephanie:</u> Because I want to be able to help people!

<u>Lois:</u> It is all right to help people who come to you and actually ask for your help, but it is not acceptable to interfere in other people's lives. Helping without permission is interference. That will bring bad karma to you, which you will have to work off over many lifetimes. It is morally wrong to interfere in other people's lives without their knowledge or permission. We do not help when we are not invited to help. What I think you really want is to help people heal themselves, right?

<u>Stephanie:</u> Yes.

<u>Lois:</u> I believe healing is what you are interested in, but when you say, astral projection, I am not certain that this is a good idea. Astral projection can actually be very dangerous unless you are highly trained. If you do astral projection, and leave your body, the body is vulnerable to being attacked by other entities invading the body. There then exists the possibility that you cannot get back into your body. So I suggest you leave the whole idea of astral projection alone until you find a teacher specifically for that. In fact, to learn more about that, and the pitfalls of doing it incorrectly, I would refer you to the Monroe Institute, or Robert Monroe's books.

What I think you might be even more interested in, however, is shamanism. It is a way of not leaving your body, but traveling into other dimensions to learn things, and to be healed and to get advice from the spirit world. You can also help to heal others like this, so long as you do it with their permission. This has been practiced all over the planet in almost the same way for 40,000 to 50,000 years. We know because we find shamanic tools in graves that are quite ancient, and the now living indigenous people use the same procedures for journeying. So I suggest you might want to learn how to do a shamanic journey. Properly trained you can do that quite safely, and you can begin to work on your own healing. There are many ways to work on your own healing that do not include leaving your body vulnerable. Astral projection is not safe without proper training and I do not recommend it, but you can achieve the same ends without leaving your body. You can see other places and other times. You can go into the past and into the future.

<u>Stephanie:</u> But what if I just want to do astral projection?

<u>Lois:</u> I have issued my warning and if you try it, then you will deal with the consequences. I am just telling you what I know from my experience and from researching the subject. If you want to do it knowing what I just said, that is for you to decide. But I am also offering another option. You can achieve the same ends without leaving your body if you study shamanism.

So if you want to know about any past lives you had where you did spiritual work, including astral projection or any other kind of spiritual work, then we can ask that question so that you get a really broad picture—not just about astral projection but about anything spiritual that you have done. Does that not sound like a better deal? Would you not like to know about a variety of spiritual lifetimes, or healing ones, from a variety of backgrounds?

Stephanie: Do most of them do astral projection? I am really interested in that.

Lois: I am saying that astral projection is not a very broad subject. I am saying let us ask for a broader perspective on it—spiritual work in general. So, are you attracted to the powerful aspect of astral. It feels quite powerful to most of us. But going after power in that way can have serious pitfalls.

Stephanie: How about going into a past life when I was able to do the astral projection successfully and see if it...

Lois: You want to know about the lifetimes where you did it safely? Is that what you just said?

Stephanie: Yes.

Lois: And are you open to hearing about any you did unsafely and in which you had a bad consequence?

Stephanie: Actually, it would be good for me. I would like to hear this.

Lois: Okay. We will ask that of your Higher Self, Guides and the Guardians of the Akashic Records, and then they will show us what they want you to see. (I then explain what I am about to do, and proceed with the reading.)

The first thing I am seeing is a cave in Tibet. There is an old man meditating. You are one of the people assigned to take care of him, by bringing him food and water, placing it before him, and removing his chamber pot and emptying it. No one ever sees when this food and water disappears, but it does. When you come back, it is gone and the bowls are empty.

This goes on for many years, until one day he comes out of his trance long enough to speak, and asks you if you want to be trained in meditation. You say yes, that is why you have been coming there. You were hoping some of his energy would rub off. He gives you a mantra and tells you to send someone else to bring in food and water. You are told to stay in a room in your home, and meditate on that mantra until he sends for you.

In that lifetime you were also male. It appears that you were meditating using that mantra for several years, and someone else was bringing you food and water. Then you began having out-of-body experiences, and they are not calling it astral traveling. Your Guides are calling it out-of-body experiences. I am not clear what the distinction is. You are connected to your body by a cord but you are moving about through many dimensions/densities not necessarily on the Earth plane, but elsewhere. This went on for many years, and you learned a lot. You had several teachers who were not in physical form. It seems you went in many different directions. It is hard to describe where these places were, but they were in many other energetic densities, but simultaneous with our own.

One day you were sitting down to meditate and the old man from the mountain cave appears before you. He just materializes and says that you have been out in many different directions, now go within. Then he dematerialized and you meditated upon going within and this was most difficult. Finally you were able to do this. You got in touch with the inner planes or inner dimensions which are many and varied. This is what increased your spiritual power. When you went within, you found yourself in other densities as well. In the middle of all this, you just left your body permanently. You had achieved a pretty high level of development at that point, and did not come back into a physical body for a long time. This was hundreds of years ago, perhaps four to five hundred years ago, and this is the first time you have actually been in a physical body since then. Prior to that you had many lifetimes, but this is the first time you have come back——so it would appear this is why you have that drive to find out about astral travel.

What you were doing was actually called out-of-body experiences, and I am not sure why there is a distinction, but my Guides are telling me there is one. When you went into your inner planes, it was almost an explosion of energy, and you left the body for good. So I think what you are feeling is in some ways a desire to go back to that form of contemplation. I am hearing that you are supposed to be doing that as part of a group. There is a group of people who will be meditating together, and you just need to find them. If you decide you want to find them, you will. The reason to do this is because the energy is magnified in a group of people meditating together. The intensity and spiritual quality of it is intensified especially if these people are of similar maturation or developmental levels as Souls.

Now there are other lifetimes being shown to me if you are interested in looking at them. Are you? (Stephanie nods yes.) (Pause)

I am seeing a woman who lives aboard a family boat. They do not live on land at all. They have all their food, furniture, clothes and tools on the boat. The whole family takes fish to market and trades it for vegetables, fruit, bread, and butter. You like butter as opposed to olive oil or anything else. You really like butter——clarified butter. You live on the boat all the time and hate walking on the land. The water has a hypnotic sort of effect. It is not an easy life. You are working hard, but when you are not working, you are going into a contemplative state looking at the water, and the sky and clouds and birds and butterflies reflected in the water. This causes you to think about reality rather than reflection——the real versus the mirrored. You spend a lot of time in a self-trained meditation, staring at the surface of the water. You were very spiritual being, and at the same time, you were birthing and raising babies on the boat. Your mother-in-law lived there as did your father-in-law, and when they got older and passed-over, it was just you and your husband and kids. They grew up and got married and got their own boats.

Your family lived along the edge of the land. This was a very peaceful life, so if you have any attraction to water, ponds and meditation ponds, and pools of contemplation, this would be why. I am seeing lotus plants, lotus along the water's edge in little ponds that had fresh water. I think you were in salt water. It was on the edge of a sea that had fresh water ponds just inside on the land. Do you have any questions?

Stephanie: No.

Lois: Let us look at the next past life, then. (Pause) I am seeing you in a very snowy climate. You are a man in this lifetime, a leader in the community; it is in perhaps Alaska or northern Canada. I am seeing dogsleds, and those igloo houses made of chunks of ice. You were a very important man in the community. You practiced shamanism. You were a healer, and people in the community came to you for their well-being.

In that lifetime, the people who are your mother and father now were your children, and you wanted one of them to grow up—they were both brothers in that lifetime—and you wanted one of them at least to follow in your footsteps, but this did not happen. They were rowdy and playful and not interested in settling down and learning what you had to teach. Somebody else came along and wanted to learn it, so you taught him instead. You were disappointed that your boys were not very mature at the time they should have been to learn shamanism from you. That was not their path. If you have a desire to heal people, this may be why. It might also explain why you feel you need to work with your parents to help them. I think you are an older Soul than they. Do you have questions about your lifetime as an Inuit shaman?

Stephanie: Both of my parents were my children and were boys?

Lois: Yes. They were very rough with each other, too. They played rough, competing with one another. They were very close in age, like maybe a year apart. They were always wrestling, competing, trying to best one another in sports, hunting and fishing, so you might observe and see if they are still competing. Cooperation works better than competition, especially within a family. (I pause to see the next lifetime.)

I am seeing another with you as a woman in what is now called Ireland. You practiced some form of spiritual practice which was Earth-based, like Wicca. Yet this is such a long time ago! Your main job was to create flags for celebrations. I see you with many long, brightly colored streamers or flags. You also danced with the flags, and you took part in religious ceremonies. The rest of the time you herded sheep and you cut their coats to sell to weavers. During special holidays, you were the flag person performing a stunning ceremony. It was something you practiced all year long, and for which you were quite famous. People traveled a long way to witness these ceremonies, and one of the main attractions was your dancing. Later on you taught other people how to do it. The dance enhanced the spiritual quality of the gathering, and the mesmerizing movements put people into a trance state, so they could come from a deeper part of themselves in their everyday lives. It was very inspiring, and colorful. Your work was appreciated, and your name was well known. Have you questions about that one?

Stephanie: I was well known in that lifetime?

Lois: Yes. I think you are going to become well-known in this lifetime, too, but you will be a bit older, in your forties. Yes, you are going to become known for something, I am not sure what it is. It seems very mysterious. They will not let me see. It is hidden behind fog. You need to discover it on your own. You may not even know you are interested in it yet.

That concludes your past life reading, Stephanie.

Lois' Notes: Sometimes people will come in with strange requests like Stephanie's coming in wanting to know about past lives with astral travel. In this case, the natural thing to think is that they need to be warned, especially if they are young, since astral travel can be dangerous. And indeed it was appropriate to warn her. Yet in this case, the client also had a very good reason for wanting to know about this particular topic. Stephanie emailed me later expressing gratitude at learning about the past lives as a shaman and Wiccan flag dancer. She said it helped her to relax a bit about doing the astral travel until she finds a teacher for that. In the meantime she is reading about shamanism and Wicca, which are very different from her upbringing, and are stretching her in a good way. She has also been meditating looking into a large bowl of water, and having very interesting experiences! Clearly, she is progressing on her spiritual path. We are both pleased with that.

Past Life Reading: Susie La Verne: August 13, 2008

Susie is a petite, attractive, perky, career woman in her mid-fifties who came to me for a reading because she needed to know more about factors contributing to a current and rather volatile situation in her family of origin.

Lois: What is it exactly that you hope to accomplish with this past life reading?

Susie: I need to know more about my family.

Lois: You mean your family of origin? (Susie nods.)

Susie: I feel like I am in the wrong family. All in all, I wonder, did the hospital send them home with the wrong baby?

Lois: Well, I think you will see that there is a reason these things happen. What else? You do not fit in. You are fifty-six years old, and it still hurts after all this time.

Susie: Well it is just horrible. And my mother now has cancer. The dynamics between me and my sister are excessively tense to the point where I am actually becoming afraid of her.

Lois: Is she an older or younger sister?

Susie: She is four years and seven months older than I am.

Lois: And her name is?

Susie: Carlotta. Friday my mother had a doctor's appointment. She has lung cancer, and I get no information from my sister. I am going to the doctor's appointment, but of course Carlotta does not need me there.

Lois: Does your mother want you there?

Susie: Yeah, my mother wants me there twenty-four/seven. We have somewhat mended our ways over the years, but then my sister "stepped into those shoes" of being the harsh and bossy one when I was younger. My family dynamics are horrible. My father is gone.

Lois: The family dynamics shifted after he died, too, right? Those dynamics change when somebody leaves.

Susie: Oh trust me, it did change. She is out of control now. And you know, I also want to understand why I do not have any intimate personal relationships.

Lois: Have you ever been married?

Susie: Once. I was married quite a number of years ago.

Lois: Do you have children?

Susie: None. I have none. Next year, next July it will be ten years since a man has asked me out on a date and come to pick me up. I want to know why I live such a solitary life. But my main thing is to give me some type of reasoning before Friday to deal with that person.

Lois: You mean before you have to see your sister on Friday. You want some understanding of what these dynamics are as they have occurred in your past which would be impacting this lifetime. This is the main thing that you want to know?

Susie: Right.

Lois: Okay, I understand. Now, here is what I want to tell you about past life readings is that probably we will cover that in some way, shape or form; however, your Higher Self and your angels and Guides may just say, "Oh my!

She is here for a past life reading, and we can tell her some information she needs to know about the past that will help her in this lifetime having to do with x, y and z," which they deem to be more important than your relationship with your sister, Carlotta. So that may jump in first, so please do not get your feelings hurt or feel like I am not doing what you asked me to do, because, you see, I am not in control here. Your own Guides, Higher Self and Guardians of the Records are. You would not want me to be in control. I do not know as much as your Guides do. These spiritual beings know more about what you need to know than I ever could. So they are going to show me what they want me to see, and it would be very strange to me if they did not tell me about the dynamic between the three of you in some past life, but they might not get to that first.

Susie: Let me share with you that I did have a past life regression many years ago.

Lois: Please do not tell me about that one. I do not want to know. Because the past life regression that you had, that lifetime may or may not show up here. A lot of people think, "Well, I am going to judge this past life reading based on whether or not she sees that same past life I already know about." But the spirits who are actually in control in this situation, would be saying, "What would be the point of that? She already knows about that one." They would decide to get you to take a look at parts of the Akashic Record of which you are not aware. And you know, the day will come in our lifetime when we can look at our own Akashic Record any time we want, but we are not quite there yet, at least not most of us.

Susie: I want different things from past life knowledge this time than I did all those years ago. At this point I cannot even relate to those past lives. Secondly, I was not all that impressed with the proceedings, so...

Lois: Oh, I see. So the purpose of finding out about past lives, and the reason that I do this, is not to entertain people. A lot of people think it would be fun to get a reading because they want to be amused, or entertained, or to hear about how important they were. But I do not sense at all that you are one of those people. I am clarifying this in case you let anyone else listen to this recorded reading so they do not think, "Oh! Maybe I was the Queen of Sheba. I want to go get a reading." I know that somebody listening to it later might have such a thought, but this is not what this is about. Rarely do I see a past life of someone famous. What I am shown are mostly unresolved issues, past lives that are eating away at you, or otherwise affecting your current life, because you do not know about them. At that point, that is when you can begin to heal—when you remember. As long as the memory remains repressed, it is a festering wound that is still coming out in strange ways. Sometimes it comes out in ways that do not even seem to be related to it. You may see changes in things you did not realize at all were related to past lives. In other words, not just how you relate to your mom and your sister, but how you feel when you are driving in traffic, perhaps, or how you feel about eating, or how you feel about relating to girlfriends or men or any relationship.

So, just be a neutral observer of your life after we do this, and I would love it if you would journal. I think that is something people can do that really helps them. You can journal online instead of typing it out and printing it, on a blog that nobody else can see. There are many different ways to do it. You can tape your observations if that is more comfortable for you. But just be a neutral observer of your own process after this reading. You may notice immediate changes, or it might take months to completely assimilate all of this. I do not suggest anybody getting a reading too often. I used to say to wait a year or more before you get another one. But the energies on this planet have sped up so much now that I tell people to wait three or four months before getting another one, because people are able to assimilate all these past lives much faster. I think that is all the groundwork I want to lay before I do the reading for you. Do you have questions?

Susie: Not right now.

Lois: Okay, then, shall we get started? (Susie nods.) At the end of each lifetime, I will give you a chance to ask questions, but if you start talking while I am still looking at the "movie" I am seeing in my head, then I lose my train of thought. Seeing the past life versus talking requires my moving from one state of consciousness to another, so I will ask you at the end of each lifetime if you have questions about that one. That way I do not have to shift back and forth between states of consciousness as often. Then I will go on to the next lifetime. (Long pause)

Sometimes past lives are difficult to look at, based either on things you did, or things that were done to you and are just vile and contain harsh imagery sometimes. I am having a very hard time with this one. It is quite painful for me to observe. But I am going to force myself to keep looking, because your Higher Self obviously thinks it is important. This is the first one that your committee of Higher Self and Guides are showing me, and so it is the most significant one for you to know about at this point in time.

(I take a deep breath, sighing.) This is in the Middle Ages and it is with your same family that you have now. You were a male, and your mother and father grew wheat, and then ground it up into flour and the family sold flour. They were millers as well as farmers. You were living out in the countryside, but your sister in this lifetime, Carlotta, was your older brother in this medieval lifetime. You were all living in what is now England. You were born mentally retarded because of a birth trauma that cut off the oxygen for a while, and it became apparent when you were about three years of age that you were never going to be normal. Because it was the Middle Ages and people were ignorant and cruel—it was a time when people were very unkind to one another—you were treated like an animal or a pet. They taught you to fetch things for them, and would give you food based on how you performed. As soon as you were big enough to do this, they hooked you up to the millstone which was pushed around by large logs hooked into something like a ball. The part they strapped you onto was made out of a log which had the bark taken off of it.

They decided they could use the mule some other way, and they would use you to push a massive grinding stone endlessly around in a circle. You slept out in the shed like an animal, and you were fed out there like an animal, and you were just in every way treated like an animal. You never really learned how to talk, but you had intense feelings, and this was an excruciatingly painful lifetime. One of the reasons you came into this particular lifetime was to teach lessons to others, especially your family. It was a sacrifice you took on for them. You knew you were not an animal. There was a certain level of cognitive ability that allowed you to realize what was happening was unfair, but not enough verbal skills—you just communicated in moans and grunts because nobody took the time to teach you to speak. Eventually this life became utterly unbearable.

One day you just lay down in the stall and no matter what they did you would not get up. You would not eat. You would not drink. And you just starved yourself to death. It took about three days. No matter what they did to you—hit you, beat you, burn you—your brother would heat up a metal object like a nail and stab you with it, trying to get you to get up, and you would scream and howl, but you would not get up, and you did die. You actually died from not drinking enough water. It was the only way you could figure to get out, because you did have brain impairment. The purpose of this lifetime was also to teach you something, not just to teach them. It was to teach you endurance in difficult situations, and you got that lesson, and when you did, your Higher Self let you know it was okay to just lie down and pass over to the other side.

You had a series of other lifetimes where you had been a person who was a quitter, and had run off, but you hung in there in one of the most difficult circumstances imaginable. You just persisted in doing the next thing that was in front of you that you had to do. And on a Soul level, you learned an enormous amount in this lifetime and at the same time, at the moment of death you thought that you must be a really bad person to deserve to be treated like this. And you thought close family ties were not safe to have. You drew the wrong conclusions. The correct conclusion would have been, sometimes life is not fair, but sometimes it is.

You had days where you were really in touch with the beauty of nature and your food tasted good, defecating felt good, and you were happy. The temperature was okay—you were not too hot or too cold; you had happy days. That was the thing you could have focused on as you lay there dying. You could have said, "I had happy days, but I am tired now. This is a rough lifetime and I am ready to go." What you need to know is that sometimes life is not fair, but what is important is to focus on the moment, the beauty that lies inherent in every moment. The joy of life is always available to us if we but focus on the beauty of nature that surrounds us, even if all we can see of that is clouds, or the workings of insects. They, too, are part of the magnificence of creation. We must focus on the beauty and let go of any self-blame. You were blaming yourself, "If I were not such a stupid person...if I were not just such a sub-human creature they would not have treated me like that." It was not your fault that they were ignorant and did not know any better than to behave like that. So this is one lesson you came to learn. Focus on the now, and the beauty inherent in every moment.

No matter how bad things get, we can just look around at any moment, and focus on the wind blowing through the trees, the sunlight glistening on dew drops, how beautiful things look in the moonlight, the clouds moving overhead, the butterflies fluttering around, bugs crawling in the bushes. We can find the beauty of the Creator in every moment if we just focus on nature. Be in the moment. So the other purpose of this lifetime was to teach you to hang in there in difficult situations and you did. Do you have any questions about that lifetime?

<u>Susie:</u> No, I can see similarities to what I feel today.

<u>Lois:</u> So you are having the same kind of feeling even though you are not retarded in this lifetime. It would appear that the contempt that your brother had for you in that lifetime transferred over into this lifetime. It was unjustified contempt, which is that Soul's lesson. It is not about you, it is about that Soul getting their lesson. You were blameless in that situation. (I pause again.)

The next lifetime is coming in for me to see. You are a "half-breed Indian" in the American West. At first I was wondering why that white guy was so good at tracking natives, and now I am seeing that you were half Indian and half white, raised in a tribe, Chatauqua. It was a small tribe. Your father was a member of the tribe, and your mother was white. In the time I am seeing you were very westernized-looking as you worked for the military. You also worked independently sometimes and would track down renegades who were off the Reservation robbing and stealing and killing people. There were some justifiably angry Amerindians around this period of time. It was the mid-1800s, I believe. It was maybe slightly earlier than that. You went off on your own like a bounty hunter after a while, and at some point, you captured this renegade upon whom everybody had been trying to get their hands. When you found him, you immediately despised him the instant you set eyes upon him. It surprised you, the intensity of this contempt. You bound his wrists painfully, and made him walk behind your horse.

The plains tribes were accustomed to walking great distances, and actually jogging great distances, so that was not particularly hard on him. Due to your massive dislike for this guy, you made his life very difficult during that fifty-five mile trek, which took a couple of days. You felt really guilty about that later in that lifetime. It actually bothered you so much, in fact, that you started drinking after you turned him in and he was hanged by the government. At the same time you felt a strange kinship with this guy, and you could not figure out why that was. It was as if you had known him before. Yet, guess who it was? It was Carlotta. So this person was not your relative in this particular lifetime, but you managed to do some getting even in spite of that—in the few days you knew this Soul again. But it truly bothered you afterward in that lifetime.

Ultimately this person was hanged because you captured him. Compassion was more appropriate, but you could not muster that. So that is part of what is at play, too, is that she, on a Soul level, is a bit infuriated about that whole event. It made the end of that life more uncomfortable than it needed to be. This fellow was being pulled along roughly behind your horse, and it was harsher than it might have been. You gave him just enough water to stay alive but not enough to be comfortable, and tied him up very tightly at night, for example. Can you think of questions about that one?

Susie: Not off the top of my head.

Lois: When I am telling you about it, do you have feelings associated with it?

Susie: Not like the first one. Only, I cannot imagine treating anyone like that regardless of what they have done.

Lois: That may be why it drove you to drink. You spent a significant amount of time drunk after that renegade was hanged. You also did not know why you felt so badly, because a lot of people would have done worse and just hanged him out on the prairie, and brought the corpse back draped over his horse. But you did not kill him yourself. That is finally what made it tolerable. You talked to a friend who was a saloon girl, and she told you that you could have done a whole lot worse to him. She started telling you horrible things you could have done to him that you did not, and she had a very gory imagination. That helped you get out of your funk. Yet Carlotta remembers this cruelty on some level.

Susie: Could that be the reason I feel so subservient in her presence today?

Lois: Because you did something bad to the captured renegade?

Susie: Yeah.

Lois: Maybe. Are you feeling like you might need to make up for that bad thing you did?

Susie: Yes.

Lois: Maybe, because the high road would have been to bring him in with compassion for him as a human being. The wonderful shift that could come of all this is if you can allow Carlotta's feelings to express and do not react to them, keeping things in perspective, knowing you are resolving karma. If you can just be a neutral observer of your own processes from day to day, that will help. There is no judgment if you do not impose it. You could get to a place where there is peace and acceptance between the two of you. That is my hope. But let us go ahead and look at the next lifetime, and see what else we have here, that may or may not have to do with this person. (Another long pause)

I am seeing a lifetime in Alaska. It is impossible to tell precisely when this was, because their costumes were the same for many hundreds of years. It is the dead of winter. You are a married woman, and have a wonderful husband whom you adore. There are two small children aged about four and two, and a baby who is a couple of months old. I see that you have become sick and feverish, and yet still nursing the baby. The baby must eat; it does not matter if mama is sick.

Your husband is bringing you food and water and taking care of you. This is happening inside an igloo, and it is storming badly outside. Falling asleep while nursing the baby in the night, you roll enough onto the baby so that your breast blocks the baby's breathing, and the baby dies. Everyone is still asleep when you awaken, and you realize what has happened, that your baby has died. Without a doubt you feel it is all utterly your fault. You cut yourself no slack for being seriously ill and falling asleep and rolling over slightly, so you get up with the baby and walk outside into the blizzard. You just walk without ceasing. Feverish, you think you are going to your grandmother's home, because she can do healing with herbs. There is a blizzard out there, and you cannot see. It is like a dense fog. You cannot see in front of your face and you are walking in clothes that are made for being inside, not outside. Finally, you get very sleepy which happens when one is freezing to death, and you fall down in the snow and die. Everybody thought the baby froze to death with you. Even though we see that you were sick and wandering in the snow, and in your mind, going to your grandmother for help, your grandmother was never anywhere around. In fact, she may already have been dead.

Nobody could fathom where you had been headed. What was going through your mind as you were walking through the snow is, "I am not fit to be a mother. I am not fit to have children. I am not fit to be a wife to anyone. I killed my own baby out of carelessness. What kind of mother rolls over on a tiny baby and smothers it?" You were unable to find compassion for yourself, and believed you deserved to die.

This was not a logical conclusion, and you made it partially because you were feverish. Secondly, this was an unhelpful conclusion because you were not the first mother who had ever fallen asleep and rolled over on their baby and smothered it while it was nursing. This is more commonplace than people realize. Occasionally what is branded as crib death is actually a case of a baby who got smothered while the mom was sleeping. They just put it in the crib and say it died in its sleep just out of sheer, deep shame. So, in that lifetime as you died you were thinking these erroneous thoughts. These thoughts stay with us; it is imprinted on the Soul until something comes along, while we are incarnated again in human form, to help dissolve that image, and those beliefs.

So that could explain in part why you have not created another family for yourself as an adult. You have had no husband for very long time, and no children, because of this deep belief that you are not fit to have all of that, and fears that you might kill another baby. Believing on a deep level that you are dangerous, and it is not safe for you to be a mother, you do not want the responsibility. At the Soul level that is what is going on. It is the kind of thing that we have to forgive, because rolling over in our sleep is not something that we can control. You were just really very sick, and there were not any other older women there to take care of you. Most of the time there would be old ladies to take care of a new mother. The blizzard came along and it was a surprise, and nobody else was there but your husband. Ideally, from that lifetime you could have learned self-forgiveness, but this did not happen. Do you have questions about that lifetime?

Susie: It sure explains why I do not have kids. How will I...I do not know how to change that.

Lois: Well, remember what I said earlier? Just knowing about it will start the healing process. It could happen spontaneously and immediately, but it may not. If not, you will process these lifetimes gradually over time and it will be healed because it is not hidden any more. And if you wanted to go to a hospital later on as a volunteer and rock new babies, or something like that, it might be healing for you. (I pause to see the next lifetime.)

I am not sure that I know yet why I am being shown this, you may know why. I am seeing a lifetime a long time ago, in an unfamiliar culture. You are wearing costumes I have never seen before, and you are doing something that looks kind of like...something that you ride waves with but it has got sort of a sail attached to it. Um... Windsurfing. Yes. That is what it looks like, but only not like any windsurfing equipment that I have seen before, because some of them have more than one person on them, and more than one sail. Apparently you were a young male who did this full-time, and it was a competitive sport. You and your team were the best at doing this in the whole country, and I see that occasionally you were parading through the streets, just this fabulous athlete, in their version of the Olympics. You frequently took awards. You never really had to "work" in the way that others did.

Your Guides want you to know that you have also had lifetimes where you had incredible successes, and a lot of fun. In that windsurfing lifetime you had brothers and sisters who were very close to you. The parents were living somewhere far away, but the brothers and sisters all lived near each other, and their children were very close. Ultimately you married and had sixteen children. Several of them became competitive windsurfers for lack of a better phrase. You had a windsurfing dynasty designing your own windsurfing boards, only they were different than the equipment used currently. You made money both from your business and in prize money. Besides, the community supported you because you were so special. They supported your whole family, and you were the patriarch of a really powerful, famous family. So, your Guides wanted you to know that—because it has not all been tortured suffering and pain. You came into this current lifetime to clear some of the karma associated with past pain and suffering, but those are not the only kinds of lifetimes you ever had, and your committee of Higher Self and Guides want to be sure you know that.

That is the last lifetime they want to show you today, and you should wait at least four months before having another session. Do you have questions?

Susie: No, but I might later, and I will contact you if I do. Thank you for this. It helps me to understand a lot of how I feel and how others have treated me in this lifetime.

Lois' Notes: I called Susie one year after the reading to talk about what has happened since her past life reading. Susie said that things were very up and down with Carlotta for a while, because their mother was dying of cancer. Carlotta was resentful because she had the bulk of the responsibility, as she was living in the same town as their mother, which was in Louisiana. Susie had a great job she was unwilling to leave, which was in Texas. Susie supported Carlotta as well as she could, sending money, and coming to visit every other weekend to give Carlotta a break, staying at the hospital with their mother all the time she was there. She finally talked Carlotta into hiring a sitter part time during the week for their mother, who seemed to go berserk near the end of each day.

One evening when her mother was especially out of it, Susie was there as the sitter for their mother, again giving her sister a break from the responsibility. To that end, she did not call Carlotta when her mother began to lose control near the end of the day. The nurses were restraining their mom in the hospital bed with wrist and ankle bindings when Carlotta called Susie to see how things were going. Susie responded that they were getting ready to restrain the mom and Carlotta became upset. She came to the hospital, giving Susie another scolding, saying, "She is my mother, too, you know."

Susie's intent had been to give her sister the break she had so often requested. At that point Susie reported she had reached her breaking point. She told Carlotta that nothing she, Susie, ever did was right according to her, and that Carlotta should be glad they were in a public place, because Susie feared she might do bodily harm to her otherwise. There was rage in her eyes. Susie walked away and called a friend on the phone, Jeanne, who calmed her down. This took about a half an hour.

After that, things were different. Susie said she had definitely drawn courage from the past life readings to finally stand up to Carlotta, and that Carlotta had seen something in Susie's eyes that day that she had never seen before. Susie really was clearly ready to stand up for herself no matter what. Everything shifted in that moment. She was not the retarded child from medieval times any longer, lying down to die.

Later that same day Susie said to Carlotta, "We have a light at the end of this tunnel. All we have to do is get to the end, and then we are done. I never have to have anything to do with you again. And you do not ever have to see me again, either."

Their mother died a couple of months later, but ever since that night of courage, Carlotta has treated Susie differently. Perhaps she realized that she would lose her sister, and did not want to, or perhaps she realized for the first time how badly she had been treating her baby sister. She got a clear dose of Susie's reality. At any rate, as Susie tells it, their relationship has turned out better than she ever could have dreamed. Carlotta had just called her a few minutes before our conversation to ask her how she was doing, and if the trip to the chiropractor had helped her back pain any. Before the past life reading, a caring relationship of any kind at all between them was unimaginable to Susie. And Susie is not nearly as alone as before the reading now that she really has a sister.

Past Life Reading: Suzanne Heinz: October 22, 2005

Suzanne has come for a past life reading. She says that she is just curious to learn more about herself. She came right to see me immediately after her sister had a past life reading. She has no specific questions.

Lois: I am seeing feudal Japan, long ago when there were warlords. I am seeing you as a male performer, a member of a team. Your first attitude toward it is like a sporting team. This is like a cross between a sporting team and an army drill team where everyone's movements are coordinated and precise. You practice this drill many hours each day; what you are practicing is hitting gigantic drums. You make ritualized, rhythmic music by beating these drums. These are ancient instruments, and even though you are making music, this is "sacred performance" at the same time. Additionally you do gymnastics in the midst of beating the drum, and it really makes for a stunning and beautiful pageant. This group was respected as if they were priests.

As I watch this, I am being reminded of coordinated swimming patterns, the way it was practiced by teams of American females in the 1950s. What you were doing, however, was ceremonial art. This practice is what you did for a major part of your lifetime.

Additionally, in between the drilling and the drumming, you were in training as a skilled swordsman and a warrior. Your biggest dream was to be a Shogun, but you never worked your way up to that, which was rather sad for you. My guess would be that it leaves you in awe, a little bit, when you watch military processions, people marching, parades and that sort of thing. You may be longing to do this, and wondering why it is not more highly valued in our culture.

You were actually supposed to become a Shogun; it was your Soul's plan for that life. Yet very secretly on the side, you had a woman whom you considered to be your wife. For some reason, because of your commitment to the drumming ceremonial group, you were not supposed to marry, so she had to remain a secret. You and she were committed to one another, and yet neither of you was ever able to be with the other in public. She became pregnant and took herbs to make the baby go away. But it did not work, and she had the baby. Because of this, she was persecuted and harassed. You tried to protect her, but it did not work. Ultimately, she ran away taking the baby with her to be safe. She went to a mountain village where she had some distant relatives. No one in your town or region knew where she went. You knew where she was, but you decided that you could not risk finding her.

There was no anonymity for you. If you went to look for her everyone would know who you were. You apparently had your head shaved in a certain way with certain identifying marks, similar to tattoos so that everyone would know that you were a member of that particular ceremonial group. These were marks of high honor, and people on the street deferred to you. That group had really high social and moral standards, so you could not risk going to see her or the child. You deeply felt a dreadful longing for her and for your child.

Deeply torn between your duty to your work, and the duty of being a father to your child and being a husband, you were coming apart at the seams. It was an unbearably difficult position to be in, and ultimately, you met with an accident and fell off a cliff. You had a premonition this was going to happen, but did not take it seriously. You were not intentionally careless, but you did slip and fall off the cliff. In a way it was a relief. Falling you were thinking, "Thank God this is finally over."

From the point of view of the Soul, the issue here was that you were unable to choose between your "priestly" calling and your love for this woman and child. So you did not make a choice, you simply had an accident. What your Guides want you to know is that not making a decision actually is a decision. It would have been better to leave your work and go with your family, leaving the societal pressures behind. But it was a matter of your lack of courage. There will be more lessons in courage for you due to this. We get the same lessons again later, until we "get" the lesson. Do you have any questions about that?

Suzanne: No.

Lois: Right after that lifetime, you came immediately into another lifetime with those two same people. This time, you came back as a man and she as a woman again, and you had that child again, and were married and were with one other every single day. The two of you would go out fishing together, and it was magnificently peaceful. You would fish with nets and you also made and mended nets for others. That is how you made your living. She made things by hand, but this was not in Japan. The feel it has to it is like South American Indians. So you balanced that karma with those people, but I do not know if they are in this lifetime with you again. That was a very calm, gentle and peaceful life. You accomplished everything you intended to in that lifetime. The reason you needed to know about that other lifetime to explain some of the feelings you have sometimes where people can just get trapped by life. Does that make sense to you? Sometimes there is nothing you can do that seems right. Things happen and you feel boxed in, and that is why you might have those thoughts. There were things you could have done to solve your dilemma in the life in Japan, but you did not feel at the time that there was anything you could do. You could not see outside the box that the culture put you in. You could have taken her and the child away to another country, but you did not see that as a possibility at the time. Your Guides decided to allow you this peaceful lifetime together, so that you would not be afraid to reincarnate. Later you would have to do the work necessary to balance not having made a decision, but having an accident instead. Have you any questions about that lifetime as a happy fisherman?

Suzanne: (Shakes her head no.)

Lois: Now what I am seeing is that you were a female butcher in one past life. Yes, in this life you were a woman living in what is now Alaska. I see your tribe catching whales, and they either come up onto the beach, or are dragged up there by the men who speared them. What you do, the job you were born to, is that you extract the most valuable part, ounce for ounce, from the body of the whale. You remove it with your knife; it has got the ambergris in it, from which so many perfumes are made. The family you came from were experts at preserving that particular essence so that it lasted a long time. That is what you did for a living. You extracted the ambergris from whales, preserved it, and made it into pastes. You gathered it yourself; there was no middle man. Acting like a wholesaler, you sold or traded it to people in large quantities who then spread out, or fanned out to a larger area and distributed it. You traveled alone. Your husband did not want you traveling with ambergris and cash, either, because he believed that it was too dangerous.

At one point you were carrying an unusually large sum of money. Actually, it was a large collection of something small, which functioned in the same manner as money. It might have been bones that were carved or etched and used like currency, but not exactly money as we think of it. Holed up in a cave during the time of year when there is a lot of snow, you fell asleep by the fire. Somebody had been tracking you, and after you were asleep, he sneaked up on you. Hitting you on the head, this robber then took all your ambergris, all your carved things, and left you to die. But the death was slow, and you faded in and out of consciousness. After a day or so, you did die from that head injury. When fading in and out of awareness, you would think, "My husband was right. My husband was right. I should never have gone this far from home." You died thinking, "I should stick close to home. I do not need to go far from home. It is not safe."

The point of knowing about this lifetime is that any fears you have about getting away from home, or the need to stay home to be safe, are unfounded. You drew the wrong conclusion during your last moments in that life. Being more careful about where you set up camp might have been a more logical conclusion, or not traveling alone, or deciding you should have set a booby-trap in the cave's entrance so that you had warning that someone was coming might have been truer conclusions. Deciding to be more careful about who knew you had valuables with you, all these would have been logical conclusions. Questions?

Suzanne: No. I cannot think of any. (Pause)

Lois: Next I am seeing wounded soldiers. The job you have is that of making armor for them, to limit their wounds. You are making shields and little round, metal things that are attached to their leather sort of clothing which is supposed to protect them from knives and swords and things. You are hammering metal and giving thought to the work. It looks like you have had several lifetimes where metal is very important to you. You have made armor or swords or sharpened scissors for a living. They all come back to this one where you became kind of famous for creating suits of armor. You are the first person who ever designs chain mail—you try to make these suits of armor beautiful as well as protective. Imprinting them with designs to make them much more interesting was one experiment that you tried. You did a really great job, and saved up your money. Later you actually loaned it out to other people, like a bank does, and they faithfully paid you back with interest. It was an extremely financially successful lifetime. You were a man, and your children were fortunate enough to travel. That was the best education anyone could get in those days. You are being shown this lifetime so you know that you have a lot of creativity in your past, and you were an inventor. You also have a great deal of business acuity and could call upon either of these talents in the present if you so choose. (Pause)

I am being told to ask if there are any particular issues that you have. Things you would like to know about?

Suzanne: Well, yes. Ted's daughter is two. I have such a connection with her. I live in Michigan now for the sole purpose of being with her. I was so excited when she was born, even though she is not my daughter. It is not logical. But I feel that there is something there.

Lois: Well, the three of you have been together numerous times. It looks like she has been your daughter before, too, which is why you have been so happy to have her in your life. She tried to incarnate a couple of times before as your child, and you have had some miscarriages or abortions when she tried to come. She desperately needed to be here now. That is why you were excited about her birth. You, she and Ted have been a trio in a few more lifetimes. There are probably five or six lifetimes where you have been together. You have come as sisters, mother-daughter, grandmother, that kind of thing and sometimes brothers. This is definitely your Soul family, and you have come back in more than one life together.

Suzanne: How about my nephew. Why do I feel such a bond with him?

Lois: (Pause) Suzanne, you have been his brother a couple of times, and you have been married to him as his wife. The karma is over about husband and wife relationships, and you are here to protect him while he is young this time. He has some very important work to do. It looks as if he is going to have trouble with school, perhaps, or other people misunderstanding him. He is different, and he needs your protection in so far as you need to have faith in him, and no matter what happens, believe in him. There will be a point in time where he will not be able to get this much-needed support from anybody but you. He is very different. He has a unique gift, and he is here make his mark on the world. He may do it quietly, or he may do it very publicly. He has several choices to make about that, but he needs you to believe in him now, unconditionally. You came into this lifetime to be there for him no matter what. Questions?

Suzanne: No, I have no questions.

Lois: Well, okay. That is it for today.

The session ends.

Lois' Notes: There were several lessons highlighted for Suzanne, but it is not clear, since she was not very communicative, whether she actually absorbed them or not. My saying something and the client truly, deeply, hearing what I am saying are two different things. I wondered afterward if she merely was unprepared for the serious nature of the past life as the shogun-trainee. Perhaps she was taken aback by the idea that we reincarnate as both men and women. Most people would have had some kind of reaction to being told that they invented chain mail, but Suzanne said nothing. In talking with her afterward, I could not get a feel for what she was thinking or feeling. Who knows, maybe she did not even believe a word of it! Sometimes people come at another person's urging, and they do not get much from a reading or healing session, if they arrive in that state of mind. Or perhaps she just needed time to absorb it all before speaking. It is not necessary for me to understand. I simply report what I see, and the client will take from it what they will.

Past Life Reading: Theodore Wong: November 23, 2008

Theodore is a Vietnamese American male in his early twenties. He has completed a tour of duty in the United States Army, and at the time of the reading had come back to the family home and was working in Houston. He initially had come to see me for a Reiki session, telling me that at one time, when he was younger, he was in a state of bliss constantly, yet he has lost the ability to be there all the time. He stated that he deeply wants to get back to the place where he is in a constant state of bliss. I told him how important regular meditation was to that process.

Several months later, he decided to come for an Akashic Records reading of past lives. Here is what transpired after I explained to him why I do these readings for people, and prepared him for the reading.

Lois: (Long pause) I believe I am seeing a culture we do not know about any more. I see many of these. This particular culture does not "ring any bells" for me. I have never seen anything exactly like this one before, although I have seen similar cultural artifacts in Tibetan rituals. This is neither Lemuria nor Atlantis but during that approximate time frame...oh, wait, actually, it is during the Lemurian time frame, but it is a different part of the planet, and a different culture. It is very tropical in this place; the land is one rich with undergrowth, damp and lush with vegetation. Located at the epicenter of your territory is a rather large volcano. You appear to have been on a large island. That island does not exist any longer. It has moved to a position under the ocean now, as tectonic plate shifts have occurred, of course, and land masses have gone under and new ones emerged. Humans have been on this planet vastly longer than our history records indicate. Every so often someone finds a remnant of one of these civilizations, and these remnants end up on a shelf in the basement in some museum marked as an "anomaly", meaning, no one knows where it came from. They are not investigated.

This land I am seeing is very warm all year round, and the people, both the men and women, were only clothed from the waist down. You are male in this lifetime and you are some kind of monk or priest or something. I am seeing you in a procession. You are one of the more high-ranking spiritual leaders of this particular culture. As they are marching in this procession, which is not marching like soldiers march, but a very gentle, slow, one foot in front of the other, their hands are to the sides of their bodies as they do an unusual kind of ritualized walking style, in sync with the drum and with each other's movements. You each are highly decorated in ornate robes from the waist down. There is some sort of twisted, colorful, rolling thing at the top—functioning like a waistband, and it is knotted in front. There are threads that look like gold and silver running through the fabric. It is quite beautiful to see.

You are all walking to a very slow drumbeat, yes, slow and deliberate, the kind of beat that sends people into a deep trance state of consciousness. Everyone in the group of priests is doing this walking or marching, up the mountain to the rhythm of this colorful, ancient, ornately decorated, ritual drum.

This group of men is planning to have a ceremony at the top of the mountain where the volcano crater is located. This particular volcano is alive, meaning that it is active. Active volcanoes give off smoke, or gasses or lava, or a combination of those. This volcano was considered to be a type of God. In this civilization it is considered that trees and rocks and plants and animals and mountains and rivers and streams and oceans all have consciousness, which is actually more accurate than our own understanding today. Scientists tell us this is true, but most people are sadly unaware of this fact. All things have consciousness. But this particular civilization I am seeing knows that fact, and considers this volcano to be very powerful in consciousness, which was at the level of Godlike consciousness. This volcano was a place where spiritual leaders and healers could recharge their energies and heal by drawing upon the power of the Volcanic God, Uhratu.

On the day which I am seeing, you are all going up to the volcano to create a type of ritual in which there was some sort of gift to be given to the God of the volcano, so it would not erupt in anger from being ignored, nor destroy anything. That may sound like a really primitive understanding, but it is not. The volcano's anger could be stirred by petty bickering between people at the expense of their awareness of the sacredness all around them, including the sacredness of the volcano. These people were extremely advanced intellectually and spiritually, but they were very clearly a shamanic-based culture, which is not well understood in our times. These people knew from going into altered states of consciousness regularly that this volcano had a consciousness that occasionally needed to be acknowledged and gifted. They did not consider it sacrifice. They considered it a gift due the volcano for its freely-given gifts of power and healing to the shamans, who then healed the rest of their clan.

There was a gift coming along behind the group of five animals, and it is not clear whether it was five goats or sheep. They also offered some grains. A percentage of the crop each year is what the volcano got—very much like we do with tithing at church today. When the procession, which was very long, deliberate and accompanied by a beautiful drumbeat and chimes, got up to the top of the volcano, you suddenly and unexpectedly tripped on your robes. This was considered to be a terribly bad omen. The head priest decided that you needed to relinquish your robes and your office for the time being, and throw the robes into the volcano as a way of appeasing or apologizing to the volcanic God, Uhratu. You hesitated. Ultimately you did it, but you paused for a little too long, and everyone thought you were about to defy the head priest. The hesitation was only because you were embarrassed to be naked in front of all those people. This was because you had an erection. There was no sexual reason, there were no women around, but it was just that you were so very excited to be part of this procession.

Apparently you were very young, and had just been promoted, and this was your first big procession. And though the men all knew that sometimes when men are excited about an event they get an erection, still, you were embarrassed. So after hesitating, you did remove the robes, and you tossed them into the volcano exactly as instructed. Unfortunately, thereafter the event became quite the big joke. Everybody teased you about it later when you got down to the bottom of the mountain. Although there had been somebody there with another type of garment you could put on, everybody teased you mercilessly about the erection. Finally, instead of bearing the brunt of the embarrassment and the teasing, and letting the clamor die down of its own accord, one day you just got into your boat, and went far away. You felt you had to get away from the embarrassment and the humiliation. This was not the best choice, since you had given up a golden opportunity. You could have had a brilliant career as a priest-like leader in this shamanic spiritual practice. Instead of riding out the ribbing and what you saw as humiliation, you ran away out of embarrassment and started over elsewhere. However, you did not live up to your full potential in the new location.

So what your Guides want to tell you is that it is extremely important to your Soul development that when you finally figure out what your spiritual practice is and you begin, you hang in there no matter what the difficulty, because you may have challenges thrown your way to make sure you have learned that lesson of false pride. It is very important to demonstrate that you are not going to give up or walk away, no matter what happens. Here is why. When you moved to the other island you became an ordinary citizen who worked rather like a blacksmith. Making objects for daily use that had to do with fire and metal and hammering, you lived a quiet, but humdrum life. You married and had children and were relatively happy, but always longed for that other lifetime you almost had. The other opportunity you abandoned was a higher calling, and you knew it. You always regretted walking away, for the rest of your days. Any questions about that lifetime?

Theodore: I am just trying to absorb it.

Lois: I know it can sound overwhelming. And remember, you will have more time to absorb it later. You can listen to this recording over and over. I know what I just told you probably does come as a big surprise. Very frequently our past lives do come as a big surprise. So you are going to need some time to integrate this. It can take as long as a few months to integrate one of your past life readings. So if you do not have any questions...you know, Theodore, having an erection publicly in that culture was not such a big deal. It was just something to joke about, whereas in our culture, it would be a much more significant issue.

Theodore: I think it was just...it was the whole process, the procedure. Everything just happened at the worst time possible.

Lois: Yes. Exactly.

Theodore: He was trying to complete the ritual, he really was trying!

Lois: Yes, it was his first big ritual.

Theodore: Yes. I can feel some of his discomfort now. It was so important to him and...

Lois: And you tripped over yourself and got horribly embarrassed.
So do not worry about not being able to absorb it in the moment. You are going to have ample time over the next few months to deal emotionally with all of this. If you have a question later, you can always email me. (There was a moment of silence.)

Are you ready for me to go on with the next lifetime?

Theodore: Yes. (Another long pause)

Lois: The next one I am seeing, you are a male again in this lifetime, although most of us go back and forth between lifetimes. We are males sometimes, females at other times, but I am seeing you as a male again this time. You are a North American Indian. This was before white men came to this continent, when things were really working pretty well aside from the occasional tribal warfare, and before horses had been introduced to the North American continent. This seems to be located somewhere which is now slightly south of South Dakota, which means you had harsh winters, but very beautiful spring times.

There was one particular spring time where you fell in love with a girl from a neighboring tribe. They traveled in for a gathering. Several tribes regularly came together in the springtime, or early summer, for a group meeting. You actually had seen this girl before, but it had been a few years, and you had both grown up a lot since you had seen her. She was like a third cousin, which is not such a close relative that you cannot marry her. You each just fell head over heels in love. When people are really in love, they are just seriously head over heels. They are tripping and they cannot remember what they said or what anybody else said when they are in the presence of the beloved. They almost feel like they are drunk, or their brains are not working quite right. That is how you two were.

The two of you went for a walk with a chaperone not too far behind. Then at some point you start trying to show off for this girl. Walking on some rocks, you slip and fall into the river, which is pretty swift. You get banged up against a rock and shattered your shoulder blade—you had been training to be a warrior, and you were really good with a bow and arrow, but you could not do that any longer. You went around with your arm and shoulder bandaged against your body for months before the shoulder blade healed enough so that you could stand the pain of not having it tied up. This bandaging and immobilization of the arm seriously restricted your range of motion with that arm. Never again could you draw the bow in the same manner.

This girl was still absolutely wild about you, and she felt as though the tumble you took was all her fault. You got hurt because you were showing off for her. She had said something like, "Those rocks are really slippery. I would not walk on those. I bet you would, though, because you are so brave." She was trying to flatter you, but you took it as a challenge. So there you were again, dealing with the theme of embarrassment, and false pride. You could not face this girl even though there were people sent from her tribe to yours telling you that she really cared for you, and that she was very interested in a family alliance. She would have been a good match for you, because her father was a chief of that group of tribes. It would have been a favorable alliance for your family, as well, but you were just too embarrassed to become involved with her, which was too bad, because you were supposed to be with this girl. Again, you got a lesson in false pride, and what that can cost a person, and the harm which it can do to others.

Much later, because you could not fight with a bow and arrow any more, you became a healer. But you floundered about, not knowing what to do with your life for a while. You eventually were taken under the shaman's wing, and he trained you to become a healer. The husband of the girl you had rejected was eventually killed in a battle. The two of you finally got together, but she already had children by her first husband. You were probably too old to have children together by then. However, you did finally get married, so it was not as bad an outcome as it could have been. But she never quite got over the fact that you were not there for her when you should have been. She really wanted to have your children, and it was most painful for her that she was not able to have them. Yet the good news was that ultimately you did get together. I think you are seeing or hearing about this lifetime because there seems to be a theme here. You need to be cautious to not let your pride get in the way of living out your life plan. In other words, do not let simple, small things derail the train of your destiny. Does that make sense to you? Or resonate with you? Do you have a tendency to do that?

Theodore: Yes. I do. I get easily upset when a lot of people are looking at me. I do not like to draw attention.

Lois: Okay. So this would be a big thing a Soul would want to learn. To swallow your pride, and go ahead and go after what it is you really want. Not letting anyone else's silliness or your own embarrassment keep you from your true destiny. Do you have any questions?

Theodore: So this lifetime was after the priest lifetime, right?

Lois: Well, here is the deal with past lives: there is really no such thing as linear time. It is just an illusion because we are on a spinning planet. These lifetimes are all occurring simultaneously, and you are getting to hear about them today in order of their significance. The first one was the most important one to learn about. The second one I described was the next most important one for you to know about today.

Theodore: I see. Okay.

Lois: I am now going to see what the next lifetime is. (Pause)

The next one is a lifetime as a Tibetan monk. It looks like the eleventh century CE and you were identified, you were a Rinpoche Lama, which means that you were identified by the monks when you were about three or four years old. When asked if you recognized anything that was yours, you went straight up to the ritual objects that actually belonged to you in that prior lifetime as a Lama. The monks knew to look for you, because the seers had said that this particular Lama had been born again in such and such a year, the year you were born. So they went looking for you and found you and a few others born around the same time. They found three or four boys they thought might be the Rinpoche, or reincarnated, Lama. You were the only one who walked straight up to the vast grouping of objects, and picked out the ones that had belonged to you in the prior life. So this is how they knew it was you. You were the only one who could do this; the only child who knew which objects had been your own.

And so, as is the custom, at the age of about four-and-a-half or five you were taken from your parents and brought to the monastery, where you were trained to be a Lama. You were a tremendously gifted child, and you passed through the ranks extremely quickly. By the time that you were about fourteen or fifteen years of age, you were ordained, or their equivalent of ordained. You had a big ceremony in which you became a full-fledged Tibetan monk. Then you were taken someplace way high up in the mountains, and given a special, sacred task, which was very similar to your task in your last lifetime as a Rinpoche Lama. In other words you had given that same job, but with a slightly different twist. It was something you had not finished in the prior lifetime, and that you wanted to finish. Your job was to guard an extremely ancient library. Most people are not aware that the Tibetans have libraries that are many thousands of years old, which are stacked with scrolls that go to the ceiling. There are only just a few monks assigned to these remote temples where these rare, priceless documents are stored. It is considered a deeply sacred duty and an honor to be there, and you spent your entire adult lifetime there. Whenever a scholar would come to study a certain topic, you were familiar with all the scrolls. You were aware how to find the one that was needed, and to help with the research. You did your job beautifully, and you executed it perfectly. This was an immensely honorable and successful lifetime as a Tibetan monk.

Periodically, you would come into Lhasa. Well, it was not exactly at Lhasa then, but it was near there. You were honored highly for your work and given a release so that you could come in and be around people and somebody else would stay in your library temple for a while. And again, you were extremely successful in all ways. This was a very powerful lifetime from the vantage point of the Soul.

Additionally, in that lifetime, you were very gifted at making cheese from yak milk. It was like a hobby. These animals I am seeing look like yaks, anyway. These are quite long haired, longhorn-looking animals, and you are extremely gifted at making a very delicious cheese from their milk. You spent a great deal of study and time growing and tweaking this particular bacterial culture which made your special cheese which was famous far and wide. In addition to being a really gifted successful Tibetan monk and scholar, you are also really good at making this cheese which you traded to other monasteries for various goods they made. You also had recipes you shared freely. People could combine the cheese with certain ingredients to make different dishes that would taste sublimely delicious. Do you have questions about that lifetime?

Theodore: Do you know my actual name as the monk?

Lois: I am not seeing what his name was. It is not very often that it seems necessary to your Higher Self that you know what the name is.

Theodore: I am just trying to learn as much as I can. So I must have gained a lot of wisdom in that lifetime.

Lois: Yes. And you experienced a lot of bliss, which is why it has been so much easier for you to experience bliss in this lifetime than it is for most of us. Very few people just go around experiencing it frequently, like you have in this lifetime. That is why it is easy for you. You have a lot of practice as a monk with bliss. This comes from meditation. I am wondering if now you went someplace where it is really cold and snowy, if it might be easier to experience bliss full time. I recall the first time you came to see me was because you were searching to discover how you could experience your bliss full time. I think you should go someplace cold and snowy like it was in Tibet up in the Himalayas, and meditate and see what happens. But meditation is the key, Theo, wherever you happen to be.

I am being told these are all the lifetimes you need to be told about at this point in time, because apparently the first one, and to a slightly lesser degree the second one, will be fairly difficult for you to integrate.

Theodore: Okay. Thank you.

Lois' Notes: Later Theodore emailed me about the reading. Here is what he wrote:

Dear Lois,

I remember the first time I had a Reiki treatment done by you, you told me that I was a very old Soul, and that I have had many past lives... one being a shaman, and a recent one being a monk. On that day did you know about my past life as that very shaman or that I have been a reincarnated Rinpoche Lama before? Just curious.

I have also been told before that I have been a Tibetan monk in a very recent past life under the Galugpa sect - the yellow hats - and in direct service to the Dalai Lama, and that I died during the Chinese communist revolution in 1966. I must of have been a Rinpoche Lama during that time too to be in direct service to the Dalai Lama.

I know I must have been a Lama more than just twice throughout my entire past lives. There must be a great significance to why my Guides wanted to show me the life I had as a Rinpoche Lama during that eleventh century CE, and not as a Lama in my other lifetimes... If I had spent nearly my whole entire lifetime in the Tibetan Sacred Library I must have gained an incredible amount of knowledge and wisdom there... I reincarnated and was given the same task again, but why... why did the seer come to look for me? What is the importance in finding me again...to put me back in the same job as before? When you accessed my Akashic Records, you saw that there were three or four other candidates whom the monks thought might be the reincarnated Rinpoche Lama, and knew I was the one because I walked up to my objects. Why find me again? Was I only a guardian or the ancient sacred Tibetan library or was I also a spiritual teacher and such?

You know, as soon as I was born, my mother and father brought me to a very high ranking monk and that monk have said to my parents that I will grow up to become a great person, and that he really favors me a lot. When I was older, like seventeen years old, that monk went on a world tour and came to Houston. He met my parents again and told them good things about me——I always get ticked off because I do not understand what he sees in me——what is it that he sees that I am not able to see in myself?

I went to see Cao Chin, an enlightened monk here in Houston, for a reading, and he also told me I was special, and invited me to come meditate with his group.

I asked my father if he also brought my older brother when he was born to that other famous monk, too. He said that he did not, but in my case they did not know why, but they felt that they were supposed to bring me to see that monk.

I always asked myself why me? What is it about me that is different from anybody else?

Now I understand. It is because I have had many past lives as a reincarnated Lama. I feel like a lot of things in my life finally make sense now.

Lois, I just want to say thank you. I finally figured out that answer... what is it that they see in me that I do not see in myself that makes them favor me so much.
Theodore Wong

Lois' Notes: The answers to Theodore's questions are as follows: It is my understanding that usually when a Rinpoche Lama reincarnates, he is located by the other monks, using an ancient technique, and becomes a monk again. But apparently not always, or Theo would have been located as a child for training in this life. There certainly were opportunities. He was taken to a high ranking monk as an infant. It would appear that his Soul has chosen a different path to follow in this lifetime. He was sent to the remote library/temple to work again in the eleventh century, because that is what his Soul had chosen, before he reincarnated, to do again in that lifetime. He had something to finish.

When Theo had come to see me earlier for a Reiki treatment, I saw brief glimpses of his having had a lifetime as a shaman and as a Tibetan monk, but only fragments, not the details I would later see in an Akashic Records reading, due to time constraints in the energy medicine session. Nor had I seen the lessons he was supposed to learn from those past lives until I did the full reading.

At the time of this writing, Theodore is still young and searching for his calling. I do hope to hear from him occasionally, to let me know how he is progressing on his spiritual journey. He has enormous potential due to his past lives, but it is entirely up to him what he does with this one. For example, it is up to him if he begins meditating on a regular basis or studies with a spiritual teacher, or follows his inner guidance to the next step in life. What we do with this lifetime involves choices we all have to make. This is true for everyone. No one gets to rest on his laurels.

Past life reading: Terri Smithers: November 18, 2008

Terri, a thin blonde haired woman who appeared to be in her early forties, came in for an Akashic Records reading. She carried an oxygen machine everywhere with her, and was connected to it most of the time just so she could breathe. She had contracted a disease from a coughing co-worker some years ago, which caused total diaphragm paralysis, making it extremely hard for her to breathe. The diaphragm is the muscle that pulls the lungs down so that air is sucked in. Without a functioning diaphragm it is almost impossible to breathe on one's own. She was using chest muscles to inflate her lungs. Terri was living on disability, yet doing her spiritual work—learning and growing—which is quite admirable.

After talking with Terri regarding why she wanted an Akashic Records readings, and asking what Terri hoped to get from the reading, I asked Terri get onto the healing table, and began the session. Terri had related that she wanted to know if there was a karmic reason for her breathing problems, first and foremost, and then anything else her Guides wanted her to know. I had Terri lie on the healing table, and then began the session. (Long Pause)

Lois: Hmmm...I see you in a lifetime as a man. I see a robe and tall staff which has a crook at the top. You are trudging through the sand in the desert. There are people following you and they are herding both goats and sheep. It is like a caravan only everyone is walking. This caravan has been going on for quite some time. (Another pause) Good heavens, I have never seen this before. You would think that in all these years I would have seen this before. This is actually the migration of the Jews through the desert for the forty years after they left Egypt. You are Moses' brother. Was his name, Aaron? I think it was Aaron. That is what I am hearing. This is very unusual. I almost never see famous people. Apparently, there was some undercurrent of dissent among the people for a long time, and it finally erupted. There was a great deal of struggle going on to keep everything under control, because people are really getting tired of what they think is turning out to be just a lot of pointlessness—everyone going around in circles aimlessly following this pillar of fire, eating the same boring thing every day. They just keep moving around in the desert, just wandering and wandering. And there was actually a purpose to it, but they certainly could not see what it was at the time.

There is a whole faction of people who decided to split off and go their own way and yet another faction of people who decided they needed to be stopped. I mean that some other faction decided that the group who was going to go their own way needed to be stopped. It was feared that if they were not stopped, the entire tribe would dissipate into tiny splinter groups that would go the wrong way, or many different ways. They would lose their identity as a Nation. Part of the purpose of the wandering, it appears, was to give everyone with slave mentality a tribal mentality. They were following their own leader, not some Egyptian, and moving together with just each other, and bonding. The younger people came into adulthood, and had no memory of slavery. This ultimately went on for forty years as we know from records in the Old Testament. The ones who were against the splinter group's leaving did not want this gigantic group they considered a family to begin to fragment. So in the middle of the night, the group that did not want the tribe to dissipate poisoned the food of the people who were going to leave the next morning. Twenty-five to thirty people were affected. They were allowed to wander off into the desert and die. Scouts were later sent out to check on them, so that the scout could come back to the entire group and relay the information of their deaths and frighten others out of attempting a similar coup.

I am unable to get any idea of who was behind this poisoning or who organized it. But I do see clearly that it was very disturbing to the leaders—to

Aaron and to Moses——in this situation. They had not known about it in advance, but Aaron had intuitively sensed something was up and had failed to look into it. He felt badly that he had not investigated his instincts. He and Moses were deeply troubled by the poisoning as well as the splinter group leaving in the first place. Do you have any questions about that lifetime?

Terri: Gosh. No, I cannot think of any offhand.

Lois: (Long pause) I am seeing you again as a male. You were a mountain climber, and it looks like perhaps you were climbing for sport. You were with a few other people who were climbing to the top——the location feels like what is now Europe, but quite some time ago. This was perhaps thousands of years ago. This appears to be yet another civilization we know absolutely nothing about, of which we have no record. (The clothes are just so interesting! Homespun, like extremely delicate muslin.)

It is becoming clear that actually, rather than a sport climb, the group was climbing in these mountains to get some extremely rare herbs which were also very sacred, to be used in their healing ceremonies. The air is so thin, and everyone is having trouble breathing. There is another herb which you always bring along that had properties which would allow everyone to exist in that environment——up high, where there is not much oxygen. You decide that somebody either dropped it along the way, or it was never packed in the first place.

When it came time to use this life-sustaining herb, it could not be found. There was a very short time frame in which the herbs at the top of the mountain could be harvested, and so the expedition continued in spite of the oxygen-producing herb having gone missing. It took a special person like you to even find the high altitude healing herbs which were so important in ceremonial applications. I think the location might have been a secret to all but a few, because the plants were so powerful. If no one knew how to locate them but the healers, the herbs were less likely to be misused. The healing, medicinal herbs were taken carefully, just like pharmaceuticals are today. An overdose could kill, and so that is one other reason why there were only a few people who knew where this plant was. You and the rest of the group——there were four or five of you——I am seeing you all climbing again for a long while. Steadily it is becoming more difficult. All of a sudden, a freak storm blows in. You are completely unprepared for it. It was unseasonably cold, and everybody finally freezes, even though they pitched tents and tried valiantly to protect themselves.

Freezing is a fairly slow death, and gives one time to ponder the situation. As you were freezing, and realizing what was happening, you snapped to that someone had sabotaged the trip. You faintly recalled that prior to the trip, one particular person had been digging around in your bags. These bags were similar to backpacks; bags that everyone was planning to carry on their bodies up the mountain. Lying there dying, you remember seeing a person you had trusted doing something with the bags before you left, and this must have been the person who removed the oxygen-enhancing herbs—the plants that made it easier to live in a low-oxygen environment. The time you wasted looking for the herb is part of the reason you were not where you needed to be when that storm blew up. You died knowing you were sabotaged, but entirely puzzled as to why. It was actually just a power-grab on the part of that other person. But you died feeling betrayed and confused as to why. You had no concept that anyone would do such a horrible thing just to get power, because you would never have done such a thing to anyone, not ever. Do you have any questions about that lifetime?

Terri: So you said that long ago, the people's clothing looked like it is made of muslin?

Lois: It was homespun, but very well done. It was not actually raggedy looking, or anything, but it was also obviously not machine-made. It looks hand-woven, and this is clearly thousands of years ago. I am still looking at the fabrics, since you mentioned them. I am amazed. These are just beautiful woven things, their clothes; very nicely woven things. It looks like real artisans did this work. I love looking at these garments of theirs...soft, gossamer-looking clothes, yet extremely warm. I wish I could touch them. The fiber is totally unfamiliar-looking to me. The fabrics are quite delicate, with intense brilliant colors. These people were really master colorists.

You know, Terri, what further fascinates me is that you were among the first in that culture to climb as far up as you had begun to go. (Pause) Questions about that lifetime?

Terri: Wow. I wish I knew where that breathing herb was located now! I would definitely go pick some.

Lois: Yes, that would be really nice to have! (Pause) About the breathing herb, I am hearing that it could only be used for a couple of weeks at a time safely, and not any longer than that. It was used as a short-term mountain climbing assist, but not for a long-term solution to anything. Okay. Let me see about the next lifetime. (Long Pause)

Lois: Now I am seeing a civilization that is actually living beneath the surface of the Earth at this time. It was a civilization of Lemurians who evolved to an ascended state, and they live in a different frequency of vibration, but actually under the Earth in caverns. They have cities there. You had a lifetime in one of those cities. This would not have been thousands of years ago, but merely hundreds of years ago. I see that you do some travel to other planets from time to time. Spaceships were coming in and out of those cities, but they went into the ocean first so that nobody on the surface would know where their entrance was. The spaceships would dive into the water and emerge into these caverns underground, and park and people would disembark. You went on several trips to other planets, but you are living in an ascended civilization inside the Earth most of the time, and you are a healer in that particular lifetime—actually in several lifetimes. Naturally your healing has spiritual overtones. These are most advanced cultures. This culture considered healing and spirituality to be different threads of the same fabric, and they are woven together very nicely in their world. It would appear that you went to training seminars for lack of a better word, off-world. That is what you were doing on the spaceships. You also communicated with the dolphins and whales. You learned some of your sound healing techniques from the "dolphin people", as you called them. That is very interesting. And you were a female in that lifetime although most people then were androgynous. They do not look terribly male or female, but I have the knowledge that you were a female, and a healer who specialized in using sound and frequency to specifically balance the endocrine glands, and thereby heal emotional imbalances. That is what she did. Your Guides and Higher Self are telling me you needed to know about that. Hmmm. Yes, I am seeing some very interesting sound frequency healing. You needed to know that you have had more than one lifetime as a healer. Any questions about that lifetime?

Terri: You said it was just hundreds of years ago?

Lois: Yes, it was just hundreds of years ago. They live simultaneously with other Spirit beings in cities inside the crust of the Earth and they are in a different dimensional frequency. Deeahnna. They keep telling me to tell you her name: I have never heard that name before. No further questions about that lifetime?

Terri: No

Lois: Do you sing?

Terri: No

Lois: She uses sound frequency in her healing practice, and a lot of times her own voice's tonal frequencies to heal, which is why I asked if you sang.

Terri: No

Lois: I will bet you could...Deeahnna. I recommend you try it, just experiment. I will go on to the next lifetime now. Names do not usually come up in my readings, by the way. Okay...Wait a minute. She is not letting me go. She wants me to see some ritualized dancing which is part of the healing process. I am seeing very precise movements. These are quick, jerky movements. (Lois watches briefly.) Okay. Let us move on to the next lifetime. (Pause)

My goodness, this seems to be yet another lifetime as a healer! This is a woman living on a tropical island not too long ago, just a couple of hundred years ago—two hundred or three hundred years ago. This body of water has the color and feel of the Pacific Ocean. Yes, it looks like it is off in the direction of Bali. I do not know the name of the island, but it is one of the former mountaintops of Lemuria, which is why in my coming from that other lifetime underground, I had the sensation that I just popped to the surface of the water, and then I saw this next lifetime. This is actually the tippy-top of the Lemurian mountain range. Fascinating!

You are working as a healer who——again, they healed with dance. There are a lot of healings with specific drum patterns that the shaman knew and the groups would dance in a circle around the sick person. The shaman would administer pats and taps and prodding to the patient during the healing process. This allowed things that look like black smoke to escape or leave the body, things that were causing disharmony or illness. This is really very interesting to watch. There was some kind of bead that you would weave into a sort of waist and hip band of a skirt. It was a grass skirt. Everybody had to wear that when they were being healed, and it gave off some sort of frequency that had to do with healing. Oh, the bead gradually emits some kind of a fluid at body temperature - that is what it is! In addition to a fluid, it releases some other kind of frequency. Again you are a healer using sound and herbs. You are healing within a group setting. It has the look and feel of a shamanic healing ceremony like those which are performed in indigenous cultures to this day.

Wow! My entire body became extremely hot when I was telling you about that healing session. There was a lot of energy going through me almost as though I were in the center of the healing circle and being worked upon myself. That is just exactly the sensation I got. I had just waves and waves of energy and heat moving through me. Amazing, I have never had that happen before in one of these readings. Do you have any questions about that lifetime?

Terri: No. But I felt really over-heated, too, while you were describing that healing session.

Lois: (Long pause) Here is another lifetime. I am seeing you as a World War I pilot in a bi-plane. Oh, this is great! It is almost comical. You guys are dropping some kind of bombs, and you are doing it manually. It only looks funny because I am seeing it in a cartoon version. You are wearing a strange-looking leather hat, and some goggles that look like swim goggles. This is one of those leather hats with ear flaps. You were a pilot who survived the war.

Your Guides just wanted you to know that you were a pilot in WWI, and you survived. You dropped bombs——I do not know why it looks so funny. (I continue laughing, and Terri giggles, too.) It rather reminds me of those old Keystone Cops films. I think you guys thought it was funny, too, because you did not know or care if you were hitting anything, you were just dropping these small bombs because the command had told you to. It was like a big joke to you. Neither of you perceived any danger. It was such a new technology, this aviation business. You were the person sitting in the back. I do not think you ever hit anything other than a cow in some barn somewhere, but still, you were a British bombardier. You and your co-pilot remained friends for the rest of your lives, drinking in the same pub, telling war stories which morphed into these quite elaborate scenarios over the years.

So, you survived the war and went on to marry and have children. You owned and operated your own business, selling carpets and oriental rugs and cleaning them. You had a carpet company which meant that you also traveled a lot to the Middle East where you sat around drinking peppermint tea while people showed you carpet after carpet. In this life you had a lot of fun, and a pretty peaceful, productive life after the war. He was happy. I am told that this is the last lifetime I am to show you.

Terri: That is the last one?

Lois: Yes. So, if you do not have any questions about that one.

Terri: So I was a pilot who went on to sell carpets? (She seems puzzled.)

Lois: Yes, not every lifetime has a huge lesson or significance. Sometimes, we simply are there to take a break, to relax and have fun. You might find it easy to pick up knowledge of Oriental rugs or running a business, if you wanted to "mine" his talents. By the way, when this man died, he was doing a lot of coughing—some sort of pneumonia it looks like. Oh, I see. He got sick by being a bit careless—you were an old man trying to do too much out-of-doors in the winter, and you became ill. So you had respiratory failure. You died coughing, unable to breathe. Your Guides are saying, "Take care in bad weather." (Terri laughs, thanking me.)

Lois' Notes: This was the end of the session with Terri. Later that day she emailed me. Here is the pertinent portion of that email.

Dear Lois,

It is with such gratefulness that I write you today. Thank you for sharing about my Soul / Moses' brother Aaron and his profound sadness regarding group dissent /poisoned food / loss of life.

While driving home yesterday, all of the sudden, I understood that it is after extreme conflict (after severe verbal / emotional abuse) that I become fearful that a person could poison me. My truth is … although Aaron did not actually cause the poisoning, I felt very responsible as a leader. Apparently, my Soul has felt guilt / profound sadness for an extremely long time. In this lifetime, I have avoided conflict at all cost and if others became extremely angry and abusive, I have been very fearful of some unknown outcome. (Apparently, to

me, others anger/conflict ends in someone else poisoning food, which equates to death to self /others). Knowing this, I can begin to process the event and finally heal from it. (I look forward to receiving the audio recording so that I can write everything down and remember it.)
Kindest regards,
Terri

And then again, few days later, Terri wrote the following:

Dear Lois,
You were so very right! Your reading provided a vehicle for my Soul to connect with my conscious mind and facilitate some much needed healing. I was fortunate enough to find a good source of information on Aaron's life, from different religious perspectives. It is amazing to see how his sense of responsibility, concerns and desires for peace and harmony are so closely aligned to what my Soul still feels today.
Thank you so much,
Terri

7

A Series of Past Life Readings for One Person: Cindy Oswald

July 31, 2008

This is the first in a series of past life readings for one individual. I am including this series, because it shows how the same issues can be worked on repeatedly over time, like peeling the layers of an onion.

These will be long-distance readings as the client lives a couple of hours away from my office. Cindy has explained in an email that she really wants to know why she has such a fear of driving. It is an absolutely debilitating terror, which is odd, since Cindy worked for a large international corporation for twenty years traveling abroad. When asked how she managed that, she stated that whenever she traveled anywhere, she made sure that someone else drove. She used public transportation, cabs and limos, but she did not drive herself. Now that she is retired and teaching in a University in the Southwest, she needs to be able to drive to get to work, visit friends, attend church, stock up at the grocery store, and so on. There is no reliable public transportation in the mid-sized town where she lives. Everything is quite spread out, with wide open spaces everywhere. Everyone owns a car and drives themselves wherever they need to go in this part of the world.

Cindy also wants to know more about her mother in this lifetime, because she spent several years caring for her mother at the end of her life. She feels this was a significant relationship, and wants to know more about it. She mentions that she thinks and/or senses that she was her own grandmother who died of Swine Flu in 1918 in the United States, and was unable to raise her daughter, who was Cindy's mom in this current lifetime today.

After a long pause, the most significant lifetime comes into focus.

Lois: In the first situation I am seeing, you are a male driving a covered wagon. Your whole family is in it. The family is part of a small wagon train, and this wagon train expedition is not very well protected. The people who are leading it do not appear to know what they are doing; it is their first trip as leaders and they have shrugged off many of the precautions they had seen other leaders take.

I see that you are crossing a river where you hit a rock and one of the wheels breaks off and the wagon tips. Before you know it, you and your entire family go down in this swift stream. The rocks have the people stuck inside the wagon, and under water. Nobody can get out of the water. The people who did manage to wiggle out of the wagon are trapped in an eddy, being sucked down over and over. You manage to pull yourself around the inside of the wagon to get people out, but the speed of the water flow and the water bashing everyone against the rocks is just too overwhelming. Ultimately everyone but the horses drown; you and your whole family die. The point in letting you know about this lifetime is that this is one of the reasons why you have this almost paralyzing fear of driving. You want to travel. You want to get to other places and see new vistas; you just do not want to be the one in charge or doing the driving. This would make sense as to why.

The other piece of information that I am getting is that during this lifetime, you had really strong intuition which you had failed to follow. You felt ever so strongly that you were supposed to be crossing the river at another point, but you had been raised to believe that you have to follow rules, do what the leader of the group says, and not strike out on your own. So you ignored your own compelling inner truth. That was a test for you and a rich experience that you learned from as a Soul, but at the same time, it left a residual which was, "I should not be driving this wagon." This is what you were thinking when you died, and, "I do not have enough sense to be doing this. I was following somebody who absolutely did not know what he was doing, and I felt his incompetence. Yet still did not do what I knew was right from my own inner knowing."

You drew a conclusion, during those powerful last few moments before death, that you were inadequate in that capacity and you should not be driving any conveyance, especially with other people inside it. However, that was absolutely not the point of the experience. The point of the experience was to help you learn how to trust your own inner guidance rather than relying on the authority figures in the world. Now that you are aware of this, this misperception can now begin to heal within your heart and Soul. (Pause)

I see a lot of lifetimes in Atlantis, because so many of us from back there are incarnated now to be here for the coming shift. And the next lifetime I am permitted to see is also during the time of Atlantis. You are the pilot of an inter-dimensional ship. This ship will take you down inside of the Earth, and it moves through solid rock. It just moves through the Earth and rock as if they were water. It also moves through the air, too, which is where you normally take it unless you happen to need to go through the Earth. Not only are you a pilot, you are also the one in charge of navigational frequency shifts which all occur within your mind. There are no machines that control this kind of thing, but it is a form of spiritual technology, controlling the frequencies. It is all a learned skill. They knew how to take advantage of the focus and computation in their minds. People still can do that but have forgotten how, due to the way it was misused in Atlantis.

Now I am seeing you are making evasive maneuvers. This appears very similar to what we would call a dogfight, say during WWII with the fighter jets. It looks like a dogfight in a way but these are not fighter jets, but rather a transport vehicle being attacked by an armed warship. The attacker seems additionally to be trying to scramble your thought waves to mess them up. In this way they hope to cause you to make a computational error and crash. These calculations are creating a vibrational energy shift so that everyone, including the ship, can move through things like Earth or rock or air or water. This kind of mental control requires an intense level of focus. At some point you are distracted by the enemy's efforts, and the ship goes into a vibratory anomaly. What then occurs is that everything and everyone in that transport vehicle just vaporizes, or dematerializes, because you could not hold your focus.

Again, when you realized what was happening, you shamed and blamed yourself and said, "I should not be in charge of anything that has to do with moving people from one place to the next. I must not be involved with anything that has to do with being in control of travel." There is nothing being held against travel, but against your actually being the one who is in charge of moving things around. The decision you made is against being the one in charge of driving.

The reason this comes up is so you know about this, and realize that the conclusion you drew is not necessarily logical, although it may have seemed so at the time. What was really going on was there were opposing forces attacking, and there should never have been anyone attacking your vehicle. The behavior was equivalent to somebody shooting down a passenger plane. You should never have been under attack. You were just collateral damage. The enemy was trying to strike fear in everyone's hearts by attacking innocent, unarmed bystanders. It was never really your fault; you were just in the wrong place at the wrong time. Yes, I am scanning, and that is all I am getting for that lifetime, all you need to know. (Pause)

Your Guides are telling me that there are a couple other lifetimes in which there was a mishap while you were driving, and because you were in charge of the conveyance or whatever, it exacerbated the belief that it is just not safe for you to be in charge of transport. They are not going to show me all those lifetimes details, because these two are the important ones. They are the major seeds of this issue in your Soul's records.

This next lifetime we are going to has to do with your being—this is France in the late 1500s or early 1600s that this occurs, just about the time of the Renaissance.

You come from a wealthy family and are an only son. Your mother dies relatively young and that leaves the family as just you and your father, all on your own. Your father is distant, and your two older sisters marry and leave early on, but you never marry. You were busy being a dilettante—drinking, carousing with gamblers, sleeping with prostitutes, the women you do go out with who are possible marriage partners you mistreat because of the attitude toward women which you developed while you were very young. As an adult male you were rakishly handsome and charming, and initially women fell for you easily. But those who became involved always ended up being heartbroken.

Your initial sexual contact in that lifetime was a prostitute so you did not have much tenderness or gentleness toward someone who was an innocent virgin. You did not have a concept of what that lack of care might feel like for the woman. Consequently, due to your rough manner, no one wished to marry you. You do not really want to marry them either. This goes back to the deep hurt you felt when your mother died, feeling abandoned, and no one else stepping up to love you or care for you. The adults told you that she was visiting cousins, and she would be back some day, but she did not return, of course. You are just going through the motions with women. You do this so nobody will think there is something weird about you and gossip. The wealthy people were a small community and gossiped a great deal.

Now your father, who had inherited all this "old money" was ignored pretty much by his father, who had been ignored by his father as well, so you never do quite feel a connection with him, or for that matter, to anybody else. You felt a strong, loving connection to your mother, but she was gone early on, by the time you were five years of age. Subsequently there was a rapid succession of nannies and governesses who were responsible for your care. Nobody had the concept that you needed to bond with anyone, and so you never really did. You spent your adulthood squandering money, gambling, and carousing. You had a lot of fun, or at least you thought it was fun, because other people envied you and you drank a lot. Inebriation is often mistaken for fun. When your father fell ill, you followed the family pattern and just ignored him. In that lifetime part of your Soul level agreement had been to see the error of your ways, and nurture and take care of your father even though he never nurtured or took care of you.

You did not do this, though. You just kept on partying and finally, when he got really sick and could not do much about it, and you realized you were about to inherit everything that was left, you just went berserk. You drank entirely too much and began having the prostitutes show up at the house; you began having hedonistic, out-of-control drunken parties, making a lot of noise and squandering disgusting sums of money. There were parasitic people who took advantage of you because you drank, and to make a long story short, you wasted every last bit of the money. There was not much of anything left to pay the servants and they left. Your father was not being taken care of and ultimately died in a very uncomfortable way with nobody to help him get to the toilet, or feed him. That happens to be part of the reason that in this lifetime, and there has been more than one life, but this lifetime, you came back together and one of your jobs was to take care of this person in old age, which you did. This person came back as your mother this life. Part of what you have been doing is fulfilling an obligation you had not fulfilled in that past life by taking care of her, and you did it this time. And you did a good job of it.

Oh, I am seeing more now from that lifetime. As you were partying and drunk you were having people over to the house for the first time to have parties. Prior to this time, you had been partying away from the house, at pubs and inns. But as they came into your home, you were never sober, and so not very discriminating about who came in. In short, you were pretty much robbed blind. Your refusal to listen to the servants who tried to warn you made things go downhill even faster. Ultimately, there were servants who robbed you, too, after they realized that if they did not grab it, then some total stranger who had never devoted themselves to working for your family would. Why you needed to know that part, I do not know, but your Guides did tell me that you needed to know that part. You had invited these thefts. (Long pause)

The next lifetime I am being shown is one almost immediately after the last one in which you come back as the illegitimate son of a very wealthy man who never acknowledges you as his son, but does provide for your education. The mother is a seamstress or something—a sweet, beautiful auburn-haired woman whom he had callously seduced. She is a good and kind person, and she raised you well. Your father paid for all your needs, including your education. Later, when you wanted to become a painter, he paid for that education abroad as well. He then provided a stipend for the rest of your life, so you would have the freedom and the money to live upon, so you could paint full-time. Again, in that lifetime, the mother was the same person who is your mother in this lifetime. You mutually cared for one another. It was just the two of you for quite a long time. And this time you turned the behavior around. You did help out and tenderly take care of her when she needed you at the end, partially pulling yourself out of the karmic hole you had dug in the lifetime as a dilettante.

Another important thing to know about this lifetime is that you were an obscure little-known painter who was really quite gifted. In your Soul is artistic ability. All of that, having the wealthy father who paid for everything, occurred so that you could not be distracted while you took care of your mother, not that she was sick the whole time, but you were just attentive and kind. You also needed to know that you do have creative abilities. If you are not aware of it, you have latent creative abilities from this lifetime because your artwork was quite good, actually. (Another pause)

The next lifetime I am seeing is you as a young mother who had a very tiny baby. This occurs in a fishing village in England quite some time ago. It is not clear when it was. Sometimes I can tell from the costumes, but it was several hundred years ago, anyway. This small baby of yours became ill and died through no fault of your own. She was the same Soul who was your mother in this lifetime, so here was another reason you needed to spend some time with her, nurturing her and tending her. Also connected with that was the lifetime you mentioned remembering earlier, in which you got the Swine Flu and died and did not get to raise your daughter. So as you suspected, you actually were your own maternal grandmother. This current life allowed fulfillment of both those lifetimes where you did not get to nurture this Soul who was your mother in this lifetime, when she was young. But in this lifetime, you did get to care for her as she was older. It truly is the relationship that is important, not at what age or stage the relationship occurs, but the way we relate to each other. The love, compassion and nurturing are all the same whether for a baby, an ageing parent or a wounded soldier.

I am being told that this is sufficient information for this time. These are enough lifetimes to try to assimilate all at once. You should wait a bit, several months at least, before you get any more past life readings because it takes time to assimilate these memories that have been brought back. And so we are complete for today.

Lois' Notes: Later Cindy revealed that even while on an airplane as a passenger she has always felt the need to remain alert and "in control" because of a deep sense that everything depends upon her. She knows this is not true, but has always felt this way. Now she knows why, the Atlantean pilot did have to stay alert at all times, and everything did depend upon his focus. Things ended badly when he lost focus.

Not too long after the reading, Cindy began yielding to a long-standing temptation to create crafts and to begin painting. She states she never would have done that without knowing about the past life as a successful, though little-known, painter.

Of course, Cindy was happy that she was affirmed to be correct in believing that she was the grandmother who died of Swine Flu as suspected, since we do appreciate confirmation when our inner vision is correct. She was grateful to understand more deeply why she felt she had needed to care for her mom while she was ill for all those years at the end of her life, and justified in having given up everything else to care for her. She had "just known" without a doubt that this was what she had to do.

About a year later, Cindy and I were talking about the reading again, and it popped into both our heads at the same time just why I had been told she needed to know about the lifetime where the wealthy, charming young man was drinking and squandering money while the father died. I had been told that the young man had been robbed blind by visitors who he foolishly and repeatedly invited to his drunken parties in his dying father's home. He had invited the thefts with his carelessness and his total disregard for his inherited money or possessions, but we did not know why she needed to know that.

In this later conversation, at the same moment, we both realized that she was experiencing repeated robberies of her vacation home located about an hour north of where she lived. This was why she needed to know about the invited thefts in the other life! Now perhaps she will be able to release the karmic "need" to be robbed.

November 3, 2008

This is the second in a series of past life readings for Cindy. Before we did this reading she asked if perhaps we might find out something about her incessant jaw pain, in her tempro-mandibular joints. This is commonly called TMJ pain. At the time of the reading, it has been with her for over fifty years. She is also curious about why she is not interested in getting married again; she is perfectly happy living with her cats and teaching college.

Lois: I am seeing a huge field of grain. This crop might be oats...and there are some wildflowers growing there too. Oh, these folks believe flowers need to grow intermingled with the grain for the emotional health of the grain. (How about that!) You are a young female with short, curly brown hair, wearing a simple, homespun dress, tending the fields, checking for pests, insects and other bugs. You pick them off, and place them in a jar with an alcoholic beverage in it. The bugs like to drink that, and becoming intoxicated, they do not leave. You are relaxed, and it is warm and pleasant out. In a peaceful, zoned out state, you are walking alone through a vast field. The wind is blowing and the grain is making rustling sounds. On this day the wind is rather noisy, actually. The field is enormous and you are a long way from any kind of house. Due to the noise of the wind you do not hear the man riding up behind you on an animal similar to a horse. He sweeps you up onto his saddle against your will. You have been abducted. Apparently he has been planning this for a long time, as he has enough provisions for a long journey. Wherever it is that he is taking you, it is far away, and they have a shortage of women there. Some kind of epidemic that killed all the women had erupted in their village, but it had not affected the men.

No trace of you is left in the field except for that jar filled with alcohol and bugs. This man takes you to the place where he lives, which is inside a network of caves in the hills. These are not primitive people in any way; they are fairly civilized. They do not like the idea of building outside; it defiles the surface, and nature looks better than structures do to them. They are deeply respectful of the aesthetics of nature. But they oddly enough, they also are very militaristic. This tribe is comprised of distant relatives of your clan, but your people are more agricultural. The cave clan lives off hunting for animals plus foraged root crops and mushrooms. So it is a very different way of life. You are forced to remain there against your will. Immediately you are compelled to have sex with several different men. They do not want to know who the father of the child is. They feel everyone has the right to father a child, and there are not enough women to go around, so they have agreed to give everyone the opportunity to father a child by sharing the women. You immediately become pregnant. One baby after another comes from your loins for many years. These men are quite concerned that their civilization may die out, since they lost all their women to that epidemic.

You kept moving back and forth between wanting to plot an escape and not being able to leave your children, because you loved them. Your life was not all that hard; you did not have to work in the fields, or clean up after anyone. They valued you because you could have children. It was in their best interest to keep you healthy and safe, so they were good to you. You did tan hides when you had time. You rather enjoyed doing that; it staved off boredom. However, you really wanted to go home and take your children with you for a visit. That was never going to happen, however.

Late one afternoon, quite by accident, someone knocked over a lantern, and a fire spread through the cave. You were trapped. As you realized you were going to die, your life flashed before you. You wondered, "What was the point in living at all, if you do not get to choose how you live, or who you make love with, or who fathers your children?" You died having a lot of deep anger at these men who took your life away from you, and gave you no choices. You also had a lot of ambivalence, because you loved your children. (Pause)

This time I am seeing a culture where people live in boats. They travel along the shore of a large island, but for some reason they live on boats, not land. (Pause) Oh, I see, they used to live on the island, but they kept having their homes wiped out by typhoons, and discovered they were better off in boats. They designed boats which they could seal off when storms came. When they were sealed up, they looked like huge dark brown seed pods. But they had devices off to the side for balance, like a catamaran does. These are quite large boats, and entire families lived in them. Apparently sea levels fluctuated a lot back then. This seems to be down in the South Pacific. (Another pause)

In this boating lifetime you are a man. You apparently did something to anger the powers that be, and they had a type of punishment where they would run a rod made from a big fish bone, through the mouth. This hook went through the masseter muscles, which are the muscles at the back of your cheeks, near the ears, which allow you to open and close your mouth. They would hook a rope to either side of the fish bone and drag people behind the boat face up, by the head. It was not intended to kill, just to inflict immense pain. This punishment was usually reserved for young men who behaved as if they might be interested in overthrowing the leadership of the clan. You were dragged for about a day when a sudden storm broke out, and they were unable to pull you back in quickly enough. So you drowned. Whatever you are thinking at death makes an imprint on the Soul, like light on a negative, and your focus and feelings were all on your jaw muscles, the masseters, which open and close the mouth. These were what were holding you attached to the ropes and unable to save yourself. The Guardians of the Records wish you to know that this is the reason for your TMJ problems in the current lifetime.

What happened to you was extremely unfair, and if a storm had not blown up suddenly and taken everyone by surprise, they would have brought you back in. Your punishment time was up already. That treatment definitely tended to whip men into shape; no one wanted to go through that again. And it branded them. The scars on the cheeks let everyone know for the rest of their lives that they had been in trouble when they were young. (I pause to see the next lifetime.)

Ah, now I am seeing a Native American lifetime in the plains states of what is now the United States. This is a very peaceful tribe. You are an elder, and a male. Again you are tanning hides, preparing them for ritual use. This time you are preparing a wolf hide for a shamanic initiation. Everyone is taken by surprise when another tribe comes rushing in on foot. Apparently this occurs during the time before horses were introduced to America. The raiders took both of your daughters, your wife, and all the women they could grab and take away with them. Most of the younger men were off hunting; you were much older by then. The invaders knew the braves were gone. You were torn as to whether to stay and watch the children or go after the women. Because you knew the women would have wanted you to watch their children, you did. When the younger men got home, they were inconsolable. They immediately took off after the raiders. But they never found the women, because the invaders had a two day start.

Torturing yourself because you did not go after the women when they were first taken, you worried constantly about what happened to them. You had been on the horns of a dilemma, because you could not abandon all those children under the age of twelve who would have been left behind. Your Guides want you to know that you did the right thing. The children needed protecting from wild animals and drowning and all the other things small children can get into, and the women never would have been found anyway. You could not have recovered them all by yourself even if you had found them.

Your Guides also want you to know that you have a tendency to beat yourself up over things you cannot control. You had violent imaginings and dreams about what happened to those women, and in reality they were only used as servants. The bottom line is this: do not beat yourself up when you are unable to do the impossible. (Pause)

I am now seeing you in Central America; you are among a tribe of indigenous peoples, in what is now Costa Rica. There is volcano-worshiping going on. I am seeing you as a shaman, or the equivalent. You do something similar to fire-walking, but it is volcano-walking on hot lava. Those around you believed that the shaman's walking on lava would ensure bountiful crops and healthy children and plenty of food. You did this every year, and every year you dreaded it, and wondered how you could have done it the year before. Yet every year you managed to do it again.

Each year the pressure built more. Everyone's expectations grew. You had learned this technique from the one person who could do it, and now you were the only one who could do it. You waited and waited for your replacement to show up, and one never did. The tension kept building until one year, a couple of days before the annual event's unfolding you went up to the volcano. There you took an extremely heavy dose of a "teacher plant" and while contacting the spirits, you decided to dive in, and go to the center of the volcano, and become one with the volcano. Your body died very quickly. This seemed like the only honorable way to end your service to the tribe.

This lifetime is about taking on an incredible burden for others; for fertility, for healthy children, for sufficient food, for peace, for the volcano not erupting, for the success of the entire tribe. The lava walking got harder every single year. And this ending was about feeling overwhelmed by the responsibility year after year until it became unbearable. So you decided to sacrifice yourself. Another option might have been to say, "I can no longer do this; it is not going to happen this year." Or you could have just packed your bags and gone away. You were attempting to do the impossible, again, and became overwhelmed.

I think you will get something else from this lifetime that I am not, but not the first time you listen to the tape, Cindy. (Pause)

I am seeing a lifetime during the Deep South in America, in the early 1800s when slaves were sold on the slave blocks. You were an African female kidnapped at about fourteen years of age, while you were young and nubile. The person who bought you decided that you would be used as breeding stock, with other slaves, so he could have even more slaves. His teenaged sons and his friends had other plans, though, and broke in to the slave quarters and raped you repeatedly over a period of few days. You had not had time to learn any of the other slave's native languages or English, so you could not tell anyone what had happened to you. Lonely and isolated, you thought you had a lifetime ahead of you of continuous rape, so you hanged yourself. It seems we are seeing a pattern here in more than one lifetime, where as a woman you are at the mercy of men, and have no control over your life. This explains some of your fears of getting married again. (I pause to see the next life.)

I am feeling the joy coming from the next lifetime. Your Guides want you to know that not all your lives have been difficult, that these are just the ones that have unresolved issues we have seen so far today. I now see a "happy gypsy", traveling from town to town across Europe in a wagon, stopping to perform for crowds periodically. You are doing a dance where you twirl and flip your ruffled skirts. I call her a "happy gypsy" because she is not the scheming kind, but just the traveling kind. She also sells handmade candy. She stops off on the side of the road on her way to the next town, lights a fire, and sets up a large copper kettle and makes candy with butter, sugar and local berries or fruit. She wraps the candies in colorful papers, and sells them to people before and after the dance performances. Quite the entrepreneur, she made fairly decent money, but decided to go to the Americas, and to the Wild West. She was just magnetically drawn by the stories she had heard.

And so she sold her wagon, took a boat to America, and went far enough west that she thought she was in the Wild West. Becoming a can-can dancer in a saloon, she had a great deal of fun, and got several proposals of marriage. She wanted to go back to Europe where she came from, and so she did not marry. Instead she just raked in a great deal of money. This seems to have been a mining town; there was money and booze flowing very freely. After five years, she accumulated enough money to go home and set up a dress shop where she and a friend designed and sold their own dresses. She entertained the clients in her shop by telling wild tales about her adventures to the American West, and how the people threw gold coins up on the stage at her because they liked her so much. She kept her shop, and finally was married in her forties to a widower who was a blacksmith, and had a nice upscale stable where he kept horses for people in town. It was a long and happy life.

This is the end of the reading for today.

Lois' Notes: In this session we see several examples of why Cindy is not that interested in re-marrying. By knowing about these, she will begin to heal of her fear of men when incarnated in a female body. We also see why she has had the TMJ pain most of her life. Cindy reported that a few days after the session, her jaw pain was almost entirely gone for the first time in fifty years. When it does rarely come back, she says to herself, "You are not being pulled behind a boat," and the pain goes away!

Cindy also has said that she has always loved to sew, and that this last lifetime with the dress shop helps her to have a point of reference as to why.

<u>January 29, 2009</u>

This is the third in an ongoing series of past life readings for Cindy Oswald. After reminding Cindy why we have past life readings, Lois begins this distance session.

<u>Lois:</u> You are male in the life I am seeing first, and it would appear that you are living on the Yucatan peninsula of what is now called Mexico. You are Mayan, and the time period is right after the Atlanteans moved to the Yucatan, bringing their teaching and wisdom to the peoples there. You are preparing for a journey, somewhat like a pilgrimage, and taking many sacred ritual objects such as carved jade objects and ritual knives. These are not knives to be used in warfare, but in religious rituals.

I see that you are boarding a large ship, leaving from approximately where the pyramid of Tulum is located. This is on the Gulf of Mexico, along the edge of the peninsula, near the island which is now called Isla de las Mujeres, or Island of the Women, and this expedition will be sailing across the Gulf of Mexico, to the point on the mainland up north where Texas and Louisiana now have their border. That is the spot where the Red River empties into the Gulf of Mexico. From the point where the river meets the Gulf, I see you are taking a land journey, walking alongside this river, going north, against the flow of the river. This is why you are walking and not in a boat, you are going upstream. It is for this reason an arduous and difficult journey compared to moving across the water. This particular land journey is headed for the crystal fields of what is now Arkansas. Your plan is to trade these exquisitely carved ritual objects, charged with power by the shamanic community, to trade with the natives whom we call the American Indians. This had been an ongoing trade route between your peoples for hundreds of years. You are on a quest to obtain more of their amazing, powerful crystals, which are so plentiful where they live.

You have a pre-scheduled meeting there with several different tribes. Everyone for miles and miles to either side of the river knew when these expeditions would be coming, and there was a great deal of planning and celebration around the visitors from Mayaland coming through. This happened only once every five to ten years. Many tribes along the way came to the river to greet you and trade with you.

The group you would ultimately be meeting with at the crystal fields included the Cherokee. This large tribe, by the way, had a written language which they had developed from the Mayans. The language later evolved so that was not the same as Mayan, but at that time it still was really close, the way Spanish and Portuguese are similar. The Cherokee and Mayan were closely related, as Cherokee were actually Mayans who had relocated to the north over a thousand years earlier. About a third to half of the way to the crystal fields, members of your party begin to fall ill. You are a highly trained, successful healer at home. You are also an important individual in the spiritual hierarchy where you lived.

In this instance, however, you are puzzled as to what this illness is. You simply cannot figure out what has happened to your people, thinking it is a disease or some kind of insect or even sorcery that has caused the illness. However, the one thing that did not occur to you was what had actually happened. A group of people about a third of the way up that trail you were on had poisoned your party. These people had been known to be friendly for centuries, so everyone assumed they still were. However, what was not known was that they had recently been overtaken by hostile forces, and destroyed. These hostile forces had donned their clothing and had fooled all of you. They knew about your sacred objects which were about to be traded with the Cherokee, and they saw only their monetary value, not their sacred, religious significance. Oddly, these were all women who perpetrated this horror. These women poisoned all of you, and just followed at a distance, waiting for everyone to die, so they could then rob your group.

As your people died off, you buried them and then you just kept carrying more heavy burdens yourself, much of it on your own back. With the help of some pack horses you carried all their sacred, ritual objects and supplies. There was one other man who joined your party as a guide when you first landed, who was not ill. He had a premonition of some kind that proffered food was not safe, he saw the people in the dream as charming Gila monsters, a type of gigantic, venomous lizard. In his dream, the Gila monsters were standing on back legs, wearing the local costumes, smiling and proffering food. For this reason he was only eating food which he had foraged himself, from nature along the way. He began to give that to you, as well, warning you not to eat anything else because it might be carrying disease. After everyone else got sick, he had realized the dream to be true. You were the only one not yet ill, so he gave you his food to eat, that which he had been collecting along the way. He saved your life, but without ever telling you what was actually going on.

He had correctly guessed that had you become aware of the truth on the way up there, there would have been a horrible war, as the Mayans and the Cherokee routed out the murderers. He knew the Cherokee would meet the killers with swift retribution. They were not ones to allow that kind of treachery to go unpunished. The net result of this for his part of the world was that he and his family would have been caught in the middle, and probably destroyed. This was short-sighted of him, not wanting the evildoers routed out of the neighborhood. But he was something of a coward, and that is his karma to bear.

You completed your mission, and the people who had brought you to the mainland by boat were waiting for you at the mouth of the river to take you back to the Yucatan. But arriving back there alone looked really bad. To make matters worse, you felt guilty because you believed that spiritually, you must have done something horribly wrong to have been punished by having everyone but yourself die. You had an overwhelming case of survivor's guilt, and that pain was on your face. You never found out what really happened; you never even guessed it. The guide never spilled the beans, since he did not want this war.

When you finally made it home, people began immediately gossiping about you. The consensus was that you must have done something wrong to be the only one alive. This belief was exacerbated by the fact that you walked around in pain, with a guilty look on your face. No one ever treated you the same after that. Your whole life changed permanently. Even your friends shied away from you. You had taken responsibility for something you did not do and over which you had no control. Living another twelve years, you were pretty miserable over something that happened that was not your fault, but for which you undeservedly assumed responsibility and were subsequently blamed. The families of the people who had not come back from that expedition especially shunned you.

The reason for looking at this lifetime is so that you are aware of what really happened, and therefore, can let go of this guilt while in human form. It has been affecting you in ways of which you are not at all aware. Your Guides feel it is time to know about this and release the guilt. It has also made you suspicious, worried about things going wrong that you cannot control, and so on.

You need to be reminded that you completed your mission, doing a lot of "heavy lifting" all by yourself. What you accomplished was heroic, actually, and you never gave yourself the proper credit for that. You allowed yourself to be undercut after you got home, due to a competitive situation which had previously existed. People had their own personal greed and agendas. So please hear this: sometimes things happen that are not your fault, and you do not have to take responsibility for that over which you have no control. You can say, "I do not know what happened," and not take the blame for everything that goes wrong. (Long pause)

In the next lifetime that I am seeing, you are coming into the Earth's atmosphere in some kind of vehicle. The energy is disguised. Your vehicle is made to look like a shooting star. You are coming in during approximately 1400 BCE from another star system. The reason that you are coming here is to covertly monitor levels of certain chemicals in the soil on Earth. There are mining operations going on at this time in very remote regions. Humans are doing mining under the supervision of certain extra-terrestrials. Humans do not know these are extra-terrestrials; however, they think they are humans from far away. There is some kind of inter-stellar treaty in place, which allows these extra-terrestrials to get humans to do the mining for them. The agreement is that this mining must be done in such a way that there are no chemical byproducts or pollutants of any kind, created by this mining project that will later damage, or in any way impact the RNA/DNA of plants, animals or humans on Earth, or in any way affect their subsequent evolution. The actual mining operation was being directed by humanoids from a different star system than you, and there were questions within the inter-galactic governing body, which is where the treaty was signed, as to whether these beings were honoring their agreement regarding keeping the Earth free of pollutants.

Because there were worried parties within that governing body who cared about what happened to the evolving, but still primitive peoples of Earth, it was decided that a covert observation mission was needed. Thus, you were sent on a stealth mission with three other people and one android, to monitor this situation without the knowledge of the group from the neighboring star system, which was doing the mining. They were not notified that you were there. It was felt by the High Command that this was the only way that you could get accurate readings. The mission directives stated that you were to take soil samples, and as the leader, you had decided it would be safer to do this undetected, under the cover of darkness.

Unfortunately, the other group of extra-terrestrials caught your people covertly taking soil samples, and one of your members was captured. Rather than going home on schedule, you determined that you would stay until you got your crew member returned. The reason that this was an unscheduled inspection was because there were suspicions that earlier inspectors had been paid off. And this was true as you all discovered. There was a huge kick-back scheme going on at the expense of the evolution of the people of planet Earth. When it was realized that you had found them out, those who had not been captured were put in the position of having to hide and move constantly. This was hard on everyone, as you were way outnumbered.

Not leaving on time, your party had to remain on Earth for an extremely long time, waiting to get your fellow inspector back, and because the planets/ stars were not lined up correctly to return, you ended up being here for years instead of days as originally planned.

Oh, here is a surprising twist. The Earthlings discovered that you were here to help, and they hid you and fed you as best they could. There was a lot of time spent in a network of caves deep underground, dodging the mining concerns. Now for the big surprise, you were a woman in this lifetime, a woman who got pregnant by an Earthling. This complicated things for your race. This was not supposed to happen.

When you were finally able to go home to your own planet, you had discovered on the trip home that you were pregnant. When you got home you gave birth to the baby, but this caused big problems for your race of people. All this may have left you with some real hesitancy, or emotional issues around the idea of having children, and with having sex, and so on. I sense that it left you feeling not-safe to engage in these activities. So of course, knowing about that will help you start to heal.

There was a big pow-wow when you got home to determine whether this child would be allowed to reproduce. It was decided by the High Council that he would not. And this was sad for him and for you as well. He was treated as though he were quite special, loved and honored, but not allowed to reproduce. He looked unusual, and so was something of a celebrity all his life. But your leaders did not want a hybrid race started anywhere, neither on Earth nor on their home world.

Here is what else you need to take away from that past life. You have a history of not knowing when to cut your losses. You did not follow protocol and should have. Protocol stated that you leave the captured party, go straight back home, and tell your superiors what had happened, but you did not. Here is the other thing you are to take from knowing about this lifetime. Historically, as a Soul, you have a problem having to do with sex, reproduction, and so on, and that knowing about this particular life will help you finally begin to heal it.

You may be wondering when you decided to incarnate on Earth, since you were from another star system. Knowing your son made you fascinated with the people of Earth and their process of karma and Soul evolution, so you decided to join us, so you could reincarnate with your son, and be with him again in the future. (Pause)

Here is a lifetime as a young, cocky male. He is tall with flowing black, straight hair. He is strong, muscular, and had quite a way with the ladies. The hormones are really pumping in him at the point in that lifetime I am seeing. He sits by the side of the river, bored, and trying to think up adventures. He fantasizes a lot about adventure that challenges him. There is not much to do in his village.

The river he sits beside is both wide and treacherous. Even while fishing, the locals are careful not to fall in, as it is fierce. It flows fast, and there are many huge boulders both in it and along the river's edge. This river is coming down at a steep grade, in between some very high mountains with sharp peaks. I am not clear which continent this is on.

One day you decide to take a boat trip down this river, which, since it is filled with large rocks, has plenty of whitewater, or "rapids". Everyone in your village said it was too treacherous, too rough to navigate, due to the heavy rainfall conditions at the time. Perhaps all that rain had fueled your boredom, too.

All of your neighbors warned you not to do this run. You decide to do it anyway, having a sense of being invincible. So two of your young men friends decide to come along. You gather up sufficient provisions one morning and take off for the unknown.

The next scene I am seeing is most strange. A few days into the trip, late one afternoon as the sun was setting, a huge bird with about a six foot wingspan, perhaps an eagle or condor, comes screaming down from above heading straight for you. This enormous raptor buzzes your head, and completely throws off your concentration, right as you are navigating some difficult rapids. It flashes through your mind that this is a very bad omen. Because of this you become terrified, lose focus, and come too close to a rock. This action flips the boat, and when it does, you hit your head on a huge rock in the river. This blow to the head kills you. The other two people with you live, but as you realized you were dying, it reinforced the notion that when you are "driving" (in this case the boat) bad things happen. The conclusion at the moment of death was again that you do not need to be the one in charge of any conveyance carrying people. This trip would all have been just fine, had you not freaked out when you saw the huge bird, thought it was an omen, and lost focus. The river was not really too dangerous to travel; you had been right about that. So this is another layer of that onion we are peeling, which is your fear of driving, which has been addressed in past life readings previously. The fear has abated, but not totally disappeared, and the Guides wanted to work on healing this issue a bit more. So this is why we have looked at that past life. (I pause again.)

I am seeing just one more lifetime today, in a culture where people only live into their thirties. You are a young female living in a community that mostly lives within caves. On the day I am seeing, you are in the middle of giving birth. It is a difficult birth; the baby gets stuck. You bleed to death, even though the baby has been removed in pieces. They just were hoping to allow you to live. Many times in ancient history when a baby was just too large for the birth canal, they would have to kill the infant to get it out at all, hoping to save the mother. They knew that if the mother died and the baby was stuck, the baby would die anyway. The Caesarian section was not an option to these people living in caves. Sometimes this method worked, and sometimes it did not. In this case it did not.

This is just a sample of another time that you died in childbirth, which was once quite a common occurrence. The experience just reinforced the idea for your Soul that having babies is dangerous, so we are furthering the healing process. In that way, hopefully in some subsequent life, you will not have this fear to that same degree, and when the Soul decides to have children, you will not be too frightened.

The first two lifetimes will be the most difficult for you to integrate, so do not forget your apple cider vinegar baths. Email me if you have any questions.

Lois' Notes: Cindy remarked that the past life where she died in childbirth helped further explain why she had no strong interest in having children in this lifetime. The lifetime where her only child was a half breed between human and another planetary race, who was then not allowed to reproduce, underscored this. That same lifetime echoed with the covert operations, her earlier experiences with secrecy in the current lifetime. Cindy had worked in a large multi-national corporation where to be on the leading edge of the industry, innovation was crucial and industrial spying was common.

The recurring theme that it is not safe to be "driving" seems to be continuing to be addressed, the more layers of that issue that are unraveled, the easier it will be for Cindy to both drive long distances and in heavy traffic. Driving is getting easier for her, and she saw a further shift after this past life, too.

Where the first lifetime was concerned, Cindy realizes she has had a tendency to worry excessively about things going wrong that she cannot control. She is looking forward to being able to relax in that regard, now that she knows about the lifetime as a Mayan.

April 29, 2009

This is another in the series of long-distance past life readings for Cindy Oswald, a middle-aged college professor who lives about two hours' drive from my office. She is also a long-distance energy medicine client of mine. Cindy is quite serious in the pursuit of doing her spiritual growth work. She has wisely made the decision at the time of this reading to just remain open to seeing whatever the Committee comprised of her Guides and her Higher Self wish to show her, in concert with the Guardians of the Akashic Records. Learning more about herself from the readings, and growing from that experience, Cindy is just being open and allowing.

Lois: I am seeing a lifetime in Spain. It is approximately during the same period of time that the Conquistadors were going to the new world. You are on a religious pilgrimage. I am seeing you in the late summer or early fall high up in the mountains. The air is clear, cool and crisp, and the scenery is breathtaking. You can see spread out before you brightly colored valleys and hills, streams and small farms as if floating in a mist. The view stretches out for miles and miles from some of the high mountain passes. There is a quite procession and you are leading it.

You are a Catholic priest with short, curly brown hair, light olive skin, and thick eyebrows. Usually you have a ready smile, but not at this period of time. You are riding a little donkey, at the head of a procession that lasts for weeks, perhaps months. Bouncing up and down, riding on this donkey, however, is taking its toll. This harsh bouncing is very uncomfortable, but as the priest, you are convinced that you need to maintain an erect spine and lead the procession. This posture is maintained so that everyone knows you are above reproach. It was a strange attitude, but something all the priests were taught back then. Therefore, you do not relax. You do not lean back or change your posture, or ever ride in the wagon. Riding all day like this was a form of torture, really, but it was self-imposed. At that time, you were having lower back and hemorrhoid problems, so you were quite miserable. But you said nothing—feeling that self-sacrifice was part of the job description.

This discomfort is going on and on, and in the beginning the procession was not through the mountains, but it gradually worked up to that. The travel through the mountains was more difficult, as the roads were rocky, and the animals lost their footing and stumbled quite a bit. There was some particular shrine or open-air chapel the group was headed toward as the culmination of the journey, where there would be a special ceremony. Therefore, you were moving up quite high into the mountains of Spain, because that was where this holy site was located. The group was on a tight schedule and you were responsible, as the leader, for maintaining that schedule. Should the snows come early at those high altitudes, people could die. This had happened to other priests before.

A child from one very tiny village you pass through becomes over-stimulated because of all the excitement in the normally quiet town, and pulls loose from his mother, running straight out into the road. Your donkey stumbles and jumps out of the way, throwing you to the ground. There is chaos as a result behind you. The child gets stepped on by other animals, and eventually the wheel of a wagon runs over him. You could see none of that. You were fairly seriously injured, and on top of the back and hemorrhoid pain you already had, you were in hideous agony. Then the grieving mother comes out screaming at you, and grabbing up her child. She seemed to be blaming you for this mishap, which was clearly unfair. You were in so much pain that you had an angry reaction to the fact that she somehow lost control of her child and then blamed you. Never having had children of your own, it ran through your mind that she was not paying attention, and that this had caused this accident and your pain. However, this was a three or four year old little boy who was killed, and that is a profound tragedy. The mother knew he was dead, but you had not yet realized this fact. You pulled yourself up, and backhanded her in the face. It was a knee-jerk reaction. You were in excruciating pain, and you also knew this accident was going to slow down the procession and prolong your agony, and even possibly cause the pilgrimage to fail by not reaching its target on time. All this flashed through your mind in a matter of seconds.

Screaming orders, you had her beaten with a whip for her irresponsibility. You were certainly not showing any compassion. This was coming out of your own intense, horrific, physical pain. It was difficult for you even to stand up unassisted by this time. The beating incident shocked everyone in the procession, and caused you to fall from grace, and you eventually lost your position in the church. After it was all over, and the whip had been applied to her back in front of everyone, she again stood up holding her dead baby, screaming and sobbing. The townspeople crowded around her to protect her from further punishment, and were shouting at the procession with raised, shaking fists. Afterward, those processions were not allowed to go through that particular location without rock-throwing protests. People were justifiably angry, and the Church Fathers were very upset with you, hence your loss of status and power. This disgrace was discussed, behind closed doors, even in Rome. The Pope actually heard about it.

Most of all, it bothered you personally for the rest of your days that you could do that to a grieving mother. But it was just out of mind-bending, intense pain that you so terribly lost control. This incident was a burden you carried for the rest of your days, and I think you lived—you were maybe in your late thirties when this happened, and you probably lived another fifteen years. You were still a priest, but with lesser duties, and spent much of the rest of that lifetime doing penance in your spare time, going around making sure that women with small children had plenty to eat. You delivered this food yourself, walking and carrying the food on the back of a donkey. You could have hired someone else to do this, priests had access to money for this kind of thing, but you chose to humble yourself and do it personally.

Some events in our lives weigh more heavily on our Souls than others, and this one has been weighing most profoundly on your Soul. Knowing about it, you can begin to heal it and forgive yourself. It is hoped that you will not ever pointlessly torture yourself like you did on the back of that donkey, so that you find yourself in a position where you react in an unreasonable manner due to discomfort or pain. Be more aware of honoring your physical limitations. Your Guides are saying not to push yourself beyond your limits, unless there is a good reason. Saving a life is a good reason, looking proper in the front of a parade is not. In this way you will never again lose perspective about who you are, and what your primary objective is. The first goal in that situation was in keeping the goodwill of the people, rather than to just hurry up and get to the pilgrimage site and get the pain over with.

You did later explain to the people in your procession that you were in a lot of pain and needed to lie down in the cart after that accident. Almost crying with relief, you were lying on some bags of dried beans for the rest of the trip. The pilgrims were eating a lot of beans as they traveled. It made a huge difference in your pain level after you actually admitted that you needed to take care of yourself, lying down made all the difference. You were surprised to learn that no one admired you for "toughing it out," and riding the donkey in excruciating pain earlier. You thought you would be admired for suffering because Jesus had suffered. This was an ego-based assumption. Your parishioners were just irritated with you for not speaking up to take care of yourself. You learned that pointless suffering is not admirable. That was a big lesson to your Soul. (Long pause)

This next lifetime would be in the Land of Mu, better known as Lemuria. This is a civilization that went on for about 100,000 years, and women were dominant then. Men were kept as slaves and they were not allowed to speak. They did not even know they could speak. They thought only women could talk. Women controlled men with their voices. It was a very strange time, long before Atlantis. Men were controlled because it was believed they would destroy the planet with war if not tightly controlled by women, who were by their inherent nature not interested in wars, since war was destructive and the female body is creative, bringing forth life. In the late stages of Lemuria, they believed that women create and men destroy by their very natures. This had not been true for the entire history of that civilization, however.

You were a tall, big-boned, rather plain woman with a ready smile, short grey hair, and relatively muscular arms for a female. You were serious about your work and had been trained by the Central Command to do a specific task, as needed. It appears you were in charge of some kind of beacon. Now this is highly unusual. I have never seen or heard of anything like this before, but the thing about past lives is that you often see and learn things about other civilizations that no one knows about. And that is a surprise. Or you sometimes see what really happened instead of what was written down in the history books.

Officially, we have no written records from Lemuria. I am aware of none, at least. I am told there are some secret Lemurian archives under the Earth in caves somewhere that some government knows about, but they cannot decipher them. The alphabet is too unfamiliar. Yet they are holding onto these writings secretly for some reason, repressing them.

Anyway, you were in charge of a beacon, which was kind of like a lighthouse. However it was not light, but rather sound that was being emitted. I am given the information now that it was sort of a shade of blue-green, like teal—a dark blue-green sound. I do not know that makes sense to most people, but it makes sense to me. Each sound has a corresponding color if you slow down or speed up the frequency. So in this Lemurian lifetime, you are in charge of making sure this sound is continually broadcast to the countryside if there is a need, because it had particular effects on the people. It could calm them, or energize them, or motivate them to action, and so on. They would vote as to how it was used, so this was not imposed on the women by "Big Brother" or anything like that.

Now this was a rural area where there had been some unrest among the males, not just the human males, but the animals that were there as well. This particular shade of blue-green sound was being broadcast to recalibrate the emotions—particularly by manipulating the pineal gland of the males. Do not ask me how they knew how to do that. I am not being shown that information, even though I would definitely like to know. This sound did not affect the pineal gland of the females, only that of the males, so this technology was very highly developed.

There was something you had to do, rather like putting—and this is an analogy, not exactly what you were doing—similar to putting wood in a stove to keep the heat up. There was something you were supposed to add to the central processing unit of this beacon. Your job was to feed into the unit some sort of glowing bars to keep it functioning. It was a delicate procedure. You had to place the bars just so, or the color of the light and the quality of the sound would vary. It had to be spot on because if it was not precisely focused, it was not going to just affect the pineal gland of the males; or it would have the wrong effect on the pineal glands of the males, so it was very exacting work.

One day you became quite ill with some kind of influenza, and remember, you were living in a rural area. I understand now that most of the Land of Mu was rural. People knew that spreading out was good for them. They were aware that human beings need to be surrounded by nature to be optimally happy and healthy. Way out where you were living, unfortunately, there was no one else who knew how to do what you were doing with the beacon. Being very self-sufficient, rather than send for help, or ask for back-up while you were sick, you kept dragging yourself out to the sound beacon. You became quite weak and feverish at one point, and made a mistake, which sent out the wrong sound. It was just slightly off, so you could not hear the difference in you weakened state. This variant on the correct sound caused a serious problem in the male animals, as well as the male humans. It interfered with the endocrine system, since the pineal gland is part of that system.

They all became depressed and lethargic, including your own male house pet, and they could not do anything, but were lying about sad and miserable. When you finally realized what was happening, you sent a message out for reinforcements. You also turned the beacon off, and suddenly all the males, both animals and humans, went back in the direction of "stirred up and making trouble." There were some fairly serious repercussions in that property got torn up. The animals destroyed fences and corn cribs and things like that. Some human males tore up the insides of houses. Many were kept much like house pets, and these were the pretty ones, chosen for the sexual pleasure of the women. Incidentally, these males were sent off to special schools when they were young men where they were highly trained in the art of pleasuring women. Therefore, because they were kept inside so their hands would remain soft to do their pleasuring tasks, they were naturally inside the houses when the beacons were turned off. Certain others were kept outside the homes, living in their own supervised compounds; they were kept around to do the heavy labor. These males wreaked havoc outside in the barns and fields, destroying crops and food storage areas in the silos and barns when the sound was turned off suddenly.

All of them got into "trouble-making" mode like they were before the beacon was turned on, only far worse, and seriously tore things up after the sound beacon was turned off. This went on for two days until the help you finally had sent for arrived.

Amazingly, you were not faulted for this incident since your superiors were compassionate. They surmised you had been overburdened, realizing that you were isolated. To be the only person who knew how to do this complicated task you had been assigned was simply too demanding. So what they did was send you an assistant after that, to keep an extra eye on things and help you out, because they realized there should not be such a heavy burden on only one person.

However, this incident bothered you enormously. You felt responsible and you spent a long time helping people repair their houses as penance; you also got out and repaired their fences and corn cribs. Rather than doing the work you were supposed to be doing, you were leaving a lot of it to the assistant, and running around repairing everyone's property that got destroyed because you felt so guilty. This was something that bothered you for quite a long period of time. It made an impression on that part of you that reincarnates. In knowing about this, you can begin to heal anything residual that remains from that lifetime. When we are talking about things like corn cribs and fences, I am talking about the current equivalent of that sort of thing...a corn crib being a place where you store corn for animals to consume, feed bins. You do not need to be doing menial labor as penance. (There is a pause as I wait to see the next lifetime.)

This is somewhat unusual for me to see. I am seeing you in a lifetime as a female dolphin. This dolphin has such sweet, loving energy! In this lifetime you had several babies, and I am being allowed to see how much intense pleasure and joy dolphins have when giving birth to their young. It was simply ecstatic! In addition to having children, you had a job having to do with dream weaving. Now, the Australian aborigines tell us that the dolphins are the "Masters of the Dreamtime". I am seeing you and your pod but particularly you. You as the leader had a specific task involving the weaving of dreams—in other words, physically carrying a stream of energy in a special way, with your body. You had to physically travel in the three dimensions, using your physical body, from Australia to the west coast of the United States so there is repeated migration over a period of years. You would go back and forth, swimming those great distances and having fun the whole way, stopping off at different islands, visiting friends along the way, talking on the sonar. Dolphins can talk over extraordinarily long distances by using sonar, by making those beeping and squeaking sounds, under the water. So "talking on the sonar phone" is what I am going to call this. (Laughing)

In carrying this beam of energy to North America and back again to Eastern Australia numerous times, and you did an exemplary job. You were in charge of this project that your pod had taken on. There were about twelve adult members of the pod in attendance most of the time. The numbers would swell and decrease, as sometimes pod members would split off and go with another pod for a while to visit, or stay. Others would join in for a while. You were the only one who had to make that trip back and forth every time, but your extended family went with you all of the time. They made sure you never had to do it alone, so that you were safe and emotionally supported.

You did a superior job of this, and the shamans from both regions, Australia and North America, were extremely appreciative to you and aware of your work. The shamans were grateful to you because your efforts increased their ability to get information from the spirit world in dreams, to communicate with each other from across vast distances, and thus to help keep the humans of the world on track. This was 700 to 800 years ago approximately. I am being shown that this particular dolphin lived to be extremely old.

So this is kind of a covert operation the dolphin was doing. It is not anything that most of the other dolphins of the world really knew about. It was just a job you did to make the world a better place. You were an unsung hero working to make the world a better place. You are going to be drawing upon that energy. As Kryon terms it, you will be "mining the Akash" for certain abilities, and this is going to be one. Working at least part of the time quietly, in a certain way, as an unsung hero is what many Lightworkers do these days. This is rather what you are going to have to do; go underground to do work that will result in making the world a better place. There are untold thousands of Lightworkers toiling as unsung heroes doing this type of work at this point in history. Just knowing they are doing a good job, for most of them, is reward enough.

In case you were wondering, you had about twelve babies over the full extent of that lifetime. Twelve little dolphin babies came to the world through you. Eight of them were males, and I do not know if this is important to you, but due to a couple of your male offspring, splitting off and hanging out in Fiji, you have a huge component of your dolphin offspring, your progeny, around the island of Fiji. They do not wander very far from Fiji because the ecosystem is so nice and clean and pristine over there. (Pause)

The lifetime that I am being shown next is back in biblical times. There is actually a story which is written in the Bible in a way that it is not exactly truly what happened. Some extremely important things were lost in translation, or else were never revealed to the public. It is not clear which. At any rate, I am being shown that when Joshua fought the Battle of Jericho and caused the walls to fall because he sounded a trumpet, you were in that army. You were one of his top ten or so people. This implies that you had others under you in your command, but it was more like a tribal rather than a strict military organization. Since it was a tribal organization, those who were working in your command were extended family members. And so here is what really happened.

You all marched around the walls of this town in a specific pattern. In other words, you marched stomping your feet in a specific pattern, and there was a drummer who constantly gave out this precise drumbeat, which Joshua had taught to them. There were two drummers, who took turns leading so no mistakes would be made due to exhaustion. This precise drumming pattern and exact trumpet tone he was to sound were given to Joshua in a dream. The drum beat sounded extremely odd to everyone, including Joshua. No one could understand exactly why they were marching to that strange pattern. And yet what happened from this odd pattern of marching was that a specific type of vibratory resonance occurred. Yes, and this is fascinating, a vibration was set up inside the physical structure of the walls. The walls were vibrating ever so slightly inside. It could not be seen, but if anyone placed their hand on the wall, they could have felt it ever so slightly. So when Joshua finally did sound his trumpet, it was the culmination of that vibration's having reached a certain level. This sustained vibration had broken down the tolerance of the wall. When he made this trumpet sound, the exact tone of which was perfectly calibrated to interfere with the wave pattern that had been set up in the walls by the marching, this then caused them to collapse into rubble. At that point your army could waltz right in and capture the city.

Your Higher Self wants you to know that you were there for that momentous occasion, and that you participated in that successful event. This deepened your interest at the Soul level in the uses of sound, which you have investigated in many other lives. At the Soul level then, you are particularly gifted in the use of sound, and the manipulation of sound frequencies. You will be using this talent again. This time, you will be using it solely to heal. You needed to know about this because this is yet another lifetime where you were involved with the uses of sound. You were using it to create an outcome that we are not normally accustomed to thinking is possible using sound, at this point in history.

There is another thing I am now seeing that happened at Jericho. When the trumpet sounded, the people who had been marching suddenly stopped dead in their tracks. When the trumpet sounded, a wave of euphoria went through the people. That was part of the vibrational frequency which decimated the wall as well. The energetic vibration that came from the people who had been marching was like a state of shamanic ecstasy, and all of that contributed to those walls disintegrating. You know that shamans will dance in a circle, and that will be part of their spiritually ecstatic experience of practicing shamanism. It is called shamanic ecstasy.

So this is what all was going on--way more than was actually going on than what is currently in the Bible. Back when this part of the Bible was written, no one could have understood that explanation about sound frequencies, anyway.

Your Higher Self and Guides are telling me that these are enough memories for you to assimilate at this time.

And so the reading ends.

<u>Lois' Notes:</u> In this set of past lives, we are starting to see that Cindy has a tendency to allow mistakes she made to eat away at her, and to go to extraordinary lengths to make up for the mistake, rather than simply forgiving herself and moving on. We see this in the hot-tempered priest lifetime, and in the sound beacon lifetime. So here is a lesson she could get from this reading.

We are also seeing that she has a distinct pattern in various lives of working with sound, as a dolphin, as a member of Joshua's army, and as the keeper of the beacon in Lemuria. It was not long after this reading that Cindy began to sing in public, something she had wanted to do for a long time. She also, several months later, began studying and practicing the use of healing humans and animals with sound, color and vibration as taught in advanced EDINA energy medicine.

Cindy also saw that she had worked at some covert operations in past lives, which explained a few things about her personal experiences with secrecy from this lifetime. She also remarked that she has always felt strongly drawn to the Fiji Islands, and now she realizes why.

Hopefully, Cindy also got from this reading the understanding, from the experience in the lifetime as the Catholic priest that it is not noble to suffer in silence for no particular reason other than ego aggrandizement. Another lesson was that there are many ways to atone, one can choose to change litter boxes in the local animal shelter, or do far more good by working to create a non-profit that raises funds to hire people to do these tasks, if we are capable of such an undertaking, which Cindy is. At the time of the reading I was unaware that Cindy had already started a non-profit to fund animal rescue shelters.

This is an important point for the reader: If we have the abilities to do the fund raising, then running around changing litter boxes is just another form of ego-building: The attitude of, "Oh, look at me, what a holy person I am to humble myself and change litter boxes for these poor stray cats," is just a way to build up the ego. Quietly and/or anonymously raising funds, to see to it that thousands of animals have homes, and get their litter boxes changed, or making certain that the funds are available to euthanize them humanely rather than brutally, as is necessary in some underfunded animal shelters, is the more Soul-based way of doing things. Posturing so that others can admire our work, or pat us on the back for our service, builds the ego. Moving away from ego-based activities and in the direction of Soul-directed behaviors is a major goal of spiritual growth. It is one which we all incarnated to experience.

August 5, 2009

This is the fifth, and final, in a series of past life readings for Cindy Oswald at this time.

Lois: I am seeing you grinding lenses, creating glass lenses that had to be shaped just so, one convex to the other. You are a male in the 1750s and you are spending all of your time grinding lenses, getting them just right; you are a perfectionist. Each one is hand cut and there is a lot of glass dust and powder around. It is all over the place and itchy, not pleasant to have on your skin, but you ignore the dust, being consumed in the grinding process. You are making them for people who need to see more clearly. You are also grinding them for people who were using them to magnify work projects, as when they were making small things like jewelry and so on.

I am being shown that you are a workaholic. All you did, all day long, was grind these lenses. Of course the work was important, and it helped a lot of people, but you never even went outside for a walk. Sometimes you would open the window and put food along the ledge for pigeons, but that was just about it for outside activity. You had one cat that you fed, and you would pet it sometimes, but mostly you were just busy thinking about lenses and grinding lenses. You were very sloppy about cleaning up the powder that came from grinding them.

What happened over time was that entirely too much of it got inside your body. There it caused massive organ failure because it was just everywhere—in your lungs, your stomach and from your stomach it could go anywhere. The point of knowing about this is not to fall into a bad habit, especially if you are working at home. This man, Gustav, was working at home, and it looks like he is in a trance all day. If you do start working at home, do not get your nose so to the grindstone so that you do not do anything but work. Be sure you get out and go for walks, go to the movies, and hang out with your friends. When this fellow's life came to an end, he realized there was so much he wanted to do that he never got around to doing. He felt like it was a wasted life. Your Guides want you to know that you do not need to repeat that pattern. You may begin to work out of your home, but you do not want to fall into Gustav's pattern again. There is something about cleaning up the details, the messes. In other words, that is just as much a part of your job. Maybe that just means filing or something like that in your case. Do not neglect the small details, and do not become an obsessed shut-in, are the only things they want you to know from this life.

Oh, wait. There was one other thing. He had one true love when he was young, and she passed away at an early age, before they ever got married. He gave up on love, and that is why he was a workaholic. They want you to know that love is possible at any age. As long as you are breathing, it is a possibility. (Long pause)

I am seeing you riding a horse, and I am afraid the word donkey would be more accurate. You are in Ireland in the 1640s is what I am seeing right now. You are a male and a traveling preacher. Moving around from place to place and teach the scriptures has become your whole life. You go to some sort of a public building, set out the times you will preach and people give you money in the collection plate. I am seeing you in a very plain, brown waistcoat. You are extremely humble and dress quite simply; no frills. You do not want to draw attention to yourself. You are questioning whether or not you want to travel constantly forever, but you just doggedly keep on doing it, not knowing how to end the cycle.

At one point you decided to stay a little bit longer in a particular town, because there was a young woman there you were interested in. You had a remarkable opportunity—because this girl really was quite special, and she cared a lot for you. She had a good family and they did not know anything about your background. You came from a very questionable background; your mother had been a prostitute, and you were illegitimate. Your mother was not even sure who your father was. That was part of the reason you were mobile, so that nobody would ever know about your background.

So, you had a remarkable opportunity to marry this genteel woman who sincerely liked you. She had an influential family and they would have built you a church. Out of low self-esteem and fear of what would happen if they ever found out about your background, you passed on this opportunity. This was the one golden opportunity of your whole life, and you passed on it because of preconceived ideas of how rich people think and act. You had all these internal conversations with yourself about what would transpire should they ever find out about you. In your fantasies you would be tarred and feathered and run out of town in shame. When the young woman pressed you to stay and marry her, you replied that you were going to think about this.

But you ran away from opportunity and disappeared in the middle of the night, which just broke her heart. She was devastated because she had no idea why you disappeared without giving her an answer. What your Guides want you to know about this lifetime is that you passed a beautiful opportunity, the biggest opportunity you had in that lifetime. The reason that you passed on it was because you had judgment in your heart about a certain group of people: the wealthy. Hearing about this lifetime is just to underscore for you the importance of getting out of judgment. While you have learned this to a very large degree, you are still in the process of completing your understanding that it is important not to have preconceived ideas about individuals based upon general assumptions about groups.

You continued to wander the Earth alone after that experience. Finally one winter you were out of doors between towns when a storm blew in, and you became cold and wet. This resulted in a bad case of pneumonia, and you died alone. It was just you and the donkey. When you passed over to the other side and were going through your life review, your Guides said, "Kick yourself in the back side, because you foolishly passed up a life-changing opportunity!" Had you married that lady you would have had children, a high regard from everybody in the region, and a family that would have protected your secret about your origins because they loved and admired you. (Pause)

I am seeing you living under water, swimming much of the time. Usually you are attached to a device much in the same way that people who are hang gliding are strapped into a contraption which responds to your movements, and magnifies them. As you move your arms up and down and pull your feet up and down, you move quickly through the water. This machine reminds me of a bicycle, but it is used underwater, and has fins. You have created this machine. This is simply fascinating. You make swimming-like movements, and the machine amplifies the movement using gears attached to fins. In this way your movements are made more efficient so that you move through the water with greater speed.

You are doing some stealthy work, actually military in nature. You have a bamboo-like reed contraption strapped to the side of your face and one end is above the water and the other end is in your mouth. And you are breathing through this bamboo pipe while moving around in the harbor of the enemy at dusk. Every now and again you come up high enough that your head is sticking out and you can peek around and see what is going on above the water. You are collecting information. Others are with you, also swimming around attached to these machines.

So here you are in the harbor of a fairly large city, commanding a group. You are in charge of organizing things, and telling everyone what they are supposed to do. Your group is collecting data, when unexpectedly someone else approaches from under water. These are members of the group upon which you are spying. They also have some sort of underwater contraptions— but different than yours.

They corner each of you individually, and capture you. They take the machine you were on, which you were not supposed to let anyone see. They then began studying the machine so they could make one like yours. They are trying to get information out of you, yet these people did not believe in torture. They believed that eventually you would tell them what they wanted to know through psychological means. They were using some sort of questioning technique which they found more reliable than torture.

Somewhere along the way as you are being questioned, you decide you really like it there. These people are very nice to you. They treat you better than your own people had. You decide that you want to defect and come to their side, because you really did not care one way or another about the politics. How did you end up being a spy? I think it just sort of happened to you. Your country had said, "He would make a good spy. Let us train him." So they trained you.

While you were a captive, and gently questioned and coerced into giving up more information than you really realized you were giving up, you decide that you definitely prefer it there. Soon you meet a young woman. Shortly thereafter, the government officials let you wander the streets because they thought they had gotten all of your information, and you were not interested in going home. They treat you like a guest. They continue to feed and clothe you, and give you a place to stay.

So, as I said, you met a young woman who took a shine to you. She decided she was going to take care of you, and that you could come and live with her. She owned a very fancy pastry shop. It is hard to tell which time period this was. Nothing looks familiar. She set you up in business, and you designed and made toys for a living. You were quite successful. You two had a couple of children. What I am getting is that the purpose of recalling this lifetime is to know that you made a fine choice walking away from being part of a warrior existence. You chose instead to serve the good, to serve the Light. Your Guides wanted you to know about this, because people who manufacture toys, which are things that make people happy, are doing important work, too. In this lifetime you made a really positive choice that was outside the box. Nobody thought you would ever do that, not even the people who captured you. You had a long and happy life with children and grandchildren.

Your Guides also wanted you to know you have a background as an inventor, and could "mine" those abilities if you chose.

It is all right—sometimes extremely desirable—to think outside the box and try something that appeals to you emotionally, even though it does not necessarily fit everyone else's pictures. This is only true if it does not harm others, naturally. (Long pause)

All right, now I am seeing a lifetime where you are a gem cutter. You are incarnated as a female in Lemuria. You use certain faceted stones to extract diseases and dark energies from people. Your specialty was clearing parasites within the physical body. There were some spiritual components, too, but you would get rid of parasites using gemstones in specific layouts and elixirs. Gem elixirs are created by taking a gemstone, soaking it in water in either the sunlight or moonlight for a certain period of time, putting a few drops of alcohol in it to preserve it , and then corking it. Gem elixirs have various different healing properties depending on the gem used to create the elixir.

You created a huge body of knowledge. You wrote books, did experiments with different gemstones, and different combinations of gemstones, using either straight gemstones themselves or elixirs. Authoring several books on these subjects, you created a large body of work used as texts for centuries. Your Guides want you to know you could do that kind of thing again if you wanted to. It would be possible for you to create healing techniques using anything you wanted to: gemstones, herbs and so on, and you could really get into that if you allowed yourself to. They are saying you could publish it all under a pseudonym. That way it would not interfere with your income from your teaching job.

I am told additionally there is something about bladder parasites. You are the only one who could get rid of them. I do not think we have those any more, but there was a really terrible bladder parasite that people would get that was just horribly painful. You figured out a way using gemstones to get rid—and this is funny, it is blue—to get rid of bladder parasites. They were seriously plaguing people.

They say that if you want to do this kind of thing again, consider yourself a researcher and write down what works and what does not. Do not assume you can remember it all.

That is it for today.

Lois' Notes: Cindy was in the process of starting to do most of her teaching/writing work at home, rather than in her office at the University, and so needed to know about the lens-grinder's obsessive behavior. This would be a past tendency for her to avoid. She was also becoming serious about her healing work, a form of energy medicine she was doing on the side. She needed to hear about the importance of taking notes during the healing session. This is especially true when one is engaging in cutting edge work—basic research in effect—it is helpful to take notes in the moment, or shortly thereafter, and not rely solely on memory.

Naturally, it would benefit anyone to hear about "outside the box" choices one had made to do good deeds in the world, such as the lifetime inventing toys instead of instruments of the spy's trade, to be used in war, especially as this was an unjust war being waged on a kind, gentle people. And the past life of missed opportunity due to low self-esteem clearly contains an obvious and universal lesson.

This concludes the series of past lives for one person. We can see that certain issues are addressed in more than one reading, as though one past life reading is insufficient to fully balance an issue. I suspect from having done energy medicine for so many years that to address too much at one time would be overwhelming to the individual, and so only as much as that person can handle is addressed at one time. So the Guides and the Guardians of the Records prioritize the lives which most need balancing/healing. The most important lifetimes to balance are always included at the beginning of any session, so it would follow logically that the Guardians of the Records and the individual's Guides would have the most important past lives to balance come up in the very first reading, and then continue with that pattern until all past lives that need balancing are eventually handled. How many readings a person needs would then depend on the individual, and how many past lives he/she has had on Earth.

Conclusion

I am both pleased and surprised to report that, in addition to helping hundreds of Souls heal, I have also learned a great deal from reading other people's Akashic Records. For example, as mentioned earlier, there are a huge number of ancient civilizations of which we have no record. These go much farther back than we dream. I have had so much fun seeing the visions of many of them over the course of doing these past life readings, starting in 1990! As we have seen, some of the civilizations had great ideas, like not building on the surface of the Earth, because it spoils Her natural beauty, but rather building below ground or in caves. Another idea I loved was that of having wildflowers growing among food crops for the "emotional health of the crops." I mean, who among us wants to eat emotionally imbalanced grains? Okay, the idea at first read may seem silly to us, but what if this kind of thing actually does affect the quality of food crops? I suspect that it may. Music does! I am constantly delighted at being exposed to some of these long lost civilization's ideas and see their architecture, clothing, jewelry, hair styles, art, conveyances and other technology.

I have learned many other things in the course of doing this work, some of them surprising. One thing I was amazed to discover is that remembering past lives allows one to release not only emotional issues and bad habits or patterns from the past, but physical ones, too. A good example of that is Cindy's experience of the bone run through her jaw muscles having been the source of her TMJ pain in this lifetime. I was quite surprised that the TMJ pain she had for over fifty years went away right after she heard about that past life...delighted, mind you, but definitely surprised.

Another thing I have noticed is that when people get past life readings, their burdens are lightened at the level of the Soul so significantly that it can be seen in their faces! Many people report feeling and looking younger after having past life readings. Their friends and family often comment on their change in appearance without prompting, and without knowing that the past life reading had occurred.

The concept of what I call "blowback" is very interesting. This is the situation in which the client has either had a spontaneous past life memory, or a regression during which they did not have the support of a good therapist. In this case, the emotions of the past life "bleed" into the current one, often causing problems. It is because of this that I do not recommend anyone use a past life regression tape and do their own past life readings all alone. One never knows what past life might surface. It might be some mild thing, or it might be one that sends one into a downward spiral. If that does happen to someone, or has happened, my suggestion is that a good energy medicine practitioner such as an accomplished BodyTalk practitioner, Psych-K facilitator, or EDINA practitioner, be contacted to balance the energies.

Also the concept of "checking out" came as a surprise to me. For every lifetime, in the planning stages prior to reincarnation, each Soul and their Advisors plan several possible "checkout points" where the Soul can choose to honorably terminate that lifetime depending upon how things are coming along. This works similar to a safety valve on a pressure cooker. It is a way for the Soul to exit safely, sans karmic penalty.

Some things the Soul seems to consider at the pre-ordained checkout points are the following: First, if you are progressing well enough according to the life plan. For example, if major goals were sobriety and taking care of a family, and at forty-five one is still single, and into serial dating and drunken debauchery, one might get "checked out." Secondly, does the Soul think that given the circumstances as they have unfolded so far, and how others are fulfilling promises which they made at the Soul level planning stage, will one be able to come anywhere near doing the work the Soul planned to do before incarnating? Third, if the Soul is concerned that difficulties being faced are too dire, and the Soul be concerned that this personality/ego will do something that will cause long-term damage to the Soul, like commit suicide or murder? In that case, the Soul may choose to opt out of the lifetime. There may be more reasons, but the last one I want to mention is that only rarely the Soul will decide if the personality is just not getting any lessons at all, and therefore the lifetime is turning out to be a waste of time and energy from the vantage point of the Soul. This happens in the case of severe, long-term addictions, for example.

These checkout points are times for review at the Soul level, and the personality is rarely aware that it has happened. We might die at a checkout point, or decide at a Soul level to continue with the life. A checkout point is never a time when suicide occurs. Suicide is seriously damaging to the Eternal Soul and must be avoided at all costs. It is always forgiven in the after-life, but then takes very time-consuming harsh, rugged, painful work and countless lifetimes on Earth to just overcome one suicide or murder. The reincarnated Soul will just face the same circumstances again in another life, only worse, until ones personality/ego lives thorough it and learns the lesson or balances the karma. A checkout point is always one where we die from an accident, or illness, or some other blameless death. A suicide by artificially causing an "accident" or any other "accidentally on purpose" death is still a suicide, and is treated as such by the Lords of Karma.

At this point, I want to mention that occasionally someone will hear about their past lives and not use that knowledge to their advantage. Instead, some will use one or more past lives as an excuse for continuing bad behavior, or for not changing or forgiving others. They will decide that they cannot help themselves, or that they have an excuse for being the way they are, based upon past lives. This is the polar opposite of why their Soul sent that person for an Akashic Records reading. This state of affairs is unfortunate. In cases like that the ego is so firmly entrenched in its control over the lifetime that no change is made at that time. It is of course possible they will encounter experiences at a later date which will allow them to benefit from the reading. In my heart I always hold that as a possibility on behalf of my clients who do not immediately reap the benefit of their reading.

Some things I have learned as a result of instruction by the Guardians of the Records while doing readings. For example, I learned that there are certain guidelines for a therapist when doing past life readings. What is crucial is that the past life therapist is compassionate, and a neutral observer, who is both nonjudgmental and unemotional about what he/she is seeing. Compassion does not mean feeling the client's feelings; compassion means the therapist must be there for the client in the way the client needs a therapist to be, in spite of how that therapist feels in the moment. The client must be allowed to express the emotions. If the past life therapist becomes emotional, and takes on the client's feelings and feels them, crying or being angry or afraid, the therapist is doing the client a disservice. For there are then two wounded people in the room, and the attention is taken from the client, who has no support at a time when they may desperately need that. In fact, many clients will try to comfort the therapist who is emoting, thereby short-circuiting the client's own healing. The therapist then becomes the center of attention, when the client is the one who has both the right and the need to be the center of attention at that moment.

So a good therapist is a neutral, non-judgmental, accepting, calm observer of the past life, and does nothing to distract the client from feeling their feelings in the moment. The therapist does not even interrupt to volunteer a tissue in the midst of an emotional release or processing, nor is the therapist patting the client and saying, "It will be okay." These are ways of distracting the client, and of demonstrating what a kind, thoughtful person the therapist is, which is just another way of putting the therapist at the center of attention. It is as if therapist is demonstrating, "Look at me, I am such a good person. I feel your feelings. I comfort you," in a moment when both parties should be focused solely on the client. Left free to cry or feel his anger, the client can begin to process these feelings and heal. A good therapist has the attitude of "I am not important in this moment, the client is." This attitude of neutrality and a supportive attitude can be expressed in a long-distance reading as well. After the Guardians told me this, I discovered that many psychologists approach therapy in this way as well.

Another thing I have learned is that up until about age five, children can often recall their past lives. This kind of information should be collected, if at all, with the utmost care and sensitivity. Usually, the child will just volunteer the information, in his own good time. During the twenty or so years I have been doing these readings, I have had the privilege of either accidentally overhearing children talking to their parents in public about a past life, or had clients who came to me telling me about a story a child or grandchild had told them, asking if I thought it were a past life. Often it is.

An example of the former was when I was in line recently at a restaurant. A tiny girl in line in front of me pointed at a photograph on the wall. The photo was of the Swiss Alps. She said excitedly to her mother, "Mommy, mommy look! Remember when I was your Daddy, we went skiing up there?" Her mother scowled at her and said something to the effect that they had never gone skiing, and jerked on her arm. The child kept trying to convince her mother that it was true, and the mother kept being obtuse and rude to her. Finally, I could not hold my tongue any longer said, "Excuse me, but your daughter is trying to tell you about a past life where she was your father and took you skiing in the Swiss Alps. Small children can recall past lives sometimes." The mother's jaw dropped and she looked back and forth a couple of times at the child, at me, and at the photo of the Alps. She never said a word to me. I do not know what she thought, but she did stop snarling at the child.

An example of the latter, of a client coming in and wondering if a child were having a past life memory, was the case of Peter. He came in for an EDINA session, and said his grandson, aged two, had just learned to talk. This two year old boy kept asking where his daughter was. He would cry and say that he missed his daughter, and did anyone know where she was? Everyone in the family just looked at him like he was crazy, poor little guy. I told Peter that yes, it was, in my opinion, clearly a past life memory which the child was having.

Here is my understanding of what happens when an individual remembers being a famous, historically significant person and so does another person. I believe that it is possible to take on some of the memories of famous or important people if your Soul comes from the same Monad as theirs. (Of course, you may actually be this person reincarnated.) These beings who have had powerful effects on many people, and who positively changed the course of history, have a huge light. If one shares the same Monad as such a person, it is possible for these lights to blend some, and for one to remember the famous past life as one's own. It is not that the two people who claim to be King Tut are mistaken or lying, it is that their Souls share light with that well-known incarnation of their Spirit, and come by their memories in that way. I mention that because this question confuses so many.

Another question is whether there actually is such a thing as individual past lives, or whether when we incarnate we take unresolved bits and pieces of past lives floating around in the collective consciousness, and agree to try to balance them on behalf of the collective. I think both are probably true. This is called a paradox, and the deeper meaning of paradox is that it is something which requires that we stretch our minds, to hold in consciousness two ideas which seem to be mutually exclusive.

I am deeply grateful to have learned so much from doing these Akashic Records readings. I feel that I have been most uniquely privileged to have witnessed both the healing and the changes resulting from these readings in people's lives over the years. It has also been an immense joy to view vanished civilizations with their very different ideas and cultural artifacts, and to see continents which have long since disappeared beneath the sea or the ground, and will be no more.

As I said in the beginning, we are Immortals, each and every one. We return again and again—in different bodies—to grow, to learn and to heal in our quest to return and merge with the Light of the Source. I am honored to have been given the Akashic Records as a sacred tool to assist others in this important work. And most of all, I am grateful to the clients who come to me for these readings, thereby allowing me to fulfill one significant part of my Soul's contract for this lifetime.

Addendum

Apple Cider Vinegar Baths

Since these were mentioned so often in the book, I want to share this simple procedure with my readers. This technique will release emotions from the body into the auric field. When we subsequently shower, the released emotions will be rinsed out of the aura and be carried down the drain.

Fill the tub with warm water and to that add 2-3 cups of apple cider vinegar. Other vinegars will not work the same. Do not add anything else to the water. Soak in this solution for thirty minutes adding warm water as needed to remain comfortably warm. If all you have is a shower stall, sit in the tub and periodically sponge or squirt a mix of apple cider vinegar and water over your body for thirty minutes.

After thirty minutes drain the tub fully and take a shower. If not washing your hair at that time, run your hands through the aura above and around your head and rinse your hands in the shower stream. Repeat this several times. This will clear the auric field around your head.

This can be used anytime you are having an especially intense emotional release, but it is not suggested that you use this consistently as a crutch to avoid dealing with personal problems which are causing intense emotional responses.

Testimonial

I knew Lois a few years before asking her for an Akashic Records reading. At the time I'd transcribed and worked with her session material, so I had a good understanding of how a session unfolded, and it didn't seem "spooky" or "weird." I was incredibly curious as to what one of my stories might be, and I also wanted to "mine my Akash," meaning that I wanted to know what skills I may have mastered in a past life so I could call forth those attributes to utilize in the "now" time. I'm a huge Kryon fan and that idea intrigued me. After all, if I was a "master baker" in another life, then it could explain my unusual attraction to anything looking or tasting like cake. I'm also a student of the Law of Attraction so I was also wondering why these seemingly random goofballs and events just showed up in my life since I don't believe in coincidence. The only life that matters to me is the one I'm in, but this could really be interesting.

After receiving my distance session notes, I made time so I wouldn't be interrupted and I listened intently. As she began, I came to realize that my guides had a different agenda for me. Instead of skills mastered in past lives, the first story explained a difficult situation I was currently experiencing and I began to see it in a different light. I immediately felt an incredible relief and compassion for all involved. I know there was no way I would have consciously attracted this situation, but knowing the karmic ties made everything easier to understand. A seeming "random" event wasn't really so random, and Lois had no way of knowing how deeply it rang true.

The next life related to an unpleasant series of events from my 30s. I didn't know why it was coming up because I felt it was ancient history and already healed. The parallels and connections offered were uncanny but I set it aside and really felt nothing more than, "I wonder what that was about."

About a month later while driving to an appointment, I actually had to pull into a parking lot and stop to catch my breath. It wasn't until later that evening that I made the connection to my Akashic Records reading.

I couldn't believe the depth of emotion I felt as I saw myself feeling the confusion, disbelief and unfairness of a situation that changed the course of my life. Instead of the shame and secrecy I felt so many years ago, I could finally see myself in a compassionate light simply caught in circumstances I didn't understand and doing the best I could at the time. I wasn't a victim and nothing was wrong. No shame, no victim, no mistake. It unfolded perfectly and it wasn't until that moment that I truly made peace with this experience. It was also as if time stopped and I just observed, then released, then forgave everyone completely—including me.

And my guides didn't disappoint when it came to showing Lois a few snapshots of my interests and talents, some of which weren't tapped in this lifetime, but knowing about my mastery once upon a time got my attention. A past life as an inventor/sculptor of functional art was evident in my current love of art and especially my connection to the annual event known as "Burning Man" where utilitarian as well as whimsical sculpture and expression is the norm. I also quilt which is another form of functional art that I shared with this past life.

I experienced another life as an illustrator for the church who hired me to illustrate the beginning of a book's chapters with ornate letters (I love to mess around with calligraphy pens) and my lifetime as a playwright/actor explained my love of writing, books and my dramatic approach to so many things.

The surprising element in all of this is that some of the information resonated immediately in that I had "aha!" realizations as she spoke and other information that seemed totally unrelated unfolded over time. I listened to my reading perhaps four times over six weeks, and each time another level of understanding and detail emerged. One relationship in particular became more compassionate and loving once I understood the underlying connection. This relationship continues to evolve and profound is all I have to say about it at this time.

Perhaps the biggest take-away is the knowledge that things really aren't always what they seem. It'll be interesting to see how knowing about my previous talents/skills might show up now that I want to explore them. I also have questions about other issues in my life, but that's another subject for another day.

Rebecca Hannah

Lois J. Wetzel, MFA

Lois conducts workshops, lectures, teaches and gives readings all over the world. Please contact Lois if you are interested in having her come to your city!

For individual clients, Lois does healing sessions as well as readings either at a distance or in person. She offers self-study classes over the internet plus a free newsletter. To get a past life reading, or to learn more about Lois Wetzel and what else she offers, please visit this website: www.hotpinklotus.com

Luminous Blessings!

1-800
760
8010
vinaprin.com

CPSIA information can be obtained at www.ICGtesting.com
Printed in the USA
BVOW081230211212

308893BV00006B/143/P